Samuel Beckett and Translation

Samuel Beckett and Translation

Edited by
José Francisco Fernández and
Mar Garre García

EDINBURGH
University Press

Edinburgh University Press is one of the leading university presses in the UK. We publish academic books and journals in our selected subject areas across the humanities and social sciences, combining cutting-edge scholarship with high editorial and production values to produce academic works of lasting importance. For more information visit our website: edinburghuniversitypress.com

Edinburgh University Press Ltd
The Tun – Holyrood Road
12(2f) Jackson's Entry
Edinburgh EH8 8PJ

First published in hardback by Edinburgh University Press, 2021

Typeset in 10.5/13 Bembo by
IDSUK (DataConnection) Ltd, and
printed and bound by CPI Group (UK) Ltd,
Croydon, CR0 4YY

A CIP record for this book is available from the British Library

ISBN 978 1 4744 8382 7 (hardback)
ISBN 978 1 4744 8383 4 (paperback)
ISBN 978 1 4744 8384 1 (webready PDF)
ISBN 978 1 4744 8385 8 (epub)

Contents

Figures

Notes on Contributors

Olga Beloborodova is a postdoctoral researcher and teaching assistant at the University of Antwerp, currently working at its Centre for Manuscript Genetics. She has published articles on the subjects of Beckett, cognition and genetic criticism in *Journal of Beckett Studies* and *Samuel Beckett Today/Aujourd'hui*. Together with Dirk Van Hulle and Pim Verhulst, she co-edited *Beckett and Modernism*, published by Palgrave in 2018. She is also Assistant Editor of *Journal of Beckett Studies* and a member of the Editorial Board of *Beckett Digital Manuscript Project*. Her monograph, *The Making of Samuel Beckett's 'Play'/'Film'*, was published with UPA/Bloomsbury in 2019. Her second monograph, *Postcognitivist Beckett*, came out in 2020 as part of the new *Elements in Beckett Studies* Series (Cambridge University Press).

Patrick Bixby is Associate Professor of English at Arizona State University and Resident Director of the University Studies Abroad Consortium Summer School at NUI Galway. He has published widely in the areas of Irish studies, modernist studies and mobility studies; his next book is *License to Travel: A Cultural History of the Passport*.

María José Carrera is a Lecturer in Irish Literature at the University of Valladolid, Spain. She has published mainly on Samuel Beckett's short prose and his English translations of poetry in Spanish, with a special focus on the manuscript notes the author took in preparation for those translations. Dr Carrera has published in refereed international journals like *Samuel Beckett Today/Aujourd'hui* and is currently preparing a monograph study on his English translation of *Antología de poesía mexicana* (*An Anthology of Mexican Poetry*, 1958).

Fábio de Souza Andrade is Associate Professor of Literary Theory and Comparative Literature at the University of São Paulo. He has published extensively on Brazilian and European Modernism, regularly reviewing fiction and poetry for Brazilian cultural periodicals. His publications on Samuel Beckett include 'Facing other Windows: Beckett in Brazil', in S. E. Gontarski (ed), *The Edinburgh Companion to Samuel Beckett and the Arts* (Edinburgh University Press, 2014), *Samuel Beckett: o Silêncio Possível* (Ateliê, 2001), as well as many articles. He has translated *Waiting for Godot, Endgame, Happy Days, Murphy* and *Watt* into Brazilian Portuguese and is presently working on the translation of Beckett's complete dramatic works.

Amanda Dennis is Assistant Professor of Comparative Literature and English at the American University of Paris. Her book, *Beckett and Embodiment: Body, Space, Agency*, is forthcoming from Edinburgh University Press in summer 2021. She co-edited the recent volume *Samuel Beckett and the Nonhuman* (Brill, 2020) and her articles have appeared in the *Journal of Modern Literature*, the *Journal of Beckett Studies* and *Samuel Beckett Today/Aujourd'hui*, among other places. She has held fellowships and visiting lectureships in France, the US, the UK and Spain, and she is the author of the novel, *Her Here* (2021).

Matthijs Engelberts is based at the University of Amsterdam, where his current research is centred on aspects of mediality in modern literature and other narrative art media. His publications include books, edited volumes and articles on Beckett, surrealist theatre, the contemporary drama text, Houellebecq, Duras, theatre sports, Molière, and other authors, mainly those working at the intersections of literature and cinema or theatre. He also contributed to the debate on the 'value of literature' (*Poétique*, 2018) and is one of the chief editors of *Samuel Beckett Today/Aujourd'hui*.

José Francisco Fernández is Senior Lecturer in English Literature at the University of Almería, Spain. His most recent work focuses on the narrative of Samuel Beckett and his reception in Spain: *Samuel Beckett en España* (University of Valladolid, 2020). He has co-edited (with Nadia Louar) Vol. 30 of *Samuel Beckett Today/Aujourd'hui* (2018), devoted to the poetics of bilingualism in Samuel Beckett. He has also translated into Spanish three novels and three separate short stories by Samuel Beckett. His translation of *Stories and Texts for Nothing* was awarded with the 2016 Best Translation Award by the Spanish Association for Anglo-American Studies. He teaches Anglo-Irish literature in the master's degree in English Studies at the Spanish Distance Education University (UNED) and has been general editor of the journal *Estudios Irlandeses*. He has published articles on Beckett's work in a number of specialised journals, including the *Journal of Beckett Studies, Journal of the Short Story in English, Babel, Anglia, AUMLA* and *Studi Irlandesi*, among others.

Gabriele Frasca (1957) is a poet, novelist and translator. He has published the following collections of poems: *Rame* (1984), *Lime* (1995), *Rive* (2001) and *Rimi* (2013); the novels *Il fermo volere* (1987), *Santa Mira* (2001) and *Dai cancelli d'acciaio* (2011); the collection of plays *Tele* (1998); and the essays *Cascando. Tre studi su Samuel Beckett* (1988), *La furia della sintassi. La sestina in Italia* (1992), *La scimmia di Dio. L'emozione della guerra mediale* (1996), *La lettera che muore. La «letteratura» nel reticolo mediale* (2005), *L'oscuro scrutare di Philip K. Dick* (2007), *Un quanto di erotia. Gadda con Freud e Schrödinger* (2011) and *Joyicity. Joyce con McLuhan e Lacan* (2013). He has translated Philip K. Dick (*A Scanner Darkly*, 1993 and 1998) and Samuel Beckett (*Watt*, 1998; *Collected Poems*, 1999; *Murphy*, 2003 and *Nohow On*, 2008) into Italian. Gabriele Frasca teaches Comparative Studies at the University of Salerno.

Alan W. Friedman is Thaman Professor of English and Comparative Literature at the University of Texas at Austin. He specialises in modern British, Irish, and American literature, the novel, and Shakespearean drama. He is the author of *Fictional Death and the Modernist Enterprise* (1995) and *Party Pieces: Oral Narrative and Social Performance in Joyce and Beckett* (2007). His most recent book is *Surreal Beckett: Samuel Beckett, James Joyce, and Surrealism* (2019). Edited books include *Beckett Translating/Translating Beckett* (1987) (co-editor) and *Beckett in Black and Red: The Translations for Nancy Cunard's Negro (1934)* (2000). He has co-edited four special journal issues on Joyce and Beckett.

Mar Garre García graduated in English Studies at the University of Almería in 2016. In 2017, she obtained her MA in English Literature and Linguistics at the University of Granada, specialising in both disciplines. Between 2018 and 2019 she collaborated with the area of English Philology at the University of Almería as a Young Researcher, in association with the I+D+i project FFI2016-76477-P 'Samuel Beckett and the Spanish Translations of his Work: A Research into the Reception of a Bilingual Writer'. Mar Garre is currently working as a Gerty Cori fellow at the University of Almería, where she combines teaching tasks with her doctoral dissertation on Samuel Beckett's poetry: 'Evolutive Analysis of Samuel Beckett's Poetry: Towards a Definition of Beckettian Poetics'. Her publications include articles on Beckett's poems in *Beckettiana, Complutense Journal of English Studies* and *Babel Afial*, among other journals.

Antoni Libera (1949) is a Polish writer, translator, literary critic, and theatre director. He graduated from Warsaw University and received his doctorate from the Polish Academy of Sciences. From 1976 onwards he was in close contact with Samuel Beckett, who advised him and gave him many production tips, and called him his 'ambassador' in Eastern Europe. Libera has translated all of

Beckett's dramas, part of his prose work, and also essays and poems. In Poland he produced Beckett's plays in theatres and for television. He has also staged Beckett's plays in the original in London, Dublin and Melbourne, among other venues. He has also translated into Polish works by Sophocles, Shakespeare, Kavafis, Oscar Wilde, and opera libretti.

Waqas Mirza is a Lecturer in French at St Catherine's College, Oxford and a doctoral student in Modern Languages at Lincoln College, Oxford. He has previously held teaching positions at Swiss state schools, the Ashmolean Museum, and Lincoln College. Waqas's doctoral thesis explores self-translation in Samuel Beckett's artistic process. It compares the English and French versions of *Molloy*, *Malone Meurt*, and *L'Innommable* by examining how self-translation affects the representation of the character's mind and consciousness. On a broader note, his research interests include French and English literature, the representation of the mind and consciousness in the arts, literary bilingualism and self-translation, Hip Hop studies, imperial history, material culture and museum studies.

Shane O'Neill is a Government of Ireland, Irish Research Council funded doctoral candidate at Mary Immaculate College, University of Limerick. His research is published or forthcoming in *Samuel Beckett Today/Aujourd'hui* as well as in the edited collection *The Golden Thread: Irish Women Playwrights (1716–2016)*. His reviews appear in *The Beckett Circle*. O'Neill's fiction can be found in various literary journals and his writing has been broadcast on RTÉ Radio One. His play *Kebabs and Hookers* was produced in Smock Alley as part of Scene + Heard Festival 2020.

John Pilling is Emeritus Professor of English and European Literature, University of Reading, UK. He is the editor of *Collected Poems of Samuel Beckett* (with Seán Lawlor) (Faber, 2012), and the author of *Samuel Beckett's More Pricks Than Kicks: In a Strait of Two Wills* (Bloomsbury, 2010); *A Samuel Beckett Chronology* (Palgrave Macmillan, 2006); *A Companion to "Dream of Fair to Middling Women"* (Journal of Beckett Studies Books, 2004); and *Beckett Before Godot* (Cambridge University Press, 1997). He has published numerous essays in *Journal of Beckett Studies* since 1976, in *Samuel Beckett Today/Aujourd'hui* since 1998, and in more than a dozen published symposia and collections over the last forty years. A study of Beckett's prose between 1945 and 1955 provisionally entitled *Strange Journeys* is in preparation. See also: *Fifty Modern European Poets* (Heinemann, 1994), *The Rilke of Ruth Speirs* (Two Rivers Press, 2015; with Peter Robinson), and essays in *PN Review* covering a wide range of topics (1978–2009).

Martin Schauss is an IRC-funded Postdoctoral Research Fellow in the School of English, Drama and Film at University College Dublin. His research project, 'The New Ecological Imaginary: Waste, Water, Energy, and the Built Environment in Twenty-First Century Experimental Prose' looks at experimental languages as a response to eco-political crisis. His wider research teases out political and historical connections between twentieth- and twenty-first-century literatures, material environments, resources and the nonhuman. Martin has a PhD in English and Comparative Literary Studies from the University of Warwick. His thesis, 'Like a Thing Forsaken: Beckett, Sebald and the Politics of Materiality' (2019), explored materiality, objects, and thingness in the works of Beckett and Sebald. Recent publications include '"With an Eye to Their Later Existence as Ruins": Language, Materiality and the Ruin in the Work of W.G. Sebald' in *Critique: Studies in Contemporary Fiction* (2021) and '"Such density of furniture defeats imagination": Beckett's Postwar Room and the Inheritance of Things' in *Modernist Objects: Literature, Art, Culture* (Clemson University Press, 2021).

Sławomir Studniarz, Associate Professor, is a Polish scholar, and has been a faculty member at the University of Warmia and Mazury in Olsztyn since 2003, where he gives lectures in American literature and conducts BA and MA seminars. He has published three monographs and several articles on Edgar Allan Poe, including two essays on his poetry published in *The Edgar Allan Poe Review*. He is also the author of numerous articles on other American writers. His recent articles are concerned with the fiction of Paul Auster. He has also written on the poetry of Samuel Beckett: 'Beckett's early verse and the Modernist long poem: A study of "Enueg I"', published in *The Journal of Beckett Studies*, and '*Echo's Bones* and Samuel Beckett's Early Aesthetics: "The Vulture", "Alba" and "Dortmunder" as Poetic Manifestos', published in *Estudios Irlandeses*. His latest book publications are the monograph on Poe's poetry *The Time-Transcending Poetry of Edgar Allan Poe* published by Mellen Press in 2016, and *Narrative Framing in Contemporary American Novels* published by Cambridge Scholars in May 2017.

Erika Tophoven has been a freelance translator of literature since 1956. She has rendered, with Elmar Tophoven, more than one hundred titles from French or English into German, most importantly, the works of Samuel Beckett and authors of the Nouveau Roman. Her publications on Beckett's German connections include a transcription of part of his German Diaries, *Becketts Berlin* (2005) and *Godot hinter Gittern* (2015). Her book on the Tophovens' translation experiences, *Glückliche Jahre: Übersetzerleben in Paris*, appeared in 2011.

Dirk Van Hulle is Professor of Bibliography and Modern Book History at the University of Oxford, chair of the Oxford Centre for Textual Editing and Theory (OCTET) and director of the Centre for Manuscript Genetics at the University of Antwerp. With Mark Nixon, he is co-director of the *Beckett Digital Manuscript Project* (www.beckettarchive.org), series editor of the Cambridge University Press series 'Elements in Beckett Studies' and editor of the *Journal of Beckett Studies*. His publications include *Textual Awareness* (2004), *Modern Manuscripts* (2014), *Samuel Beckett's Library* (2013, with Mark Nixon), *The New Cambridge Companion to Samuel Beckett* (2015), *James Joyce's Work in Progress* (2016), the *Beckett Digital Library*, a number of volumes in the 'Making of' series (Bloomsbury) and genetic editions in the *Beckett Digital Manuscript Project*, which won the 2019 Prize for a Bibliography, Archive or Digital Project of the Modern Language Association (MLA).

Pim Verhulst is a postdoctoral researcher and teaching assistant at the University of Antwerp. He has published various articles in *Samuel Beckett Today / Aujourd'hui*, *La revue des lettres modernes*, *Genetic Joyce Studies* and the *Journal of Beckett Studies*, of which he was an assistant editor from 2014 to 2020. His book chapters have appeared in *Beckett and BBC Radio* (Palgrave 2017), *Beckett and Modernism* (Palgrave 2018, co-edited), *Pop Beckett* (Ibidem 2019) and *Beckett and World Literature* (Bloomsbury 2020). He is the co-author and co-editor of the *Molloy, Malone meurt / Malone Dies* and *En attendant Godot / Waiting for Godot* modules in the Beckett Digital Manuscript Project (www.beckettarchive.org), of which he is also an editorial board member and which received a Prize from the Modern Language Association (MLA) in 2016–2017. His monograph *The Making of Samuel Beckett's Radio Plays* is forthcoming with Bloomsbury and University Press Antwerp in the BDMP series.

Introduction

José Francisco Fernández and Mar Garre García

There is no doubt as to the vitality of Beckett Studies in the new millennium. In the words of Anthony Uhlmann, there exists 'an ecosystem of creative activity named Beckett that remains very much alive' (Uhlmann 2018: xiii). A growing surge of interest around the world for this austere and enigmatic Irish author who avoided public exposure and who wrote equally in English and French might seem surprising if it were not for the fact that he provided the template – in his bluntness and in his precise description of the void that surrounds human existence – for the posthuman times in which we currently live. New and updated editions of companions and readers of his work are regularly published, such is the demand for explanations that his writing continues to generate. The now-established structure of these collections of essays around Beckett is exemplary in their attempt to leave no aspect of his literary production unaddressed. Let us take, for instance, *Samuel Beckett in Context* (2013), edited by Anthony Uhlmann. The admirable scope of this book well illustrates the contemporary ambition of leaving no stone unturned, examining as it does virtually anything that may provide 'new and illuminating ways of addressing Beckett's oeuvre and our changing relationships with it', as P. J. Murphy (2016: 16) wrote in another notable collection published in recent years. In Professor Uhlmann's edition of collected essays, geographical landscapes connected to Beckett's life are visited, social and political contexts are examined, literary movements that the author frequented at some point of his career are studied, as are the assortment of foreign literatures with which he was acquainted. A variety of artistic forms (painting, music, cinema . . .) are examined, and the established systems of knowledge in Western thought of interest to Beckett are also considered, ranging from the Bible to mathematics. As befits so comprehensive a volume, a section is devoted to Beckett's peculiar handling of language, and additional chapters examine the importance of his letters and manuscripts for a full understanding of his work. The paradox of this and other similar volumes lies in that such a wide variety of approaches is needed to study the writing of an author who tended towards silence, who reduced the language of literature to its minimal expression. It is as if only by making broad circles of the area containing Beckett's literary production can the elusive meaning of his novels, poems and plays be pinned down. The combination of critical perspectives, therefore, is what distinguishes contemporary publications on Beckett. As Dirk Van Hulle puts it in a new edition of the Cambridge Companion devoted to the 1969 Nobel Prize winner: 'what makes Beckett studies so vibrant today is the interaction among different approaches, ranging from theory to contextual, historical and archival research' (Van Hulle 2015: xviii).

One of the aforementioned perspectives that has been consolidated in Beckett criticism is the study of his lifelong practice of translation, both of his own work and that of others. Invariably, a chapter on this facet of his oeuvre finds its way into every manual in which the broad scope of his work is embraced. Indeed, over time, more and more attention has been paid to Beckett's unique brand of bilingualism. The ease with which he was able to switch languages seems to underline the belief that his creative realm was not really English or French, but rather that 'perilous zone' in between, in the words of Van Hulle (2008: 99), the tension generated by 'every deletion, every variant . . . in the life of the text'. Recent developments in Beckett studies, however, suggest that this is not just an ancillary feature of his activity, but a central aspect of his essence as a writer, one of the pillars of his poetics and a method to engage in a practical and fruitful way with his texts: 'the structure of translation' notes Erika Mihálycsa, 'is embedded in his work, written in whichever language, even in the earlier English-language texts that precede the birth of the bilingual *oeuvre*' (Mihálycsa 2013: 343). This view is certainly endorsed in the present collection of essays, *Samuel Beckett and Translation*, and in what follows, the main guiding principles for the collection will be set out.

At the beginning of his impressive bilingual edition of Samuel Beckett's *Comment c'est/How It Is*, Edouard Magessa O'Reilly claims that *Comment c'est* 'could probably only have been written by someone for whom French was a second language' (O'Reilly 2016: ix). What he means is that the stylistic arrangement of the fragments and the distortion applied to the syntax in this novel is inimical to the French literary tradition and to French discourse in general. Only an outsider, it is implied, could have been bold enough to write in French in that way. Extending the argument further, it might be possible to wonder whether the whole of Beckett's literary production could have been written by anyone without his extensive knowledge of a second language. Equally, only someone with a daring vision, verging on recklessness, would have taken the risk of presenting almost the totality of his writings in two languages. Indeed, it is reasonable to imagine that if Beckett had not been a bilingual author, the shape of his work would have been quite different. Take, for instance, Beckett's most famous play, *En attendant Godot*, which he translated into English in two periods during 1953 (May–June and November–December). The act of translation became an occasion for revision. At the time, he was also working with Elmar Tophoven, and the translation into German left its mark on the final text in English: 'Since he had now seen the play performed multiple times, in French and in German, and having revised translations of it in German and Spanish, naturally this prolonged exposure affected the English version' (Van Hulle and Verhulst 2017: 278). Translation was, therefore, very much part of the creative process, even becoming a source for metaphors and images throughout his work: 'Beckett's trademark of unidentifiable voices pervading the whole of his fictional and dramatic landscapes' (Louar 2014: E115) can be seen in his practice of translation.

The intimate relationship between the two versions of all of his works, translated by himself in most of the cases; the way they both complement and diverge from each other; the way the translation into one language influences the original version; the palimpsestic quality of many of his books . . . all of this leads us to think that the origin of Beckett's strangeness and profound originality lies, for the most part, in his work at the intersection of English and French. This volume certainly capitalises on the rising awareness of and interest in translation for Beckett studies and aims to offer new approaches to lines of enquiry concerning Beckett's bilingualism, along with the associated areas of translation, self-translation and translation as a poetics. The contributions herein, then, aim to highlight the nuances, contradictions and intricacies that lie behind what for many years was considered an exotic feature of the Irish writer.

What has really generated an interest in translation within Beckett studies as a solid line of enquiry is the realisation that the more we know about it, the more questions arise. Thanks to the publication of his letters and other manuscript evidence, there now exists quite precise knowledge as to the date on which Beckett composed each of his works and also when he began their translation into English or French (simultaneously, immediately after composition, or long after). There are also rigorous studies that examine what elements he introduced or deleted in each case. The 'mirror canon or self-translation canon' which, according to Van Hulle, exists 'next to what Ruby Cohn called *A Beckett Canon*' (Van Hulle 2015: xxv), has been properly classified, together with the list of works by other authors that he rendered into French or English. Hence, it can be safely assumed that an understanding of the extraordinary nature of his status as a bilingual writer is beginning to gain ground. The fundamental aspects of his artistry have been aptly summarised by Corinne Scheiner, among others, stating that Beckett is responsible for a fully bilingual corpus, that he wrote in both languages throughout his life, and that he is considered an integral part of two different traditions and cultures. However, the matter is far from being settled. Nothing so simply stated as the following description of Beckett's scope in literature can fail to resonate with possibilities for research: 'Beckett actually created four different sets of texts: those written in English, those written in French, the French translations and the English translations' (Scheiner 2013: 370). He nurtured his writing through the frictional force of these spheres and actively endowed his discourse with the traces left by the bidirectional movement of words between languages. We are dealing with 'two texts united by their similarities, but always differentiated by their language' (Astbury 2008: 189), or, as Rainier Grutman has put it in a most revealing image, Beckett's oeuvre is 'a diptych with parallel panels in each of his two languages' (Grutman 2013: 196). Beckett took pains to maintain the connections between each set of texts and strove to open the languages he worked with so that sounds, patterns and semantic associations could travel freely and nourish new settings. Bilingualism in Beckett, argues Anne Beer, 'functioned as a medium for artistic self-renewal' (Beer 1994: 210). That is why it is necessary to speak of a poetics of bilingualism or self-translation as one of the motives that make his texts work: 'More than an activity, the process of translation and the manipulation of two languages is part of his poetic inspiration' (Almeida and Veras 2017: 103).

However complete the catalogue of works written and translated by Beckett is, even a cursory review makes it clear that this was far from a mechanical process. The object of study becomes gradually more complex when it transpires that many factors were at work in each case. From a psychoanalytical point of view, Patrick J. Casement argues that when Beckett translated from French, he was able to address personal issues that he could not deal with in his native language, particularly the tensions generated by the suffocating influence of his mother. He also points out that only when Beckett's mother died could he render his writings in French into English: 'Maybe the work of translation included working at this delayed confrontation with himself' (Casement 1982: 41). This would explain, in Casement's view, that the English versions are usually far livelier and more playful than the French originals, although in fact many exceptions can be found if this proposition is subjected to scrutiny.

There is also the question of Joyce. If it is true that 'Writing-as-translation is very much at the heart of Joyce's artistic endeavour' (Wawrzycka 2010: 516), it remains to be explored how much Beckett's practice of translation was due to the example set by his mentor, what he learnt from Joyce and in what sense he tried to supersede him by maintaining a habit that continued for a lifetime. In his contribution to this volume, Pim Verhulst suggests that writing in English continued to connect Beckett to Joyce's linguistic exuberance. Curiously enough, when he translated the radio play *Embers/Cendres* into French, by paring down words and by weakening the stylistic effect of the text, it 'served as a strategy to better defend himself against the danger of Joycean wordplay'. There are, thus, various fruitful and challenging areas of enquiry here that are important to clarify in what is still a fairly recent field of research.

What we know for certain is that Beckett did not follow a fixed course of action in the act of (self)translating, and hence it is impossible to state general rules. Apart from the peculiarities of the work he was turning into English or French, there was also the question of the very medium he was using, the demands imposed by each language: 'What if Beckett's lengthier writing in French language was constrained by language itself?' – Waqas Mirza asks in his contribution to the present volume. 'What if it was a reaction to this "weakening effect", which required him to be more explicit, which required him to write *more* in French?' As Lance St John Butler has aptly noted, 'It was the languages that wrote him, not he the languages' (Butler 1994: 131).

As a tentative synopsis, we might say that when translating his own work, Beckett was doing something other than writing his texts in one language and making them available in another. He was, on the one hand, stating the unfinished quality of his writing. On the other, he opened language to multiple possibilities of interpretation. Seen in this way, when the whole process of translation is problematised, it becomes a methodological approach with enormous potential, because an individual analysis is required for the study of each specific work: 'All this should caution us against the idea that, with Beckett, the relationship of text to translation is constant and reliable, or that a general poetics of Beckett's translation work may be inferred from any particular text. Each pair of texts is a *cas d'espèce*' (Long 1996: 315). By translating his own writing, Beckett was clearly indicating the kind of writer that he wanted to be. Regardless of the numerous reasons that he adduced for doing this (his dislike for others handling his work or the ominous prospect of time wasted revising someone else's translations), he was anchoring his work in the realm of indeterminacy. No one version is to be deemed more original than the other: both are to be considered equally valid. Although each one should be sufficient for

an understanding of his particular cosmology, the perspectives of interpretation that open up in a new version may amplify the meaning contained in the
first original, which is something liberating and truly innovative. By translating his own work, he was issuing a statement of intent similar to a declaration
of principles: he was advocating the porosity of language and the multiple
resonance of written expression.

Ever since the emergence of Beckett criticism in the 1950s, the author's
double allegiance to English and French has been of interest, appearing first
in the form of discreet remarks in reviews and early critical appreciations. The
fact that he was considered as both an Irish author who wrote in English and as
a foreigner who was part of the canon of French postwar literature testifies to
the intermediate position among languages and cultures that he occupied since
his narrative and theatrical works gained worldwide attention. That he also
translated most of his plays or novels into one or the other language was also
considered a curious feature of his artistry. Early studies on Beckett and translation focused on the differences that could be found between the two versions
of a work. In her pioneering article 'Samuel Beckett Self-Translator' (1961),
Ruby Cohn, for instance, observed that there were far more obscenities in
the author's translation into French of his 1938 novel *Murphy* than in the first
version written in English. Cohn's article is relevant since through the analysis
it transpires that no consistent pattern could be discerned in Beckett's translations of his own texts; sometimes he added more things when translating,
whereas deletion was sometimes the norm. The first mappings of Beckett and
translation, then, revealed an unstable terrain with blurred boundaries which
defied entry into his work by scholars and yet, at the same time, it was too vast
a territory to ignore.

The first notable study on Beckett and translation appeared in 1987, co-
edited by one of the contributors to our present volume, Alan W. Friedman.
With the benefit of hindsight, *Beckett Translating/Translating Beckett* reads now
as if the different participants had jumped to the conclusion that Beckett's
bilingualism and (self)translation simply demanded a central placement in
Beckett's criticism: 'How can one write a biography of Samuel Beckett and
totally ignore these fundamental aspects? This baffles me.' wrote Raymond
Federman in the opening chapter of the collection (Federman 1987: 8). The
questions that he asked himself regarding the role of translation in Beckett's
writing can still act as a guide for the student of the author's bilingual output:
'Is Beckett's French simpler than his English? Is Beckett funnier in French
than in English? Is he more poetic in English than in French? Is Beckett more
vulgar, more scatological, more blasphemous in French than in English? Are
there more cultural and literary references in English than in French? And

what happens to these references, allusions, quotations, misquotations, when they pass from one language to the other? Is Beckett's French more slangish than his English?' (Federman 1987: 8). Indeed, throughout the decades that followed, dozens of articles focused precisely on answering the kinds of questions posed by Federman in his seminal chapter. The idea that gradually imposed itself was that for a full study of Beckett's creativity, the analysis of just a single version – as if the other member of the pair, normally translated by the author himself, did not exist – was essentially untenable. This is the principle taken as the basis for another influential study published a year after Alan W. Friedman's book. In *Beckett and Babel* (1988), Brian T. Fitch stated: 'It is my belief that the study of a bilingual corpus inevitably involves, for the critic, certain methodological considerations that cannot be ignored without completely betraying the work in question. In other words, I maintain that whatever the critical approach and procedures that are adopted for the analysis of a particular unilingual work, these cannot in themselves prove adequate for the analysis of Beckett's work' (Fitch 1988: 12). It is interesting to detect in the essays on Beckett and translation that were published in subsequent years an echo of this recently discovered truth, namely, that each version in a Beckett pair had a dynamic of its own; yet the series of interconnections between the two versions also merits due attention, in that the two pieces are complementary. It was as if through such repetition that the study of Beckett's writings was heading for a new turn. Let us recall, for example, Julian Garforth describing Beckett's translations of his theatre plays into German, in the capacity of supervisor of the work of Elmar Tophoven: 'More importantly, each text exists in its own right, providing significant linguistic and stylistic variants. Merely to describe one as a "translation" of another seems to be doing an injustice, both to Beckett and Tophoven' (Garforth 1996: 63).

In the decades around the turn of the millennium, a number of studies emerged, mainly in the form of research articles in specialised journals, that examined individual cases of Beckett's translations and the implications that this had in the interpretation of the particular novel or play in question. However, the coming of age for Beckett translation studies occurred in 2011 with the publication of Sinéad Mooney's *A Tongue Not Mine*. For a start, Mooney's book is systematic, in that she catalogues, analyses and explores the whole translational activity of the author throughout his life, from the early French-to-English texts for avant-garde journals in Paris in the early 1930s, to his self-translations of late texts. Such ample coverage of his bilingual work allows Mooney to consider Beckett's role as a translator as his true self: 'recoiling from the role of omniscient author, he projected for himself instead an image of authorial impoverishment, indigence, and impotence, a diminished authority more akin to the conventionally "invisible" second-order role of the translator' (Mooney 2011: 1).

The characteristic and widely noted strangeness of Beckett's work, might thus be traced back to his awareness of the multidirectional nature of language and the certainty that every time we speak and write we are handling somebody else's words. This is the uncertain territory in which Beckett set his creative universe. 'His texts' meanings are intimately bound up with their exceptional meta-linguistic position astride two languages, and his recognition of translation's systematic and inevitable infidelity' (Mooney 2011: 3–4). In her study, Mooney reveals how much of the rootless quality of Beckett's writing stems from the practice of translation: one of the main assets of her book lies in the discovery of traces or 'textual birthmarks' (Mooney 2011: 67) from a previous language that can be found under the surface of almost every Beckett text.

In developing a rationale for *Samuel Beckett and Translation* we are greatly indebted to Mooney's groundbreaking monograph. In her book, she argues that both the study of translation and the reading of Beckett 'involve a willingness to suspend a tendency to believe in textual surfaces, in linguistic "housedness" and monolithic works of art'; this activity, she claims, being 'a fruitfully uncomfortable affair' (Mooney 2011: 25). In our present collection, we want to immerse the reader in this abrupt territory identified by Mooney. Once the systematic knowledge of Beckett's translation has been mapped out, our aim is to explore the contradictions and the inconsistencies that remain to be analysed. Beckettian translation, described by Mooney, constitutes 'a form of narrative rupture' (Mooney 2011: 25) in his work, and the essays in this book are fuelled by a desire to carefully unpick established assumptions and in this way contribute to new readings of Beckett that may add complexity to an already multilayered work. If we follow, for instance, the arguments developed by Olga Beloborodova in Chapter 2 of the book, 'Tracing Translation: The Genesis of *Comédie* and *Film*', her findings resonate with a transgressive spirit: 'Still, despite a clear bias towards the visual and the abstraction in the originals, Beckett did invest a lot of effort in translating both texts . . . their self-translation often results in enhancement and enrichment rather than impoverishment'. Likewise, in Chapter 8, 'Translation's Challenge to Lyric's Immediacy: Beckett's Rimbaud', Amanda Dennis revisits one of Beckett's most accomplished translations of another author, his English version of Arthur Rimbaud's 'Le Bateau ivre', and looks beyond what other critics have said about it. It is well-known that in 'Drunken Boat' (published in 1976) Beckett 'combined a faithful translation of the poem with an audacious rendering into English. He scrupulously respected the lines which could be translated with full effect, yet gave free rein to his creative impulse when literal translation proved inadequate' (Fernández 2018: 136). Little, it might seem, is necessary to add to existing analyses of this translation by scholars such as Gerald Macklin and Damian Love. However, Dennis detects a tone of ironic distance on the part of the translator towards the French poet's apparent insouciance with regard to his society and the French literary tradition.

To mention one further example of the kind of break from stereotypical representations of Beckett and translation that we have sought to present in the chapters of this volume, Dirk Van Hulle offers a startling approach to understand translation in Beckett in Chapter 11, 'A Poetics of the Doppelgänger: Beckett as Self-Translator'. The motif of the double in Beckett has been studied extensively, but it has never been applied to the study of his versions in two languages. When he slightly modified an original poem, for example, the second text became a kind of non-identity that undermined the notion of self. This is the kind of one-step-further approach that the present collection aims to achieve, continuing the examination of Beckett's translations from the point that Mooney's seminal monograph had already taken it.

After the publication of *A Tongue Not Mine*, the existence of a solid approach, based on translation, towards the understanding of Beckett's work became an established fact. It was the beginning of specialised research which explored hitherto unknown collaborative work or which analysed Beckett's decisions when translating. In 2018, Nadia Louar, of the University of Wisconsin–Oshkosh, and José Francisco Fernández, one of the coordinators of the present collection, edited a special issue of *Samuel Beckett Today/ Aujourd'hui* 30 (2018) on *The Poetics of Bilingualism in the Work of Samuel Beckett*, in which they reiterated the need to explore new lines of enquiry that had opened up, thanks to new developments in Beckett research and translation: 'At the heart of this volume', they stated in the introduction, 'lies the idea that Beckett's bilingualism implies not only the comings and goings between the two main languages of the writer's composition, French and English, but also all the other forms of passage that characterise his creative journey as an author, translator, poet, playwright and director' (Louar and Fernández 2018: 1). In fact, 'Beckett's linguistic restlessness', they claimed, triggered 'the comings and goings between different genres and different media' (Louar and Fernández 2018: 1). The celebration of the 5th International Conference of the Samuel Beckett Society at the University of Almería, Spain, on 9–11 May 2019, did much to consolidate this state of opinion. That event was entitled *Samuel Beckett and Translation* and scholars from around the world sought to answer questions such as 'How does Beckett sound in other languages?', 'What is the approach followed by translators of his work?', and

'Are the words in a Beckett text resilient enough to endure the transposition of languages?'

Our current collection, *Samuel Beckett and Translation*, shares the same international and multidisciplinary spirit of the Almería conference and contains contributions by scholars from different continents in an attempt to ascertain how the 'waves of innovative energy' released by Beckett's bilingualism, in the words of Anne Beer (1994: 209), inform the intricacies of his literary production.

The book is divided into four parts and comprises thirteen academic papers by scholars from various universities around the world, plus four short pieces in which translators of his work and a leading scholar in Beckett Studies reflect on what it means to translate Beckett.

The realm of Beckett's self-translations is explored in Part I. In the opening essay, Shane O'Neill reveals the subtlety that Beckett applied to his translation from English into French of *Not I/Pas moi*. O'Neill recreates the author's act of translation in three successive drafts so that 'the original text's breathlessness and its complex rhythmic patterns' could be replicated in the second language. Keeping the frantic pace of English in French was paramount for the author, so that if there was an excess of words in the translations of certain expressions, or if the sounds in French produced a different effect from the original, Beckett kept on working, looking for a better solution. It is very revealing how, according to O'Neill, Beckett himself opted for 'Beckettian' terms, as if his work with the language generated its own critical discourse.

The need to analyse each problem individually is forcefully suggested in the second chapter, by Olga Beloborodova. She argues that in the case of *Play* and *Film*, texts belonging to Beckett's mature period and which he translated from English to French, he did not follow the path of austerity that has been always considered his trademark. On the contrary, as we have already noted, he produced much richer versions in the second language, adding intertextual elements and additional resonances that were not there at the moment of original composition. This is especially prescient in that it reminds us that aspects surrounding Beckett's life should also be taken into account when studying the author's two versions of a particular text. In the case of *Play/Comédie*, Beckett's translation was influenced by the play's premiere in Germany. Changes he made when preparing the manuscript for performance can be correlated to the final version of the piece in English and French. With regard to his only incursion into film, the self-imposed obligation to translate the script was an opportunity to revise the original text and to make changes which otherwise he would have not done.

In the third chapter, as if following the lead taken by Beloborodova, Waqas Mirza confirms that 'the study of Beckett's translation process is far from being an exact science'. His paper deals with the study of personal pronouns in French and English. Using examples from *Molloy* as a cue in each version, Mirza shows how in the French original the narrator is much more assertive than in the English one. Because of the nature of the grammatical systems in the two languages, English readers may feel that they are closer to the narrative voice, the fragmentation of self allowing for the inclusion of the reader, while this is not possible in the French version. Translation is, thus, considered a point of entry into Beckett's ontological concerns.

Chapter 4 applies the same inquisitive spirit of the previous essays to Beckett's poetry, a genre which in Beckett's case has not frequently been addressed from the perspective of translation. Sławomir Studniarz brings into sharp focus the differences between the French and the English versions of a number of poems written by Beckett in the period immediately before and after the Second World War. His conclusions leave little room for ambiguity: the verbal texture, the acoustic correspondences and even the semantic echoes are more subtle, profound and carefully crafted in the original French than in the author's translations into his mother tongue. Studniarz pays special attention to sound patterns, demonstrating that the richness and sophistication achieved by Beckett in French were not maintained in the English translation. The final chapter in Part I, by Pim Verhulst, is a study of Robert Pinget's translation of one of Beckett's pieces for radio, plus Beckett's role in the translation process. Verhulst examines the case of *Embers/Cendres* which, by its very definition ('collaborative self-translation'), reveals how intricate the catalogue of Beckett's versions in a second language can be. Through an exhaustive study of the documents that survive (mainly manuscripts and letters) Verhulst explores the process of translation of his text from English into French. While Robert Pinget proved to be an efficient translator, Beckett nevertheless revised his friend's work and modified the script, always bearing in mind that it was a text meant to be listened to. Verhulst reveals the added difficulty of working on Beckett's translations, in that it is not always possible to identify the changes made by Beckett or by his collaborators. In any case, what is certain in the case of *Cendres* is that Beckett removed expressions that simply did not work for him, and he toned down the strength of the images introduced by Pinget. The resulting paradox, Verhulst claims, is that it was the author who tampered with the text, 'significantly altering its hermeneutic potential'.

As regards Beckett's translation of other people's work, all accounts, including the chapters in Part II of this book, confirm that when dealing with the texts written by others, Beckett was diligent, pragmatic, efficient and, in many cases, brilliant. He was able to be imaginative and bold when the situation required, and he showed the ability to set aside expected solutions and to reach for the most striking and dazzling alternatives. Cecilia Weddell, for instance, has studied his translations of Mexican poetry in depth, and has coined the expression 'Beckett-ification', meaning the process by which he did not allow certain expressions to enter his texts, at the same time introducing certain changes that suited 'his particular idiom' (Weddell 2020: 207). As far as possible, and within the limits imposed by the source text, he tried to modulate his translations of other writers' work to his own interest, worldview or ethics. Here also translation was never the act of simply putting the same words in a different register; he involved himself in every aspect of translation.

The first two chapters in Part II focus on Beckett's work with poems in the Spanish language: an extraordinary but usually neglected facet of his translation work. In Chapter 6, Patrick Bixby examines a precedent of Beckett's 'Mexican poems': specifically, his rendering into English of 'Recado terrestre', a poem on Goethe by Nobel prize winner Gabriela Mistral. At that time in his career, in the late 1940s, Beckett was aware of the power of translation to modulate the meaning transmitted in the source text, or at least to enter into a subtle dialogue with its author. In the case of 'Message from Earth', Bixby demonstrates that Beckett maintained a critical distance from Goethe's ideals regarding the value of humanism, as reflected in Mistral's original poem. In her verse, Mistral entreats the great German author to come to earth again and renew a faith in mankind, which had been lost after the devastating experience of the Second World War. Beckett reduced the positive expectations implied by the Chilean author and showed, instead, a veiled scepticism on the beneficial powers of Goethe's influence. For her part, in Chapter 7, María José Carrera asks how much Beckett was aware of Mexican culture in his translation of the anthology compiled by Octavio Paz and commissioned by UNESCO, finally published by Indiana University Press in 1958. As her object of study, Carrera chooses a group of haikus written by avant-garde poet José Juan Tablada which were included in the *Anthology of Mexican Poetry*. As usual, Beckett was far from being a literal translator and infused his versions with his own flavour. He strove to maintain the sonic patterns of the original poems and, most importantly, he reinforced their political meanings, unearthing references to the Spanish conquest that otherwise would have remained unnoticed.

In Chapter 8, as noted above, Amanda Dennis examines one of Beckett's most celebrated translations, Arthur Rimbaud's 'Le Bateau ivre'. The critical discussion presented by Dennis dwells on the supposed subjectivity of lyric poetry, the natural and instant contact that it provides with the author's conscience, and in this sense 'Le Bateau ivre' is indeed a paramount example.

When translating the poem, according to Dennis, Beckett revealed the way it had originally been built, showing the mediated nature of Rimbaud's extraordinary verbal construction. In the translation of the poem, Beckett is shown to be an attentive reader who took his decisions after a close study of the structure of the original. He was also fully aware of the limitations of the English language regarding, for instance, the rich mosaic of verb tenses in French. Dennis considers the consequences that this particular task had on the translation of his own work in general.

Matthijs Engelberts, the author of the last essay in Part II, discusses Beckett's translations of Sébastien de Chamfort's maxims. Prior to this, he introduces an important caveat: Beckett never fostered or encouraged a bilingual reading of his work. There are hardly any editions of narrative prose, playscripts or poetry that were originally presented to the reading public in both languages, which reveals yet another paradox of the author generally considered to be amongst the most accomplished bilingual writers of all times: his work was always presented in print as the product of a monolingual conscience. 'Long after Chamfort', Beckett's adaptation into English of eight maxims by the eighteenth-century French aristocrat, would be, according to Engelberts, the only bilingual text that Beckett ever published during his lifetime. Engelbert's analysis of Beckett's translations of Chamfort's maxims centres on the way he creates a 'spectral version' of the original text. He shortened the pieces, versified them, and seemed at times to enter into a discussion with them. The result serves to update a set of old aphorisms for the modern reader: 'By reusing and restating Chamfort', writes Engelberts, 'Beckett shows that the maxims still appear to hold'.

Part III of the volume aims to provide a real and accessible guide to the parameters in which the poetics of translation in Beckett may be situated. If there is general agreement on the crucial position of translation in what has been named the 'Beckett continuum' (Van Hulle 2015: xxv), it is important to give substance to those general statements which proclaim such a central role for translation, and to map out the ways in which translation informed the execution of his work. In Chapter 10, John Pilling begins his essay with an examination of Beckett's perpetual dualism in his literary production. From the beginning of his career, argues Pilling, Beckett was 'caught in the indecision of language' and even his writing in two languages could be considered another form of the dualism that permeates his work. Beckett may have realised that the separation between subject and object found a provisional solution in the act of translation, thus attenuating the division in irreconcilable spheres that he saw everywhere. The well-known danger of identifications that Beckett warned about in the essay 'Dante . . . Bruno.

Vico.. Joyce' might, for Pilling, also have been successfully superseded by his activity between languages: 'translation did not so much change the rules of the game as subvert it by virtue of demonstrating non coincidence'. Pilling examines Beckett's articles and reviews in *Disjecta* and reveals that in many of his critical writings he was actually thinking in terms of translation: 'Every "occasion" of translation offered Beckett an opportunity to address and reassess the apparent fixity of a priori conditions of possibility'. From a different perspective, Dirk Van Hulle, in his essay on the 'poetics of the Doppelgänger' (Chapter 11), also argues that self-translation was far from being a mere technical ability in Beckett and that it was closely connected to his existential preoccupations. Like Pilling, Van Hulle recognises the fragmented self, or divided conscience, as a common trope in Beckett's writings and for him it is in the author's translations of his own work that the *dédoublement* is most powerfully enacted. Van Hulle relates the dismantling of identity in Beckett's work to the two versions that he made of most of his texts. Self-translation is revealed as stemming from the need to express the ambivalence that Beckett detected at the core of being.

Fábio de Souza Andrade, the author of Chapter 12, takes as a starting point for his discussion on the poetics of translation in Beckett, a famous episode in the novel *Watt*: the Gall's piano-tuning at Mr Knott's house. Although, in the narrative, the tuning of the old piano is carried out without further complications, Watt is unable to create a coherent story from it, and ponders instead on the tangle of sounds, impressions and movements in his mind. De Souza Andrade reads this episode as one more example of the rupture between subject and object that has been discussed before, and believes that translation in Beckett should be considered as an imaginative impulse and an opportunity for inventiveness. If a perfect, definitive expression was impossible to achieve in the original, translation should be stressed as a constituting element in Beckett's indeterminacy as a writer: 'The changing matter of experience is analogue to the moving textual meanings the translator faces'. In the final chapter of the book, Martin Schauss examines the political implications of Beckett's act of self-translation, focusing on the writing that Beckett produced immediately after the Second World War, mainly the *Nouvelles* and the Trilogy, looking with special attention at the tramps who populate these narratives. Beckett sought to maintain an attitude of political resistance without aligning himself to a particular ideological project. What was then at stake in the political arena, Schauss argues, was the question of the property of language, and Beckett reacted to the appropriation of language by a nationalistic discourse through having his destitute characters mimic the idiom of respectability. Schauss examines the strategies adopted by the Irish author in his writing, finding that when

Beckett translated his stories into English, the historical burden was somehow lessened or alleviated. It is in the language choices Beckett made in these cases that translation can be most clearly seen as an act of political intervention: 'Translation and Beckett's multilingualism play a key role in registering the very problem of politics in his work, displacing the already unstable cultural referents once over'.

The volume ends with a 'Commentary' section, in which a number of translators who worked with Samuel Beckett (Antoni Libera, Gabriele Frasca and Erika Tophoven) examine an aspect of their work with Beckett's texts. There is also a personal reflection by Professor Alan W. Friedman. These short texts have been especially commissioned for this project. Finally, the editors would like to express their gratitude to all the contributors to the volume for their enthusiastic support. We would also like to acknowledge the assistance provided by CEI Patrimonio, University of Almería. We want to thank the members of *Lindisfarne* research group for their unstinting commitment to Irish Studies and to the promotion of Samuel Beckett's work. We hope that this 'occasion of wordshed' honours that commitment and the efforts of all who have contributed to this volume.

José Francisco Fernández and Mar Garre García

Works Cited

Astbury, Helen (2008), 'Killing his Texts Dead: Beckett's Hiberno-English Translations', in Paulo E. Carvalho and Rui Carvalho Homem (eds), *Plural Beckett Pluriel*, Porto: University of Porto, 2008, pp. 189–97.

Almeida, Sandra Regina Goulart and Julia de Vasconcelos Magalhaes Veras (2017), 'From Samuel Beckett to Nancy Huston: A Poetics of Self-Translation', *Ilha do Desterro: A Journal of English Language, Literatures in English and Cultural Studies*, 70.1, 103–12.

Beer, Ann (1994), 'Beckett's Bilingualism', in John Pilling (ed), *The Cambridge Companion to Beckett*, Cambridge, UK: Cambridge University Press, pp. 209–21.

Butler, Lance St John (1994), 'Two Darks: A Solution to the Problem of Beckett's Bilingualism', *Samuel Beckett Today/Aujourd'hui*, 3, 115–35.

Casement, Patrick J. (1982), 'Samuel Beckett's Relationship to his Mother Tongue', *The International Review of Psychoanalysis*, 9, 35–44.

Cohn, Ruby (1961), 'Samuel Beckett Self-Translator', *PMLA*, 76, 613–21.

Federman, Raymond (1987), 'The Writer as Self-Translator', in Alan Warren Friedman, Charles Rossman and Dina Sherzer (eds), *Beckett Translating/*

Translating Beckett, University Park and London: The Pennsylvania State University Press, pp. 7–16.

Fernández, José Francisco (2018), 'Between "Little Latitude" and a "Discreet Liberty". Beckett's Bilingualism and the Translation of his Work into a Third Language', *Samuel Beckett Today/Aujourd'hui. The Poetics of Bilingualism in the Work of Samuel Beckett*, 30.1, 127–40.

Fitch, Brian T. (1988), *Beckett and Babel. An Investigation into the Status of the Bilingual Work*, Toronto: University of Toronto Press.

Garforth, Julian A. (1996), 'Translating Beckett's Translations', *Journal of Beckett Studies*, 6.1, 49–70.

Grutman, Rainier (2013), 'Beckett and Beyond. Putting Self-Translation in Perspective', *Orbis Litterarum*, 68.3, 188–206.

Long, Joseph (1996), 'The Reading of *Company*: Beckett and the Bi-Textual Work', *Forum for Modern Language Studies*, 32.4, 314–28.

Louar, Nadia (2014), 'Book Review. *A Tongue Not Mine: Beckett and Translation*, by Sinéad Mooney', *Modern Philology*, 112.1, E114-E117.

Louar, Nadia, and José Francisco Fernández (2018), 'Introduction', *Samuel Beckett Today/Aujourd'hui. The Poetics of Bilingualism in the Work of Samuel Beckett*, 30, 1, 1–2.

Mihálycsa, Erika (2013), '"Writing to the self-accompaniment of a tongue that is not mine": The Figure of Translation in Beckett's Work', *Hungarian Journal of English and American Studies*, 19.2, 343–74.

Mooney, Sinéad (2011), *A Tongue Not Mine. Beckett and Translation*, Oxford: Oxford University Press.

Murphy, P. J. (2016), 'Saint Samuel (à) Beckett's Big Toe. Incorporating Beckett in Popular Culture', in P. J. Murphy and Nick Pawliuk (eds), *Beckett in Popular Culture*, Jefferson, NC: McFarland, pp. 3–18.

O'Reilly, Edouard Magessa (2016), 'English Introduction', in Samuel Beckett, *Comment C'est/How It Is and/et L'Image*, New York: Routledge, pp. ix–xxxv.

Scheiner, Corinne (2013), 'Self-Translation', in Anthony Uhlmann (ed), *Samuel Beckett in Context*, Cambridge, UK: Cambridge University Press, pp. 370–80.

Uhlmann, Anthony (2018), 'Foreword', in S. E. Gontarski, *Revisioning Beckett. Samuel Beckett's Decadent Turn*, New York: Bloomsbury Academic, pp. xi–xiii.

Van Hulle, Dirk (2008), 'Bilingual Decomposition: the "Perilous Zones" in the Life of Beckett's Texts', in S. E. Gontarski, William J. Cloonan, Alec Hargreaves and Dustin Anderson (eds), *Transnational Beckett*, Tallahassee, FL: Jobs Books, pp. 97–109.

Van Hulle, Dirk (2015), 'Introduction', in Dirk Van Hulle (ed), *The New Cambridge Companion to Samuel Beckett*, New York: Cambridge University Press, pp. xvii–xxvi.

Van Hulle, Dirk and Pim Verhulst (2017), *The Making of Samuel Beckett's En attendant Godot/Waiting for Godot*, Brussels: University Press Antwerp and Bloomsbury.

Wawrzycka, Jolanta (2010), 'Introduction: Translatorial Joyce', *James Joyce Quarterly*, 47.4, 515–20.

Weddell, Cecilia (2020), 'Beckett's Mexican Translations: Resistances of Literary Diction and Conviction', in Bernardo Santano Moreno, Concepción Hermosilla Álvarez and Severina Álvarez González (eds), *Samuel Beckett: Literatura y traducción/Littérature et traduction/Literature and Translation*, Bern: Peter Lang, pp. 203–18.

Part I
Beckett's Self-Translations

Part 4

Hockey's Self-Translations

1

'. . . bouche en feu . . .': A Genetic Manuscript Study of Samuel Beckett's Self-Translation of *Not I*

Shane O'Neill

Introduction

This chapter is a genetic manuscript study of Samuel Beckett's self-translation process of his play *Not I* into *Pas moi*. Throughout this analysis, I will examine manuscripts of the translation to determine how the playwright preserves and recreates the intricate rhythms of the English text in French. *Not I* is an extremely technical composition, very much akin to a complicated piece of classical music. The musicality and technicality of *Not I* is frequently stressed by those who have performed it. Recounting her experience of playing Mouth, Billie Whitelaw explained that 'I've been practicing words at a tenth of a second . . . No one can possibly follow the text at that speed but Beckett insists that I speak it precisely. It's like music, a piece of Schoenberg in his head' (Knowlson 1997: 598). The play script is punctuated only by ellipses, question marks and exclamation marks, and is intended to be performed in one almost breathless flow. The French translation, thus, must reproduce the original text's breathlessness and its complex rhythmic patterns. It seems that Beckett did indeed find this translation particularly arduous. In *Damned to Fame*, Knowlson notes: 'On 1 March [1973, Beckett] decided to make an attempt to translate *Not I* into French but broke down, twelve days later, after only five pages. Fragmenting the syntax and transposing the verbal ambiguities presented more daunting problems' (Knowlson 1997: 599). His failure to complete his first draft of *Pas moi* demonstrates the difficulties he faced in translating the musical/rhythmic cadences of the English version. I will thus examine in detail the solutions found by Beckett throughout the translation process which would ultimately allow him to recreate the musicality of *Not I* in another language.

Translating *Pas Moi*

Comparisons are frequently made between *Not I* and Beckett's novel *L'Innommable/ The Unnamable*.[1] In their discussion of the genesis of *L'Innommable/ The Unnamable*, Dirk Van Hulle and Shane Weller write that this novel 'is a work in which readers can very easily lose themselves, and this is arguably an experience that Beckett sought to provoke' (Van Hulle and Weller 2014: 94). The same can be said for the script of *Not I/Pas moi*. When preparing for the first performance of *Not I*, Beckett told the actress playing Mouth, Jessica Tandy, that he wanted the play to 'work on the nerves of the audience, not its intellect'.[2] Even the most attentive audiences can find themselves lost in the relentless stream of words. Beckett was aware of the complexity and challenges posed by this performance piece. In the Billie Whitelaw collection at Special Collections at the University of Reading, there are four pages of directorial notes handwritten by Beckett for Whitelaw. At the top of these four pages, Beckett has written Whitelaw's name and marked each sheet as 'important'. The Special Collections website describes these pages as follows:

> Directorial notes on for *Not I*, notes written by Samuel Beckett
> Notes made by Samuel Beckett after rehearsals before the Royal Court production, providing a synopsis, dividing the play into sections, with a list of pauses, headed stationery of the Hyde Park Hotel, London. 3 docs. Undated [1972–1973]. (Special Collections website)[3]

As indicated, Beckett divided *Not I* into five sections in order to facilitate Billie Whitelaw's learning of this difficult monologue. To better structure the study of this fractured text, I will identify the separate sections, as noted by Beckett in the English version, and divide the French text in a similar manner. This will make it possible to examine the text in a more structured manner and help make it clear when I am referring to specific passages from the text.

Sections

In the published text of *Not I*, these five sections, as denoted by Beckett, are as follows:

1. From opening words 'out . . . into this world . . .' to 'found herself in the dark' (Beckett 2006: 376–7).
2. From 'and if not exactly . . . insentient . . .' to 'imagine! . . . words were coming . . .' (Beckett 2006: 377–9).

3. From 'a voice she did not recognize . . .' to 'so far . . . ha! . . . so far . . .' (Beckett 2006: 379–80).
4. From 'then thinking . . . on long after . . .' to 'could that be it? . . . something she had to . . . tell . . .' (Beckett 2006: 380–1).
5. From 'tiny little thing . . . before its time . . .' to the final lines of the play (Beckett 2006: 381–3).

These five sections correspond with the following five sections of *Pas moi*:

1. From opening words ' – monde . . . mis au monde . . .' to 'la voilà dans le . . . le noir . . .' (Beckett 1963: 82).
2. From 'et sinon exactement . . . privée de sentiment . . .' to '. . . imaginez! . . . des mots! . . .' (Beckett 1963: 82–7).
3. From '. . . une voix que d'abord . . . elle ne reconnaît pas . . .' to 'jusque là . . . ha! . . . jusque là . . .' (Beckett 1963: 87–8).
4. From 'puis se disant, . . . oh bien après . . .' to 'si c'était ça . . . quelque chose qu'il faut qu'elle . . . dise . . .' (Beckett 1963: 88–92).
5. From 'petit bout de rien . . . avant l'heure . . .' to the end of the play (Beckett 1963: 92–5).

Documents

There are three documents in the *Pas moi* dossier at Special Collections at the University of Reading – two manuscripts (BC-MS-UoR-1396-4-25 and BC-MS-UoR-1396-4-26) and one typescript (BC-MS-UoR-1396-4-27). For the purposes of this study, I will refer to BC-MS-UoR-1396-4-25 as *Pas Moi* 1 (PM1), BC-MS-UoR-1396-4-26 as PM2 and BC-MS-UoR-1396-4-27 as PM3.

The *Beckett at Reading* catalogue describes PM1 as the '[u]ntitled original manuscript of Samuel Beckett's translation of *Not I* into French. 27 × 21 cm. 5 leaves' (Bryden et al. 1998: 68). Each page is crossed through with a large 'X'. This text is drafted in black ink. Corrections made to the text are also in black ink. The text is unfinished and has been abandoned by Beckett in section four, at the point in which the protagonist is sitting in Croker's Acres staring at the tears on her hand: 'no sound . . . just the tears . . . sat and watched them dry . . . all over in a second' (Beckett 2006: 381). The text is heavily corrected throughout and there are striking variants between this draft and the published text. The text does not include stage directions.

The second manuscript, PM2, is described as follows in *Beckett at Reading*: 'Untitled original manuscript of Samuel Beckett's translation of *Not I* into French. Dated 2–19 May 1974. 27 × 21 cm. 8 leaves' (Bryden et al. 1998: 68).

This manuscript is the first complete draft of the translation. It was drafted fourteen months after the first draft was abandoned. There are many variants throughout this manuscript, but it resembles the published text much more closely than PM1. There are marginal references to biblical passages from St John's Gospel and the Book of Lamentations. Stage directions have been incorporated into this draft.

PM3 is an untitled typescript draft of *Pas moi*, containing manuscript additions and corrections throughout. Changes to the draft are made in black ink. *Beckett at Reading* notes that there are '7 leaves. Various sizes: f.1 21 × 12 cm, f.8 36 × 21 cm (extended with attached sheet) [t]he attached portion of f.8 carries notes regarding the staging (Mouth, Auditor, curtains and lighting)' (Bryden et al. 1998: 68). The text is similar to the published play script with small changes mostly being made to words and short phrases, as well as the order in which certain words appear.

Inspiration, Notable Productions and Translation

Not I was written in 1972. James Knowlson links the origins of this play to two distinct experiences. The first was Beckett's viewing of Caravaggio's 'painting, the "Beheading of St John the Baptist" in the Oratory of St John's cathedral in Valletta, which he described as "a great painting, really tremendous". He sat for more than an hour in front of it, allowing the painting to work on his imagination' (Knowlson 1997: 588). The second experience occurred while in El Jadida, a coastal Moroccan city; citing Enoch Brater, Knowlson recounts the story of Beckett seeing a figure in a djellaba who 'appeared to be in a position of intense listening' (Knowlson 1997: 589). He later realised that the figure was simply a woman waiting to pick up her child from school. Knowlson believes that:

> What probably happened is that the image of the djellaba–clad figure coalesced with his sharp memories of the Caravaggio painting. For perhaps even more striking than the partially disembodied head of John the Baptist in the Caravaggio are the watching figures. Most powerful of all is an old woman, standing to Salome's left. She observes the decapitation with horror, covering her ears rather than her eyes. This old woman emerges as the figure in Caravaggio's masterpiece whose role comes closest to the Auditor in Beckett's play, reacting compassionately to what he/she hears. (Knowlson 1997: 589)

The last date that appears on the first manuscript of *Pas moi* is 'Él Jadida 13.3.73' (PM1, 4r). Thus, Beckett attempted to translate this complicated text during another visit to El Jadida, the place that initially inspired much of the imagery of *Not I*. Perhaps he anticipated his struggle with the self-translation of this script which in so many ways resembles the text of *L'Innommable*. It could be suggested that Beckett was hoping to find motivation for the task in the same location that had initially inspired the English version of the play.

One other influence for *Not I*, as acknowledged by Beckett himself, came from his Irish background:

> I knew that woman in Ireland . . . I knew who she was – not 'she' spe-cifically, one single woman, but there were so many of those old crones, stumbling down the lanes, in the ditches, behind the hedgerows. Ireland is full of them. And I heard 'her' saying what I wrote in *Not I*. I actually heard it. (As quoted in Bair 2002: 662)

Memories of these women who obviously suffered from mental health issues were also a source of inspiration for the traumatised words spewing from Mouth.

The first performance of *Not I* took place in New York on 22 November 1972. The text was performed as part of a double bill alongside a production of *Krapp's Last Tape*. Jessica Tandy performed the role of Mouth, confessing that 'the panic [was] so dreadful, that I didn't enjoy it' (Knowlson 1997: 592). In 1973, Billie Whitelaw took on the role of Mouth for the Royal Court Theatre production of the play. Billie Whitelaw's performance is often considered the definitive production of the play. Perhaps this is due in part to Beckett's direction of Whitelaw who succeeded in delivering his vision of the play. Michael Billington, reviewing the play for *The Guardian*, wrote: 'Although the words stream out with scalding intensity, the text works on one like a poem' ('Royal Court', 17 January: 8) (Beckett 2016: 325n2). Beckett himself seemed surprised by the positive critical response to his play: in a letter to Sheila Page on 26 January 1973 from Paris, he writes:

> [a]stonished by reactions to <u>Not I</u> which I thought would be damned with faint praise by even the most open-minded as anti-theatre and unintelligi-ble. Let's say they couldn't resist Billie! Have now to pull up to the horrible job of translating it into French and to releasing it for general production, i.e. massacre 9 times out of 10. (Beckett 2016: 325)

In the same letter he also mentions that he will be off to 'Morocco for most of March' (Beckett 2016: 325). As I have suggested, Beckett seems to have anticipated the difficulty of translating *Not I* and perhaps is waiting to begin his translation in the place where he first received inspiration for *Not I*. However, this draft would ultimately be abandoned by the writer and remain unfinished. Fourteen months later, on the 16 May 1974, Beckett writes to Herbert Myron, claiming that he is '[a]t last à la tête of a foul draft of Pas moi (il)' (Beckett 2016: 370). The seventh page of PM2, the end of the second manuscript, is dated 12 May 1974. The eighth page, the page attached to this manuscript containing the stage directions, is dated 19 May 1974. Despite his description of this draft as 'foul', this version of *Pas moi* quite closely resembles the published text, and it seems that the temporal distance between the first and second draft allowed Beckett the time to begin recomposing the text in the French language. The first French production was also part of a double bill with *Krapp's Last Tape* (*La dernière bande*). Madelaine Renaud played the role of Bouche at the Théâtre d'Orsay in Paris in 1975. Beckett does not seem to have been very enthused about the prospect of staging the play: 'Just back from 2 months in Berlin directing Godot for the Schiller. Now more effing theatre here with French Not I and yet another Krapp. Then take leave of the stage' (Beckett 2016: 392). Beckett's exhaustion with theatre at the time seems to have affected his enthusiasm surrounding this play and Renaud's performance does not seem to have satisfied him, stating simply that: '[Madelaine] has made a great effort' (Knowlson 1997: 617).

Most recently, a bilingual performance of *Not I/Pas moi* by Clara Simpson was commissioned by the 2016 Paris Beckett Festival. Simpson performs the full text in French before performing it again in English. Ian Patterson describes Simpson's bilingual narration of the texts at the 2019 Happy Days Enniskillen Beckett Festival as 'an urgent, complex musical score'.[4] Performed in the chapel of Enniskillen Royal Grammar (formerly Portora Royal School, Beckett's alma mater), the proximity of the audience to Simpson meant 'that her sharp, micro-gasps for breath sound like percussive rhythms'.[5] Notably it is the musicality of the texts that is once again highlighted by Patterson, emphasising its importance in both the French and English incarnations of the play. The recent commissioning of this performance also highlights the current interest in Beckett's bilingual oeuvre, and Simpson's ability to merge the two texts into one performance piece is a clear indication that Beckett managed to preserve the complex rhythmic patterns of the original in his self-translation. Simpson believes that by knitting the two versions of the text together, the audience gets 'closer to the truth . . . even if they don't know the language, they get the rhythm of it, everybody is warmed up'.[6] Feargal Whelan writes that Simpson's performances allowed the audience 'to assess questions of difference and change in Beckett's self-translated works in real time . . . allowed for a deeper meditation on the nature of Beckett's own linguistic experience' and 'provoked deep questions of the journeying from mother tongue to adopted tongue, and back again'.[7]

Genesis of *Pas moi*

To begin my analysis of *Pas moi*, I separated the text of the manuscripts into five sections that were equivalent to the sections outlined by Beckett in his rehearsal notes for Billie Whitelaw. It was then necessary to examine these sections individually, noting the changes made from draft to draft. By analysing each of the manuscripts in this manner, patterns of translation began to emerge. The following analysis will consider some of the most notable patterns that emerge from such an examination of the manuscripts, as well as the most notable translation techniques employed by Beckett.

The playwright struggles to translate the opening words of *Not I*. The English text begins '. . . out . . . into this world . . . this world . . .' (Beckett 2006: 376). This opening, with its focus on short words and broad vowel sounds, emphasises the text's breathless pace. Translating the opening word 'out' poses an immediate problem. Beckett first translates it as 'bas' (PM1, 1r). This is effective as, similarly to 'out', it is a short, monosyllabic word allowing Beckett to establish a similar rhythm to *Not I* from the outset. The word 'bas' can be interpreted in many ways. It can simply mean 'low' or 'downcast'. It can be used figuratively to mean 'low-down' or 'base' character traits. Finally, the word can evoke the idea of a 'low' voice, such as that of the woman speaking. Having chosen to open his text with this word, the opening reads thus: 'bas . . . mis bas . . . ici bas . . .' (PM1, 1r). The past participle 'mis' suggests that the woman has been literally 'put down'. The word 'ici' suggests that she has remained down, is still down. In this way the meaning differs from the English version. The assonant 'a' sound is in contrast to the broad 'o' sounds that permeate the opening of *Not I*. In his second attempt to draft *Pas moi*, Beckett considers another translation for this line by putting parenthesis around his original translation and introducing a second variant: '(bas . . . mis bas . . . ici bas)^{au monde . . . mis au monde . . . ce monde}' (PM2, 1r). The second variant works as a more effective translation, both sonically and in terms of meaning. By PM3, he removes the opening 'au', and the writer chooses the monosyllabic word 'monde' to open his play. This translation places emphasis on the 'world' the woman is being cast into rather than the action of casting her 'out'. Similar to *Not I*, an 'o' vowel sound now pervades the opening moments of Bouche's monologue, and this translation will appear in the type-script and published text (PM3; Beckett 1963: 82).

In the English version of the text, the titular word 'not' appears thirty-six times. In contrast, in the French text the word 'pas' appears fifty-one times. It is interesting to examine the ways in which Beckett increases the frequency with which this word appears throughout the self-translation process. The playwright attempts to preserve the syntax and rhythms of the line in

section four 'as if it hadn't heard . . . or couldn't . . . couldn't pause a second'
(Beckett 2006: 380). In the typescript, the sentence appears as 'comme si elle
n'entendait pas . . . ou ne ~~pouvait . . .~~ pouvait pas . . . pas une [illeg.] seconde'
(PM3, 5r). At first, Beckett emulates the repetition of 'couldn't' from the
original text. However, he realises that it would be more effective to delete
the first 'pouvait' and instead, repeat the innately negative, titular word 'pas'.
In the English text, the word 'not' is merged into the contraction 'couldn't',
making this section of the text less explicitly negative than its French counterpart. However, this contraction preserves the 'panting' pace of the play which
results from the relentless stream of words. The deletion of 'pouvait' disrupts
the desired rhythms of the French play. Thus, the line that appears in the published version is 'comme si elle n'entendait pas . . . la bouche . . . ou ne pouvait
pas . . . pas une seconde' (Beckett 1963: 89. My emphasis). The assonant 'ou'
sound of 'la bouche' recreates the necessary rhythm and highlights the role of
the mouth 'panting' out this complicated verbal composition.

Beckett's first attempt to translate the phrase 'parents unknown . . .'
(Beckett 2006: 376) is noteworthy. In PM1 these words are translated to
'parents inconnus . . .' (1r). This literal translation appears again in the second
manuscript draft and is reminiscent of his tendency to preserve, and indeed often
increase, the number of negative affixes in self-translation. Writing about the
genesis of *The Unnamable*, Dirk Van Hulle and Shane Weller note that Beckett
enacts 'self-decomposition in the very language of the text . . . One of the most
obvious ways in which this linguistic self-decomposition (or unwording)
is enacted in the novel is through the use of negative affixes' (Van Hulle and
Weller 2014: 191). By the third draft of *Pas moi*, however, he reconsiders
this translation: '~~parents inconnus~~ père mère fantômes' (PM3, 2r). This is a rare
occasion where Beckett removes a negative affix, in this case 'in-', in a self-
translation and a clear example of Beckett's 'authorial' style of self-translation.
The French text's meaning does not change drastically but one cannot imagine
another translator offering such a translation when the obvious literal translation seems to serve the purpose of the text. But this new translation makes
sense if we are to consider the intended effect of the original text. The trochaic
noun 'parents', beginning with a jabbing 'pare-' sound and ending with a
breathless '-rents', creates a panting sound that the French noun 'parents' does
not accurately replicate. In contrast, the juxtaposed monosyllabic words 'père
mère' force the performer to pause between each word. The 'pare-' sound
of the original text is barely compromised and 'mère', beginning with a soft
consonant 'm' sound is the least harsh-sounding of the two words. The hoarse
'r' sound at the end of both these words forces Bouche to pant these words,
much in the same way as Mouth. In addition, the French word 'fantômes'
quite accurately recaptures the rhythms of the English 'unknown'.

Likewise, the translation of the following words 'unheard of' (Beckett 2006: 376) is no less notable. They are first translated as 'jamais su parler^{inouï}' (PM1, 1r). The open variant immediately highlights Beckett's difficulty in translating these words. The first option he considers, 'jamais su parler', does not accurately represent the meaning of the English text. The second variant considered, 'inouï', perfectly translates the original meaning but is perhaps rhythmically a little more stunted. Despite preserving the negative prefix of the original, the juxtaposition of the words 'inconnus' and 'inouï' in PM1 does little to recapture the harshness of the English version. In particular, 'inouï' is very lyrical-sounding due to the number of vowels in this short word. Unlike the rhythmic 'un-' sound in 'unknown' and 'unheard' which is identical, the 'in-' sounds in 'inconnus' and 'inouï' are pronounced differently, producing a sonic discord within the text. In the second manuscript, PM2, Beckett translates these words as 'jamais entendu parler' (PM2, 1r). This retains the meaning in *Not I* but the rhythms still seem compromised by an excess of words to express the idea. In the third draft, Beckett finally finds a way of translating the text in a way that pleases him and which subsequently appears in the published version of *Pas moi*: he translates 'unheard of' into 'pas trace' (PM3, 2r; Beckett 1963: 82). This succinct, negatively constructed phrase fits neatly into the rhythms of the text. The number of words necessary to translate the original idea has been minimised, helping to preserve the breathless pace of the original.

Beckett's translation of the words 'and now this stream . . . steady stream' (Beckett 2006: 379) in section three is of particular interest in the context of negative affixes. His first instinct is to translate the words as 'et maintenant ce flot . . . ininterrompu' (PM1, 3r). The negative 'in-' prefix is most notable because of its position in front of a word already containing this prefix. However, despite working accurately as a translation for 'steady', this five-syllable word fits awkwardly into this script which contains few words more than three syllables in length. Beckett revises the word, thus, in PM2: '~~ininterrompu~~ continu' (PM2, 3r). This is another rare example of an occasion where Beckett decides to choose a word with positive connotations rather than one that is constructed with a negative affix. However, the verb 'continuer' is also a very 'Beckettian' verb, again recalling the novel *L'Innommable*, in particular, the final words of the text: 'il faut continuer, je ne peux pas continuer, je vais continuer' (Beckett 2009: 211). On Beckett's second attempt to translate *Not I*, a text which in so many ways resembles his earlier novel and poses similar problems in translation, the choice of the word 'continu' seems particularly apt.

The word 'speechless' appears numerous times in the text. In section one of PM1, Beckett leaves an open variant for his translation of 'speechless infant'

(Beckett 2006: 376): 'sur l'enfant sans défense^{privé de parole}' (PM1, 1r). The alliterative 'privé de parole' suggests that the child is denied or deprived of the ability
to speak. However, Beckett decides that the first variant best suits his text: the
child is literally 'without defence' because of her inability to communicate. The
playwright finds a different translation for 'speechless' when it appears again in
section three. The context in which the word reappears is in the line 'practically
speechless . . . all her days . . . how she survived!' (Beckett 2006: 379). This sentence is particularly sibilant and the hushing 's' sound that prevails emphasises
the 'speechlessness' and silence of the life led by Mouth. Beckett's translation
in PM1 reads thus: 'pratiquement ~~sans parole . . .~~ muette . . . ~~la vie se passa~~ . . .
toute sa vie . . . miracle qu'elle ~~ait pu surviv~~^{ait tenu}' (PM1, 3r). 'Sans parole' is perhaps Beckett's attempt to combine the two variants from his earlier attempt at
translating the word in section one but this solution seems a little too literal and
stunted; instead, Beckett chooses 'muette' which perfectly preserves the sense
of the original word but has different sonic properties. The feminine inflection
of the adjective 'muet', with its emphasis on the conclusive '-ette' ending, captures a sense of finality. This ending, juxtaposed with the word 'toute', forces
the actor playing the role of Bouche to pause between words in order to make
sure these words are clearly distinguishable from one another. These pauses for
breath create the 'percussive rhythms' that Ian Patterson refers to in his review
of Clara Simpson's bilingual performance of *Not I/Pas moi*.

The rhythms of the text can be preserved by lengthening and elongating
certain passages and separating them with an additional ellipsis; however, these
new 'mutated' phrases must match the rhythms of the speech fragments that
proceed and follow them for the text to retain a sense of rhythmic consistency.
An example of one of these situations is Beckett's translation of the phrase
'how she survived!' His first two attempts in PM1 show us that he attempted
to recreate this sense of astonishment by establishing a 'que' clause: 'miracle qu'elle ~~ait pu surviv~~^{ait tenu}' (PM1, 3r). The deletion suggests that Beckett
believed that attaching a three-syllable word 'survivre' to the end of an already
lengthy phrase would have disrupted the text's pacing. His best solution at this
stage of drafting, is to replace 'ait pu survivre' with 'ait tenu', a more concise
alternative than previously considered. Fourteen months later, while reworking the second draft of the play, it seems that Beckett's impulse was still to
translate the past participle 'survived' using the verb 'survivre'. However, his
new translation was successfully achieved by further fragmenting his phrasing
and inserting additional ellipses. This is an important breakthrough in Beckett's
second attempt at translating the text and is arguably one of the main reasons
he was able to successfully complete his second draft of *Pas moi*. His new
translation thus reads: 'à se demander . . . quel miracle . . . elle a pu survivre'.

The additional ellipses break the phrase into three rhythmically cohesive fragments. The ellipsis separating 'miracle' and 'elle' removes the need to preserve
the 'que' clause and hence the verb 'pouvoir' is inflected in the perfect tense.
In fact, the only change made from this point on in the drafting is to change
this perfect tense into a pluperfect inflection: 'elle avait pu survivre' (PM3,
4r; Beckett 1963: 87). This change reinforces the idea that this speechlessness
was in the past, accounting for the current torrent of words flowing from
Bouche and recaptures the incredulity of the English phrase: 'how she
survived!' Having a voice now, she wonders how she survived never being
able to express herself verbally. It is clear now why Beckett wished to preserve
the word 'survivre' in *Pas moi*. The construction using the verb 'tenir' − 'ait
tenu' − does not suggest the sheer desperation that the verb 'to survive' does.
Using 'tenir' implies that she was not able to 'hold up' or 'maintain' herself;
this is less striking than the preferred translation in which Bouche reveals the
horror of living a speechless life, barely able to survive.

As Beckett redrafts his text, he often reconsiders the position of words
that seem almost inconsequential to the overall meaning of the text. These
changes emphasise how much attention the playwright pays to the minutiae
of the translation. One of the clearest examples of this practice is his *jeu* with
his translation of the words 'spared that' (Becket 2006: 376). This phrase
occurs five times in the published text of *Not I*. The first translation of these
words in section one is 'ça au moins' (PM1, 1r). This first manuscript of the
translation demonstrates that even at the early stages of drafting, Beckett was
unsure how best to position these words, as they appear also as 'au moins
ça' in section two (PM1, 3r). Throughout PM2 and PM3, they appear consistently as 'ça au moins'. However, throughout PM3, Beckett has made a
manuscript note in each case to change the positioning of these words back
to 'au moins ça', and this lexical arrangement appears in the published text of
Pas moi. Beginning the sentence with the word 'ça' makes the phrase sound
slightly harsher. Leading with the low, panting vowel sounds generated by 'au
moins' emphasises the breathlessness of the words being spoken. By swapping
the position of the words thus, Beckett also puts emphasis on the negative
construction of the sentence. Of note in this regard is that in two of the five
cases where this phrase appears, 'au moins' is preceded by the word 'non'.
The assonant juxtaposition of these two phrases, separated only by an ellipsis,
further highlights the breathy rhythms.

Beckett vacillates between using 'dans l'oreille' and 'dans les oreilles' to
translate 'in the ears'. His initial compulsion in the original manuscript is to
use the former option. However, he then crosses this out and replaces it with
the latter choice: 'l'oreille ~~les oreilles~~' (PM1, 1r). He preserves this translation in

PM2 but decides to go back to his earliest translation after some deliberation in the typescript: 'dans ~~les~~ l'oreilles . . .' (PM3, 2r). This translation loses little in terms of meaning but is one syllable shorter, which again allows the French text to more closely recapture the frantic pace and rhythms of *Not I*.

As he begins to draft the passage beginning with 'dismissed as foolish' in section two, Beckett writes: 'la rejeta comme ~~sottise~~^{bêtise} . . . oh longtemps après . . . cette idée rejeté comme ~~sottise~~^{bêtise}' (PM1, 1r). The oscillation between using the past historic participle and the perfect tense participle is worthy of mention when we consider the subsequent translation: 'puis chassée . . . l'idée chassée . . . oh longtemps après . . . chassée comme bêtise' (PM2, 2r). Beckett dismisses the verb 'rejeter' in favour of the sibilant verb 'chasser', conjugated into a perfect tense past participle, which better captures the sonic qualities of the verb 'dismissed' than its past historic counterpart. This translation also reveals the extent to which Beckett played with the syntax of these lines in an attempt to create a rhythmically and textually coherent translation. Yet, the translation of three fragments of English speech into four fragments in French seems a little clunky in this context and is revised again in PM3: 'puis chassée . . . l'idée chassée . . . ~~comme~~^{~~en tant que~~ comme} bêtise' (PM3, 2r). Despite displaying some hesitancy over the very direct 'comme', considering 'en tant que' as an alternative, he decides to go with his first choice, noting his preference in the left-hand margin of the typescript PM3.

The words 'sudden flash' posed problems for Beckett throughout the translation process. In his first attempt at translating this phrase, he considers two options, as demonstrated by an open variant: 'brusque étincelle^{brusque illumination}' (PM1, 1r). Beckett seems unsure about these solutions and when this phrase recurs, on the same page of the manuscript, the words are translated to 'soudain illumination' (PM1, 1r). Of these three variants considered by the playwright, 'brusque illumination' is the one that Beckett favours throughout his first draft of *Pas moi*. The playwright will eventually settle on this solution. However, throughout the second manuscript he continues to experiment with other variants, alternating between using the past participle of the verb 'éclairer' as a noun, 'un éclairé' (PM2, 1r), and the noun 'un éclair' (PM2, 2r). Finally, in the typescript, Beckett reverts back to his early translation, 'brusque illumination', only to cross it out again on each occasion and replace it with 'éclair', an addition which is also consistently deleted throughout this phase of drafting: '~~brusque illumination~~^{éclair St.}' (PM3, 2r). The final addition to this translation is the letters 'St'., shorthand for the marginal addition 'Stet', which Van Hulle and Weller note is used by the writer to indicate 'that a deletion is to be ignored' (Van Hulle and Weller 2014: 53). Thus, the addition 'St'. indicates that the second translation he considered, 'brusque illumination', are the words that should appear in the published play.

The translation of the phrase 'realized . . . words were coming . . . imagine! . . . words were coming . . .' (Beckett 2006: 379) gives us an insight into Beckett's meticulousness as a translator to recapture specific rhythms by reworking the syntax and structure of the phrase in another language. His first translation of this segment reads 'sentit . . . des mots venir . . . rendez- vous compte . . .! des mots venir' (PM1, 3r). By the next stage of drafting, he has changed the tense of the verb 'sentir' from the past historic to the present tense, one of the more frequently occurring patterns of translation throughout. He has also removed an ellipsis after this verb. The words 'rendez-vous compte!' appear consistently throughout the first manuscript as Beckett's choice of translation for 'imagine!', but by PM2 are replaced by the more simple, literal translation 'imaginez!' This change seems to be rhythmically more congruent than its alternative, this French word not being far removed sonically from its English counterpart. Like 'rendez-vous compte', the imperative 'imagine'/'imaginez' implores the audience to actively play a role in the performance. However, the more concise 'imaginez' gives the text a more authoritative, commanding tone. In PM1, 'words were coming' is simply translated as 'des mots venir'. However, with the aforementioned introduction of the present tense, Beckett begins to experiment more with the syntax of the line in PM2: 'sent venir des mots . . . imaginez! . . . des mots!' (PM2, 3r). The deletion of a second 'venir' in this revision puts extra emphasis on the word 'mots', which is more effective in conveying Bouche's astonishment at hearing her own voice again. This is compounded by the exclamation mark that follows these words, an exclamation mark that does not appear in the published text of *Not I*. Realising the importance of the word 'mots', Beckett makes another notable change during the typescript phase of drafting. He inserts an ellipsis between the words 'des' and 'mots'. This addition does not disrupt the intended rhythms of the translation because of the previous deletion of an ellipsis in PM2, thereby reproducing the syntactical spacing that exists in the English play. To put further emphasis on the word 'mots', he also introduces another 'des' after this ellipsis. The passage now reads: 'sent venir des . . .des mots . . . imaginez! . . . des mo mots!' (PM3, 4r). Beckett's translation of the phrase is now complete and these final revisions appear in the published version of *Pas moi*.

The phrase 'always winter some strange reason' (Beckett 2006: 379) recurs three times within the text of the play. Beckett's first attempt at translating this phrase into French is almost what he is looking for. He writes 'toujours l'hiver savoir pourquoi' (PM1, 3r). These words together are successful in conveying the meaning of what Beckett wants to express; however, they are not so successful in recapturing the rhythmic flow. When juxtaposed thus, the words 'l'hiver' and 'savoir' have a staccato quality that is contrary to the rhythms of the fragment of speech it is attempting to reproduce. The writer finds a solution in his subsequent draft: 'toujours l'hiver[allez] savoir pourquoi' (PM2, 3r). The addition of the imperative 'allez' ties together the sentence in a much more fluid and lyrical manner and, like the original, the phrase now has a legato quality that, without this addition, did not exist.

Moments of the play recall Beckett's short play *Breath*, written three years previously in 1969 during which the audience hears an '[i]nstant of recorded vagitus' (Beckett 2006: 370). In Beckett's self-translation of *Not I*, Beckett's initial self-translation of the fragments 'just the birth cry to get her going . . . breathing' (Beckett 2006: 380) read 'le *vagissement* un point c'est tout . . . ~~la mettre en r~~ la faire démarrer . . . le soufflé démarrer' (PM1, 5r. My emphasis).

'Vagissement' appears in the three drafts of *Pas moi*; however, the final translation in the published text reads: 'vagir un point c'est tout . . . la mettre en route . . . le souffle en route' (Beckett 1963: 90). Despite crossing out 'la mettre en route[sic]' in the first draft, Beckett decides that it is more effective than the alternative he has considered, 'démarrer'. The translation of these lines is another example of the playwright adding in additional ellipses so that the speech fragments in the French text better fit into the pre-existing rhythms already established. This is aided by Beckett's clever use of repetition and assonance. An assonant 'ou' sound permeates the translation ('tout', 'route') which helps to determine the rhythm and pacing of the speech, and the repetition of 'en route' establishes an effective refrain within this highly composed translation.

The final words of *Not I* are 'pick it up' as the curtain descends and the voice 'continues behind curtain, unintelligible' (Beckett 2006: 383) These words in conjunction with the stage directions suggest that the torrent of words will continue indefinitely after the close of curtain. One of Beckett's first instincts when self-translating the text is to simply write 'reprendre—' (PM2, 7r) which suggests a similar idea. However, when drafting the typescript, Beckett finds a more rhythmically interesting way to conclude. The solution, which will appear in the published script, is to write 'reprendre là . . . repartir de' (PM3, 7r). This translation suggests that the text is beginning again from an early starting point, such as when Mouth/Bouche was sent 'out . . . into this world . . .' (Beckett 2006: 376). This addition reinforces the idea that Bouche, like the characters of *Play*, is trapped in purgatorial space from which she will not emerge until she fully manages to express her inner trauma in a coherent manner. The text thus ends in a very balanced, musical manner: the concluding verbs both begin with the prefix 're-'. There is a prevailing assonant 'e' sound in these last two fragments; indeed, the text ends on this sound which gives the composition an inconclusive feel, suggesting that Bouche will continue to speak long after she is out of earshot of the audience. Beckett's ending to

Pas moi is comparable to the volume of a piece of music being faded out before it ends – listeners know instinctively that the piece has been interrupted leaving them without a satisfying sense of conclusion.

Conclusion

It is clear that the translation of *Not I* into *Pas moi* was not an easy task for the self-translating playwright. Recapturing the cadences and rhythms of such a composed, musical text in another language posed serious challenges. An examination of the manuscripts reveals patterns demonstrating that Beckett only achieved the translation by means of several, very innovative, translation techniques. Most notable among these are the rearranging and redistribution of ellipses throughout the French text, the restructuring of certain phrasal constructions, the constant use of assonance and alliteration, as well as the insertion of extra words to produce a legato effect within this composition. Having worked out ways to recreate these rhythmical intricacies, Beckett was able to successfully translate the words of a character whose speech, like that of the narrator of *The Unnamable*, was able to express 'three things, the inability to speak, the inability to be silent, and solitude' (Beckett 2009: 396).

Notes

1. See for example Tubridy 2000: 93–104; Van Hulle and Weller 2016. I wish to gratefully acknowledge the support of the Irish Research Council. I also want to thank the staff at Special Collections at the University of Reading and my colleagues at Mary Immaculate College, University of Limerick, in particular Dr David Clare. Samuel Beckett's *Pas moi* manuscripts cited as with kind permission of the Beckett International Foundation, the University of Reading. © The Estate of Samuel Beckett 2020. Excerpts from Samuel Beckett's unpublished self-translations of *Not I* (held at the University of Reading) reproduced by kind permission of the Estate of Samuel Beckett c/o Rosica Colin Limited, London, UK.

2. Beckett to Jessica Tandy, quoted in Brater, E. (1974), 'The *I* in Beckett's *Not I*', *Twentieth Century Literature*, 20.3, 200.

3. Billie Whitelaw Collection, University Museums and Special Collections Service, University of Reading, https://collections.reading.ac.uk/wp-content/uploads/sites/9/2020/04/Billie-Whitelaw_BW-.pdf (Accessed 15 July 2019).

4. Patterson, Ian (2019), '*Pas Moi/Not I* @ Happy Days Enniskillen International Beckett Festival'. The Thin Air.net. https://thethinair.net/2019/08/

pas-moinot-i-happy-days-enniskillen-international-beckett-festival/
?fbclid=IwAR1yFkn6nn0rNi1lcTIpmh1kg49DDlcBxGrk9U9SQ2fl
A1P478BBAUrmzEo (Accessed 22 November 2019).

5. Patterson, Ian (2019), 'Pas Moi/Not I @ Happy Days Enniskillen International Beckett Festival'. The Thin Air.net. https://thethinair.net/2019/08/
   pas-moinot-i-happy-days-enniskillen-international-beckett-festival/
   ?fbclid=IwAR1yFkn6nn0rNi1lcTIpmh1kg49DDlcBxGrk9U9SQ2fl
   A1P478BBAUrmzEo (Accessed 22 November 2019).

6. Whelan, Feargal (2019), 'Stop It at Once: Performing Beckett in French
   and English. Interview with Clara Simpson'. The Beckett Circle. https://
   thebeckettcircle.org/2019/12/24/stop-it-at-once-performing-beckett-
   in-french-and-english-interview-with-clara-simpson-by-feargal-whelan
   (Accessed 9 May 2020).

7. Whelan, Feargal (2019), 'Stop It at Once: Performing Beckett in French
   and English. Interview with Clara Simpson'. The Beckett Circle. https://
   thebeckettcircle.org/2019/12/24/stop-it-at-once-performing-beckett-
   in-french-and-english-interview-with-clara-simpson-by-feargal-whelan
   (Accessed 9 May 2020).

Works Cited

Beckett, Samuel (1963), *Oh les beaux jours suivi de Pas moi*, Paris: Les Éditions
   de Minuit.
Beckett, Samuel (2006), *The Complete Dramatic Works*, London: Faber and Faber.
Beckett, Samuel (2009), *Three Novels: Molloy, Malone Dies, The Unnamable*,
   New York: Grove Press.
Beckett, Samuel (2016), *The Letters of Samuel Beckett: 1966–1989,* Vol. 4,
   George Craig, Martha Dow Fehsenfield, Dan Gunn, Lois More Overbeck
   (eds), Cambridge, UK: Cambridge University Press.
Bryden, Mary, Julian Garforth and Peter Mills (eds) (1998), *Beckett at Reading:
   Catalogue of the Beckett Manuscript Collection at the University of Reading*, Reading:
   Whiteknights Press.
Knowlson, James (1997), *Damned to Fame*, London: Bloomsbury.
Patterson, Ian (2019), 'Pas Moi/Not I @ Happy Days Enniskillen International
   Beckett Festival', https://thethinair.net/2019/08/pas-moinot-i-happy-days-
   enniskillen-international- beckett-festival (Accessed 22 November 2019).
Tubridy, Derval (2000), 'Words Pronouncing me Alive: Beckett and Incarna-
   tion', *Samuel Beckett Today/Aujourd'hui*, 9, 93–104.
University of Reading website, 'Billie Whitelaw Catalogue', Reading.ac.uk
   https://collections.reading.ac.uk/wp-content/uploads/sites/9/2020/04/
   Billie-Whitelaw_BW-.pdf (Accessed 15 July 2019).

Van Hulle, Dirk and Shane Weller (2016), *The Making of Samuel Beckett's L'Innommable/The Unnamable*, London: Bloomsbury.

Whelan, Feargal (2019), 'Stop it, at once! Performing Beckett in French and English. Interview with Clara Simpson', *The Beckett Circle*, https://thebeckettcircle.org/2019/12/24/stop-it-at-once-performing-beckett-in-french-and-english-interview-with-clara-simpson-by-feargal-whelan (Accessed 9 May 2020).

Manuscripts relating to *Pas moi*

PM1: French manuscript of *Pas moi*, Beckett International Foundation, University of Reading (BC-MS-UoR-1396-4-25).

PM2: French manuscript of *Pas moi*, Beckett International Foundation, University of Reading (BC-MS-UoR-1396-4-26).

PM3: French typescript of *Pas moi*, Beckett International Foundation, University of Reading (BC-MS-UoR-1396-4-27).

2

Tracing Translation: The Genesis of *Comédie* and *Film* (fr)[1]

Olga Beloborodova

Introduction

As is well known in Beckett studies, one of Beckett's reasons for switching to French was to shed the cultural baggage his mother tongue burdened him with, with impoverishment as the intended result: as he famously put it to Niklaus Gessner in 1957, 'it is easier in French to write without style' (quoted in Cockerham 1975: 156). Although this may indeed have been his original intention, one should exercise caution in applying this argument to Beckett's oeuvre across the board: whereas his initial writing in French after the switch is less overtly intertextual and allusion-laden than his earlier work in English, the question is whether this still applies to Beckett's later period, when he systematically 'turned his manuscripts into bilingual laboratories' (Grutman and Van Bolderen 2014: 327). In particular, this question can be raised with regard to Beckett's systematic self-translation of his later texts, of which *Play* and *Film* are good examples, each in their own way.

The present chapter analyses the genesis of Beckett's self-translations of *Play* and *Film* vis-à-vis the 'impoverishment' strategy that underpinned Beckett's decision to write in French in the first place. Both works were originally written in English around the same time (1962–64). What makes them interesting from the translation point of view is that the text they contain is stripped of its habitual prominence. In both cases, Beckett banished the text to a secondary, more auxiliary role, foregrounding instead the visual element. In *Play*, the genesis of the English original is marked by a clear shift from text to image, with speeches increasingly obscured, truncated, fragmented and in the end nigh on unintelligible. In *Film*, entirely silent from the outset, the text is merely a script with – at least on the surface – little promise of hidden gems waiting to be brought to the surface. Moreover, that script was left untouched after the film had been made and deviates significantly from the end product (that is, the actual film as it was released). Still, despite a clear bias towards the visual and the abstraction in the originals, Beckett did invest a lot of effort in translating both texts, and, as this essay aims to demonstrate, their self-translation often results in enhancement and enrichment rather than impoverishment.

Play

It has been widely noted in literature that unlike prose fiction, works for other media such as stage theatre, radio, film or television are translations in their own right, albeit of a different, non-linguistic kind. Brian Fitch, for one, steered clear of 'the even more complex problematic of Beckett's dramatic texts' in his ground-breaking study of Beckett's bilingualism, due to 'language being, of course, but one of their components' (Fitch 1988: 32n26). Even if examined purely on a linguistic plane, the rendering of a drama text into another language has to take into account extra factors such as rhythm, prosody, duration of speeches and is in general more attuned to oral delivery, with all the restrictions it implies. In this sense, the translation of *Play* is no exception, as it features a number of alliterations and rhythmic patterns that the French language affords where the English original contains none.[2] However, as mentioned above, the role the text plays in *Play* as a conveyer of linguistic meaning is much reduced, and Beckett was of course keenly aware of this. As a self-translator, or someone who had full access to his creative intentions with regard to the source text, he would be expected to continue or perhaps even intensify the impoverishment strategy in *Comédie*, especially given the fact that the translation developed more or less alongside the original. As it turned out, the opposite was often the case.

The genesis of *Comédie* has been previously explored by Richard Admussen (1973) and Maurice Blackman (1985). Admussen has concluded that the target text is funnier than the English original, discerning 'a transformation from somewhat staid English into hilarious French' (Admussen 1973: 26). His conclusion corroborates Ruby Cohn's appraisal of the French originals of *Godot* as the more colloquial and hence the more comic one as compared to the English translation (Cohn 1962: 268). The more general conclusion of Cohn's pioneering study of Beckett as self-translator is that whatever the direction (from French to English or vice versa), the English version typically represents a reduced version of the corresponding French text in terms of richness, humour, vulgarity, colloquialisms, and the sheer nature of authorial interventions. To illustrate her point, she notes that in both *Godot* and *Endgame*, there are more deletions than additions in the English translation of the French original, whereas the opposite happens in the translation of *Murphy* (Cohn 1962: 265–70). In a later study of Beckett's bilingual plays, Harry Cockerham questions some of Cohn's findings and claims instead that there is no real difference between the originals and the translations of Beckett's plays in terms of rudeness or economy, although he does concede that the French variants are consistently more colloquial than their English counterparts (Cockerham 1975: 151–2). It may just as well be that the difference between the two studies is conditioned by the fact that Cohn had at her disposal only Beckett's early bilingual work (namely *Murphy*, *Godot*, *Endgame* and *the Trilogy*), whereas Cockerham had the opportunity to develop his argument based on a much larger body of Beckett's bilingual oeuvre. Indeed, one could argue that by the time Beckett wrote *Play/Comédie*, he had already established the self-translation routine as an inseparable part of his poetics, and as a consequence, if any stylistic discrepancies marked his early efforts, they would have gradually disappeared by then.[3]

Beckett's self-translation routine manifests itself in *Play* before the English source text is well and truly finished. *Play* is therefore a good example of 'simultaneous self-translation' (Grutman 2009: 259), a privilege only self-translators enjoy since they do not have to wait for the original to be finished before they can start the translation job. The translation process began while the original English text was still very much under revision, creating a kind of parallel genesis for the two texts.[4] Two different conclusions can be drawn from this fact (as indeed they have been): on the one hand, Admussen contends that 'the two works developed independently' (Admussen 1979: 30); on the other, he suggests elsewhere that 'there may have been influence of one language upon the other' (Admussen 1973: 25). Maurice Blackman (1985: 97–104) builds on Admussen's latter hypothesis and demonstrates in greater detail the cross-pollination that ostensibly occurred between the original and the translation during the rehearsals of *Play*'s German premiere in Ulm in June 1963. Among other things, *Comédie*'s genetic dossier shows convincing evidence that the revisions to the stage head note around the time of the Ulm premiere were first formulated in French and subsequently transferred into the English version.

Beckett began his translation of *Play* in April 1963, presumably using the eleventh typescript (ET11) as the source text. It is important to note that unlike the English original, *Comédie*'s early genesis was strongly influenced by the performance element, since it largely coincided with the preparations of the play's premiere in Germany. This is why the stage directions are the most heavily revised part of both the source and target text, and those revisions were taking place more or less simultaneously, with occasionally the French being emended first and the English following suit. The stage head note of the first French typescript is virtually identical to the original typed text of its

English counterpart and still mentions large white urns and multiple spots, but the autograph emendation in the English typescript on the details about the blackout is already part of the typed text in the French one:

ET11: No blackout (i.e., return to **almost** complete darkness of opening) except where indicated (03r; *BDMP8* 227).
FT1: Pas de noir (obscurité **presque** totale du début) (03r; *BDMP8* 227).[5]

In a letter to Deryk Mendel, the German director of the play's premiere, Beckett described his insight: 'Translating it into French last week I realised that 'black out' – "Finsternis" – is imprecise. In French it becomes "noir = obscurité presque totale du début", i.e. when curtain goes up stage in almost complete darkness' (13 May 1963; Beckett 2014: 542). Here we witness a nice case of trilingual cross-pollination, with the original impetus for a revision coming from the French and affecting both the German and English texts.

The two manuscript versions of *Comédie* were written in the same notebook within a few weeks between 11 April and 8 May 1963. By June 1963, the time of the Ulm premiere, three typescripts followed suit, and the latter was revised in November 1963 together with its English counterpart, in the aftermath of the Berlin production. The final revisions on the typescripts took place during the preparation of the Suhrkamp trilingual edition and after a long and exhausting period of intense rehearsals in Paris in the first three months of 1964. In the next section, I shall examine the genesis of *Comédie* according to the following points of interest: (1) translating the title, (2) translating ambiguity, (3) reinforcing formal patterns, and (4) translating cultural context.

Translating the Title

Unable to convey all the facets of the polysemous English 'play' in French, Beckett was immediately faced with the need to make an important choice. In a letter from Paris postmarked 11 April 1963, he sends Barbara Bray what could be seen as the first attempt at translating the title together with one of the core fragments of the text: 'Expect to let the film lie [now] for a bit & translate Play. Comédie I suppose. "Oh je sais maintenant, tout ça n'etait que comédie. Et tout ceci . . . quand est-ce que tout ceci n'aura été que comédie"' (MS-TCD-10948-1–226, quoted in *BDMP8* 209).[6] Two months later, the problem is not yet solved, as Beckett writes the following to Jérôme Lindon: 'For the title, I have been hesitating between *Comédie, Que comédie,* and *Que jeu, . . .* What do you think?' (30 June 1963; Beckett 2014: 553) It is interesting to note that at that point Beckett was considering giving up the metatheatrical title, foregrounding instead the element of play ('Que jeu'). In opting for *Comédie* in the end, Beckett shifts the balance back to something more explicitly theatrical, possibly because his mind was so set on the play's production at the time. *Comédie* also retains the metatextual, self-referential element (albeit in a less dazzling fashion than in the English counterpart), with the title pointing to the play being exactly that – a theatre play (in this case, a comedy). Besides, unlike the English title, it adds an element of irony to the play: despite a few comic moments, designed to offset the tragic fate of the three protagonists, there is not much comedy in their past or present situation.

Another possible reason for Beckett's choice for *Comédie*, and one that would signify an introduction of a major intertextual element into the otherwise extremely sparse text, is the link to Dante. Though not documented in the genesis, the link is not implausible, given the purgatorial setting of the play (its 'Hellish half-light', the three figures being suspended in limbo between life and death, the endlessness of their trial, and so on). More generally, Dante is never far away in Beckett's work, and Rosemary Pountney makes a convincing case for similarities between *Play*'s formal properties and *La Divina Commedia* (see Pountney 1988: 27–37). Another famous 'comédie' in world literature is *La Comédie humaine* by Honoré de Balzac, but, although the plot of a love triangle is a frequent trope in this lengthy collection of novels and short stories, Balzac would be an unlikely source of inspiration, considering Beckett's well-documented aversion for his modus operandi as a writer.

Translating Ambiguity

One of the problems Beckett seemed to have with Balzac's authorship is the absence of ambiguity in his treatment of the story and the characters. As the English title immediately indicates, there is no lack of ambiguity in *Play*, carefully crafted by a progressive fragmentation of speeches and obfuscation of meaning during its genesis. This creative strategy works well for the original but clashes with the very essence of translation, namely the need to explain the meaning of the words written in a different language. The obvious difficulty for Beckett was conveying the ambiguity contained in the original text without explaining it away by translation.

A good illustration of this difficult task is the opening of the Meditation part.[7] 'Quand **ce changement** –' (FM1, 06r; *BDMP8* 220) is the literal rendering of M's opening line 'When first this change –', augmented by 'la première fois' ['the first time'] in his following speech. It is not immediately obvious which change M is referring to in the English original, but just before his speech the lights are dimmed to 'half-light' and the voices are reduced to 'half previous strength', according to the stage directions. In the first typescript version, 'La première fois –' is the typed layer of H's opening réplique, revised as follows: 'H: ~~La première fois – Quand ce changement~~ **Quand ça baissa** –' (FT1, 08r; *BDMP8* 220). H's expanded speech was also duly revised: 'La première fois ~~qu'il y est ce changement quand ce changement~~ **quand ça baissa** je louai Dieu, ~~hé oui~~ je le jure' (FT1, 08r; *BDMP8* 220). This change is both more evocative and literal at the same time, since the verb 'baisser' means 'go down, descend' but also (of light) 'grow dim, dwindle'. The use of 'baisser' at the opening of the Meditation to render the 'change' points much more explicitly to the stage image, as the spots are effectively dimmed seconds before H's speech. This revision was probably inspired by Beckett's direct experience at the theatre during the Ulm rehearsals during the translation process. The enigmatic 'this change' in the English text, despite the deictic marker, remains vague as to its nature, whereas the French revision, under the influence of Beckett's experience at the theatre, adds a more direct link between the stage image and the text.

Reinforcing Formal Patterns

As *Play*'s original text became more and more ambiguous and hence less and less meaningful, the emphasis increasingly shifted to its formal properties. Throughout the genesis of the English text, the increasingly abstracted and incomprehensible speeches have been cast into an impeccably crafted formal mould grounded in symmetry and repetition, and the translation not only upholds but also at times enhances this formal scaffolding. As a means to achieve the neat symmetrical structure, a number of utterances appear twice, albeit always in a slightly amended fashion. For instance, at some point W2 retells the story of W1's visit to her home: 'I smell you off him, she [W1] screamed, he *stinks of bitch*' (Beckett 1964: 11). This sentence is echoed by M's 'I smell her off you, she [W1] *kept saying*' (Beckett 1964: 11). Both are in fact quoting W1, who never utters the sentence herself. In the translation, the 'twin' sentences read like this: 'F2: Vous l'avez empesté, hurla-t-elle, *il pue la chienne*' (Beckett 1966: 12)/'H: Elle t'a empesté, disait-elle toujours, *tu pues la pute*' (Beckett 1966: 13). Instead of literally translating the second half of M's sentence ('she kept saying'), Beckett has opted for an additional element that echoes F2's speech ('il pue la chienne'/'tu pues la pute'). This way, both halves of H's sentence reiterate both halves of F2's sentence, thus adding an extra element of symmetry to the text.[8]

Translating Cultural Context

In a play that is so stripped of worldly elements, the few remnants that have been retained inevitably draw attention. Some of those references, such as those to the

Riviera and 'our darling Grand Canary', are left as they are in *Comédie*, as both are immediately recognisable as popular holiday destinations in both linguistic communities. Other, more locally anchored elements have received a different treatment – a common practice in Beckett's self-translations (*Happy Days* being arguably he best-known case in this connection). For instance, at some point W2 recalls how she disposed of M's things: 'I made a bundle of things and burnt them. It was November and the bonfire was going. All night I smelt them smouldering' (ET11, 8r; *BDMP8* 224). Most English readers and theatregoers would automatically think of Guy Fawkes Day/Night (5 November), traditionally associated with bonfires and (in earlier days) burning the effigies of unpopular public figures. Considering W2's feelings of resentment and frustration about what she believed was her lover's defection to his wife, such associations are indeed not difficult to make. However, in a letter to his Danish translator Christian Ludvigsen, written on 22 September 1963 (so with the bulk of the translation work behind him), Beckett explicitly denies any cross-reference: 'Bonfire: associated with Nov. 5th (Guy Fawkes Day) when they "burn the guy". But no allusion to this here. It is a simple fire lit in gardens at this season to burn fallen leaves and which commonly smoulders on for days' (Beckett 2014: 573. My emphasis).[9] Despite this assertion, it is hard to believe that Beckett had no 'allusion' in mind when he changed 'October' in the second and third English typescript to 'November' in the fourth. For a non-English audience, however, the link to Guy Fawkes is much less obvious, so Beckett introduced 'la Toussaint' ('All Saints'), with 'un feu de joie' ('fire of joy'), into the French text instead (FM2; *BDMP8* 224). The first French manuscript still contains the literally translated 'novembre', and in the second you can see Beckett hesitate between 'octobre' and 'novembre', both eventually crossed out and replaced by 'la Toussaint'. Although the change to 'la Toussaint' was all but necessitated by translation (or any other) constraints, Beckett did make that change anyway. By doing that, he undermined his own argument of 'no allusion' in the Ludvigsen letter, since the French text unequivocally refers to a religious and cultural event rather than a much more neutral name of the month. The religious connotation is not present in the English original, and the evocation of 'saints' ('la Toussaint') resonates with the 'infernal' theme that will pervade the Meditation, the second part of the play that immediately follows F2's speech.

Another intervention that was entirely superfluous (and therefore interesting) from the translation point of view is a change of the butler's name from Arsene to Frontin in the second French manuscript. Something similar also happens in the English original, but there the name change (from Arsene to Erskine) was prompted by a request from Alan Schneider in the run-up to the American premiere of the play. Schneider's concern was that the French Arsene would sound too strange to the American audience, and Beckett duly emended the name to Erskine, thus maintaining the Wattean connection in the text. However, the name Arsene is by no means strange or incomprehensible to the *French* ear, so why did Becket decide to use a different name? And not just any name, but Frontin, the archetypical wheeling and dealing butler in seventeenth- and eighteenth-century French comedy, used by authors such as Alain-René Lesage and Pierre de Marivaux. Beckett would have encountered Frontin the butler during his studies of French at Trinity College Dublin (henceforth TCD), with plays by Marivaux listed in his student library (see *Beckett Digital Library*, http://www.beckettarchive.org). It is possible that introducing Frontin was meant to boost the comedy factor of the play that was called *Comédie* but despite that fact was not particularly funny. Whatever Beckett's reasons were, adding an inter-textual reference to a text supposedly stripped of all 'worldly' properties is an unusual strategy that differs from the way the English original was composed.

Apart from the additions, the translation process of *Play* also entailed a number of cuts, the most obvious ones being the omission of after-text explanatory notes on the light, the urns, and the chorus from the final rendition of *Comédie*. Cockerham explains the excision by 'the general progression in Beckett's the-atre towards an ever-greater concision and density' (Cockerham 1975: 151). Without disputing Cockerham's assertion on the evolution of Beckett's drama, the omission of the notes from the target text is not as straightforward as his explanation suggests. Beckett also considered leaving them out from the *English* text and eventually had them removed for the Suhrkamp trilingual edition as mere 'aide-mémoire à l'usage des théâtres' (MS-TCD-10948-1-272, *BDMP8* 110). Besides, he did bother to make the translations of the three notes, even though they never made the final cut of *Comédie*, which indicates that he was at the very least considering their inclusion in the text at some point in the genesis. The last page of the fifteenth English typescript bears an autograph translation on the note on the urns (titled 'Jarres') in the bottom margin.[10] The translation was later crossed out and never appeared elsewhere. The notes on the light and the chorus made their brief appearance in the second French typescript as part of the typed layer – no autographs of these translations have survived. The ver-sions that follow the second French typescript omit all after-text notes except the note on repeat, which was added to the source text after the London National Theatre production in April 1964 and duly translated by Beckett. Rather than being a translation issue, the status of after-text notes as part of the play text was something Beckett clearly struggled with in both languages.[11]

Film

At a first glance, the story of the French translation of *Film* is the polar opposite of that of *Play*. Whereas *Comédie* came into being while *Play* was not yet completed, the translation of *Film* was written more than seven years after the original. This temporal gap provided an opportunity for Beckett to revisit the original text and the film project in general with the benefit of hindsight. The translation process itself was a swift one (begun and completed in the month of January 1971), which is more than can be said of the genesis of *Comédie*. This in itself is hardly surprising, given the fact that it was only a translation of a short film script.

Beckett undertook the translation task at Jérôme Lindon's request (Knowlson 1996: 581) and announced it in a letter to Alan Schneider: 'Starting to translate *Film* into French & reading again your so generous account of proceedings' (14 January 1971; Harmon 1998: 244). By 'proceedings' Beckett means Schneider's essay 'On Directing *Film*', which was part of the 1969 Grove Press edition (Harmon 1998: 244). It is interesting to note that Beckett not only felt the need to review the film and his own script, but also to read again Schneider's text, as if to refresh his memory of the actual shooting all the way back in 1964. This may indicate that the genesis of the shooting, captured by Schneider in his essay, was on Beckett's mind while he set out to translate the script and therefore had some influence on the genesis of the translation. Besides, the material at the Grove Press archive points to Beckett doing more than just rereading.[12] It seems that he used the 1969 Grove Press edition to proofread his *English original* of the script and to make corrections to it, based on the film as it turned out to be in the end and in the light of the impending translation job. This implies that, just like in the case with *Comédie*, the performance element also had an effect (albeit deferred) on the genesis of *Film*'s translation.

Despite the careful pruning of the English text and translating this freshly revised version, Beckett's autograph revisions of the English original in his copy of the 1969 Grove Press edition never made it into any subsequent editions of *Film*. This means that the source text and the target text are two different versions in a very literal sense. A good example of this discrepancy is the fate of Note 12 of the notes that follow the main body of the script. The English original reads: '12. Chair from front during photo sequence' (Beckett 1967: 43) and is accompanied by a small drawing of O sitting in the chair and E's point of view on him. In his copy of the Grove edition, Beckett crossed out both the note and the drawing, adding a handwritten justification for his action: 'impossibly seen' (Beckett 1969: 61). Having actually seen the end result, Beckett realised that such a shot was impossible, as it would prematurely reveal E to O. Therefore, though it still featured in version 1 of the translation ('12. Berceuse vue de face pendant la séquence des photos', FM, 15r; *BDMP8* 326), the slightly rephrased Note 12 was eliminated in version 2, and the numbering of the subsequent notes adjusted accordingly.

Of all the documents comprising *Film*'s translation dossier, the manuscript containing the first version of the translation is by far the most interesting one. Barely legible and heavily revised, it shows Beckett's usual struggle with rendering his original text into another language. That struggle begins already in the very first sentence (after 'esse est percipi'). The English original reads as follows: 'All extraneous perception suppressed, animal, human, divine, self-perception maintains in being' (Beckett 1967: 31). The first translation attempt renders it thus: 'Perçu de soi subsiste l'être que nul ne perçoit, **ni semblable**, ni animal, ni Dieu'. (FM, 01r, *BDMP8* 327; emphasis added). Apart from the interesting reversal of the order (from animal – human – divine to human – animal – divine), the translation of 'human' as 'semblable' catches the eye. The use of the word 'semblable' (meaning the same, of a similar kind) could be read as an intertextual reference to Charles Baudelaire's poem 'Au Lecteur', which ends with the line '– Hypocrite lecteur, – mon semblable, – mon frère!' We know that Beckett had a copy of Baudelaire's collection of poems *Les Fleurs du mal*, of which 'Au Lecteur' is the opening poem, even though the poem itself is unmarked in that copy,[13] and we also know that he used it in an oblique reference in *Malone meurt*.[14] Sadly, this rendering does not survive for long, as the sentence is immediately crossed out, and the revised version is much closer to the English original: 'Perçu de soi subsiste l'être soustrait à ~~la~~ perception d'autrui, **humaine**, animale, divine' (FM, 01r). In the second version, the order will also be adjusted to the English original: 'Perçu de soi subsiste l'être soustrait à la toute perception ~~d'autrui~~ étrangère, animale, **humaine**, divine' (FT1, 01r; *BDMP8* 327). That said, even this brief infusion of intertextuality at the earliest stage of the translation process points to the enrichment rather than impoverishment of the target text, even though this reference is soon undone. Moreover, more cases of enrichment in the translation of *Film* do survive the revisions and end up in the published version after all, as the following example will show.

Apart from the deleted Note 12, version two bears a trace of Beckett's hesitation about some words in the script. On page 01r, there is a marginal note above the text that reads 'investissement? 4 | occultation? 5' (FT1, 01r; *BDMP8* 328). Although they are both executed in black ink, the rendition tool seems different (that is, the word 'occultation?' and the number '5' are thicker and more intensely black). The latter word is Beckett's attempt at translating the English 'occlusion' and appears on page 05r:

> ? 1. Mise en état de la chambre (occultation de la fenêtre et de la glace,
> ? expulsion du chien et du chat, destruction du chromo, occultation de la
> cage et du bocal). (FT1, 05r; *BDMP8* 328) [Preparation of room (occlusion
> of window and mirror, ejection of dog and cat, destruction of God's image,
> occlusion of parrot and goldfish]. (Beckett 1967: 35)

In both cases, the word 'occultation' is underlined (manually) and marked by a question mark in the left margin (in the same writing tool). It is not clear why Beckett considered the translation to be problematic, and he does not suggest any variants to it in this or the next draft. The same happens with the word 'investissement', Beckett's translation of 'investment':

> 3. La chambre. [The room]
> ? E doit manœuvrer tout au long de cette scène, jusqu'à l'inverstissement proprement dit, de manière à ce que O soit toujours vu de dos, . . . (FT1, 04r; *BDMP8* 329). [E must so manoeuvre throughout what follows, until *investment* proper, that O is always seen from behind . . .]. (Beckett 1967: 35)
> ? 3. Investissement de O par E et dénouement. (FT1, 05r; *BDMP8* 329) [Final *investment* of O by E and dénouement]. (Beckett 1967: 35)

In this case, it is even more surprising that Beckett seems to hesitate about his translation, because the English and the French words are nearly identical. However, unlike its English counterpart, the French word 'investissement' harbours an additional connotation related to psychoanalysis. It is the rendering of Freud's term 'Besetzung', which in turn derives from 'besetzen' ('occupy a place by military force'),[15] like the English archaic meaning of 'investment'. The English equivalent of Freud's term is 'cathexis', and it refers to 'the investment of psychic energy in an object of any kind, such as a wish, fantasy, person, goal, idea, social group, or the self. Such objects are said to be cathected when an individual attaches emotional significance (positive or negative affect) to them'.[16] The term 'psychic energy' denotes 'the instincts or drives that are located in the id and seek immediate gratification according to the pleasure principle'.[17] Applied to *Film*'s dénouement, this means that E not only 'invests' O in terms of physical confinement, but also in terms of his emotions and drives, turning him quite literally into the Object of his desire. This psychoanalytical connotation ties in with E's pursuit of O throughout the film and underscores O's being the Object of E's obsessive attention.[18]

The link to psychoanalysis resonates with Beckett's own interest in the subject during his London years in the mid-1930s, when he underwent psychoanalytic treatment by Wilfried Bion (Knowlson 1996: 174–82). At that time, he also made a large number of notes on psychoanalysis (known as the 'Psychology Notes' and now preserved at TCD) in order to get to the bottom of it while undergoing it as a patient. In particular, he enters the term 'cathexis' in the Glossary section of the notes and defines it as 'affect **investing** idea' (MS-TCD-10971-8-19, *BDMP8* 330. My emphasis). In the section called 'True Symbolism', he mentions 'affect **investing** concept' in connection to the process of symbolisation (MS-TCD-10971-8-11; *BDMP8* 330; My emphasis).[19] There are other instances of the verb 'invest' in the notes, meaning that the psychoanalytical connection may have already been present in the English original of *Film*. However, it is only by looking at the French translation that the connection becomes more explicit, pointing once again to the enrichment effect of Beckett's self-translation.

Conclusion

The translation history of *Play* and *Film*, although different, contains a number of interesting parallels. Both source texts are characterised by a significant degree of abstraction, obtained in their own genesis, and could be seen as auxiliaries that serve to create and supplement an image, be it a stage performance or a film. Despite their ostensibly lower status than their visual rendering, the texts of *Play* and *Film* seemed important enough for Beckett to invest a significant amount of time and effort into their translations. In both cases, the translation has also had a direct bearing on the English original, albeit in different ways. Due to their parallel genesis, *Comédie* influenced the evolution of *Play*, and the need to translate its ambiguity sometimes helped uncover what it was that Beckett meant to say in the original. As to *Film*, its translation triggered a long-overdue revision of the English original script in the light of the film's final cut. Because these emendations never made it into any subsequent editions of *Film*, the French translation is the only published text that incorporates – albeit indirectly – Beckett's epigenetic revisions of the English original. Moreover, these revisions would have never taken place if it had not been for the translation. Once again, just like in *Play*, the (self-)translation proves to be more than just that – it is a constitutive part of a bilingual work's genesis as a whole.

Both the French *Film* and *Comédie* have also added a number of cultural and intertextual elements that the English originals did not have. The addition rather than reduction of textual elements in the translations seems at odds with Beckett's composition strategy of 'undoing' and 'vaguening' for the originals (see Gontarski 1985 and Pountney 1988). Perhaps paradoxically, the self-translation of the English *Play* and *Film* into French has resulted in the enrichment rather than impoverishment for the source texts that were not only supposed to be secondary to their visual rendering but had also been consistently reduced and abstracted in their own genesis.

Unlike other translingual writers (such as Joseph Conrad, Vladimir Nabokov or Paul Celan), Beckett was not compelled to adopt a different language due to exile or forced emigration.[20] The original intention was, by his own admission, writing 'without style', even though we must also consider the more down-to-earth reasons that have to do with Beckett's move to France. French was – certainly at the time – a major world reading language, a fact that Beckett was no doubt well aware of (Grutman 2013: 197). In Beckett Studies, it was Stephen Stacey who drew attention to the pragmatic side of Beckett's decision, since the market opportunities for English-language prose in postwar France were quite limited (Stacey 2013, quoted in Slote 2015: 120). Whatever the reasons for his decision were, it is quite possible that Beckett never intended to return to English when he made it (Fitch 1988: 7). However, as his authorship in the new language evolved, Beckett adopted (either consciously or not) an even more revolutionary strategy, namely the systematic bi-directional self-translation of his oeuvre. By that time, his French had acquired a style of its own, at the very least equally idiomatic and 'rich' as his mother tongue. The resulting enrichment, not only of content but also of style, creates a tension with the impoverishment Beckett aspired to in his initial switch to French. Needless to say, this does not mean that he would ever return to his early, 'Joycean' way of writing. Instead, the enrichment in Beckett's bilingual works is much more subtle and complementary, as we have seen in the examples of *Play/Comédie* and *Film*. Moreover, in some cases it is only visible in the genesis of the translation and not in the published text, which underscores the interpretative value of the genetic approach to Beckett's poetics of self-translation. More generally, the cases discussed in this chapter foreground the importance and relevance of genetic translation studies (cf. Cordingley and Montini 2015; Nunes et al. 2020), an emerging yet vibrant field that harbours an enormous but hitherto largely unexploited hermeneutic potential for literary criticism with regard to translingual authorship.

Notes

1. This chapter draws on the genetic study of *Play/Comédie* and *Film* (Beloborodova 2019), henceforth abbreviated as *BDMP8*.
2. An illustrative example is the translation of M's 'Some fool was cutting grass' (Beckett 1964, 13). As it usually was the case with Beckett's translations, the first version of the translation was just a literal rendering of the original: 'Un **imbécile quelconque** tondait sa pelouse (FM1, 05r; *BDMP8* 219). In the second version, it became 'Un **con quelquepart** [sic] tondait sa pelouse', to be emended to the brilliantly alliterative 'Un **con quelconque** tondait sa pelouse' in in the third version (FT1, 07r; *BDMP8* 219, also discussed in Admussen 1973: 26). Perhaps unexpectedly, Beckett reverts this emendation back to 'Un con quelquepart' in the next version (FT2, 06r; *BDMP8* 219n242), but ultimately reconsiders yet again and goes back to 'Un con quelconque' from the third typescript onwards.

3. An entry on Beckett in the *Encyclopaedia of Literary Translation into English* points to a more or less equal distribution of idioms, colloquialisms and additions and deletions between English and French (Guest 2000: 122–5).

4. Also noted by Admussen 1973: 25; Admussen 1979: 30; Blackman 1985: 88; Pountney 1988: 264.

5. In the *Beckett Digital Manuscript Project*, ET stands for 'English typescript' and FT for 'French typescript' (so EM/FM would denote 'English' and 'French manuscript', respectively). The number following the abbreviation indicates their place in the chronology of the writing process.

6. Among other things, this letter is a good illustration of the extent to which Beckett oscillated between writing *Play/Comédie* and *Film* at the time.

7. 'Meditation' is the second part of the play, in which the characters muse on their present state and their future; in the first part, dubbed 'Narration', they are mostly talking about their past (the actual love triangle). Beckett himself referred to the play's parts in those terms.

8. The addition is also noted in Cockerham 1975: 152. Admussen also discusses the alliteration effect of the change from the original 'Elle t'a empesté, disait-elle toujours, tu pues la **chienne**' in the manuscript to 'tu pues la **pute**' in the final rendition of H's sentence. This means that the correspondence between F2's and M's quotations of F1 was even greater in the first draft, with 'la chienne' featuring in both sentences.

9. The letter to Ludvigsen is interesting in its entirety, as it is one of the rare occasions when Beckett engages in explaining his work in considerable detail, probably in order to avoid translation errors due to misunderstandings.

10. The fact that the French rendering of the note on the urns is to be found in the fifteenth English typescript is as another indication of the parallel genesis of the two texts.

11. The only edition of *Comédie* that does contain the notes on the light, the urns and the chorus is the 1972 Aubier-Flammarion Bilingual Edition (Beckett 1972), in which the notes are translated by the editor, Jean-Jacques Mayoux, probably for the purpose of maintaining the symmetry between the English and French texts, printed in parallel (on facing pages).

12. Syracuse University (SU), Grove Press Records, Beckett-Film-24446-c2, 12 pp.

13. See *Beckett Digital Library*, http://www.beckettarchive.org/library/BAU-FLE-1.html.

14. See Van Hulle and Verhulst 2017: 162.

15. Encyclopaedia Universalis, https://www.universalis.fr/encyclopedie/investissement-psychanalyse/.

16. The American Psychological Association (APA) Dictionary of Psychology, https://dictionary.apa.org/cathexis. Note the word 'investment' in the definition.

17. APA, https://dictionary.apa.org/psychic-energy.
18. At the same time, the reference is subtle enough not to be seen as a sole explanation of E's actions – this would substantially reduce the film's rich hermeneutic potential.
19. The idea is that the symbolisation process is unconscious and will enter consciousness when psychic energy is released from repression (this is my interpretation of Beckett's notes). I thank Dirk Van Hulle for supplying me with the information from the Psychology Notes.
20. Although Beckett did move to and finally settle in France, he could have continued writing in English, as, for instance, Joyce did.

Works Cited

Admussen, Richard L. (1973), 'The Manuscripts of Beckett's *Play*', *Modern Drama*, 16:1 (Spring), 23–7.

Admussen, Richard L. (1979), *The Samuel Beckett Manuscripts: A Study*, Boston: G. K. Hall.

Beckett, Samuel (1964), *Play*, in *Play and Two Short Pieces for Radio*, London: Faber and Faber.

Beckett, Samuel (1966), *Comédie*, in *Comédie et Actes Divers*, Paris: Les Éditions de Minuit.

Beckett, Samuel (1967), *Film*, in *Eh Joe and Other Writings*, London: Faber and Faber.

Beckett, Samuel (1969), *Film by Samuel Beckett: Complete Scenario, Illustrations, Production Shoots*, New York: Grove Press.

Beckett, Samuel (1972), *Comédie*, in *Words and Music – Play – Eh Joe/Paroles et Musique – Comédie – Dis Joe*, Paris: Aubier-Flammarion Bilingue, pp. 180–231.

Beckett, Samuel (2014), *The Letters of Samuel Beckett: 1957–1965,* Vol. 3, George Craig, Martha Dow Fehsenfield, Dan Gunn, Lois More Overbeck (eds), Cambridge, UK: Cambridge University Press.

Beloborodova, Olga (2019), *The Making of Play/Comédie and Film (BDMP8)*, Brussels/London: UPA/Bloomsbury.

Blackman, Maurice (1985), 'The Shaping of a Beckett Text: "Play"', *Journal of Beckett Studies*, 10, 87–107.

Cockerham, Harry (1975), 'Bilingual Playwright', in Katharine Worth (ed), *Beckett the Shape Changer: A Symposium*, London/Boston: Routledge and Kegan Paul, pp. 141–59.

Cohn, Ruby (1962), *The Comic Gamut*, New Brunswick/New Jersey: Rutgers University Press.

Cordingley, Anthony and Chiara Montini (2015), 'Genetic Translation Studies: An Emerging Discipline', *Linguistica Antverpiensia*, New Series: Themes in Translation Studies, 14.

Fitch, Brian (1988), *Beckett and Babel: An Investigation into the Status of the Bilingual Work*, Toronto/Buffalo/London: University of Toronto Press.

Gontarski, S. E. (1985), *The Intent of Undoing in Samuel Beckett's Dramatic Texts*, Bloomington: Indiana University Press.

Grutman, Rainier (2009), 'Self-Translation', in Mona Baker (ed), *Routledge Encyclopedia of Translation Studies*, London: Routledge, pp. 257–60.

Grutman, Rainier (2013), 'Beckett and Beyond: Putting Self-Translation in Perspective', *Orbis Litterarum* 68.3, 188–206.

Grutman, Rainier, and Trish Van Bolderen (2014), 'Self-Translation', in Sandra Bermann and Catherine Porter (eds), *A Companion in Translation Studies*, Hoboken, NJ: John Wiley & Sons, Ltd, pp. 323–32.

Guest, Harry (2000), 'Samuel Beckett', in Olive Classe (ed), *Encyclopedia of Literary Translation into English*, Vol. I., London/Chicago: Fitzroy Dearborn Publishers, pp. 122–26.

Harmon, Maurice (ed) (1998), *No Author Better Served: The Correspondence of Samuel Beckett and Alan Schneider*, Cambridge, MA and London: Harvard University Press.

Knowlson, James (1996), *Damned to Fame: The Life of Samuel Beckett*, London: Bloomsbury.

Nunes, Ariadne, Joana Moura and Marta Pacheco Pinto (eds) (2020), *Genetic Translation Studies: Conflict and Collaboration in Liminal Spaces*, London: Bloomsbury.

Pountney, Rosemary (1988), *Theatre of Shadows: Samuel Beckett's Drama 1956–76*, Gerrards Cross and Totowa, NJ: Colin Smythe/Barnes and Noble Books.

Schneider, Alan (1969), 'On Directing *Film*', in *Film by Samuel Beckett: Complete Scenario, Illustrations, Production Shoots*, New York: Grove Press, pp. 63–94.

Slote, Sam (2015), 'Bilingual Beckett: Beyond the Linguistic Turn', in Dirk Van Hulle (ed), *The New Cambridge Companion to Samuel Beckett*, Cambridge, UK: Cambridge University Press, pp.114–25.

Van Hulle, Dirk and Pim Verhulst (2017), *The Making of Malone meurt/Malone Dies*, Brussels/London: UPA/Bloomsbury.

3

The Self-Translation of the Representation of the Mind in Samuel Beckett's Trilogy

Waqas Mirza

In the opening paragraph of the Trilogy, Molloy exposes the cryptic motives which lie behind his narrative. Voicing his discontent with an anonymous visitor's editorial feedback, he repeatedly claims authorship of his writing: 'Voici mon commencement à moi' (Beckett 1951: 8). This rich incipit has prompted many critics to comment on its formal,[1] intertextual,[2] logical,[3] and narratological[4] aspects. Others have read it on an ontological level. Éric Wessler, for instance, interprets it as an 'évocation implicite de la naissance du sujet' (Wessler 2009: 258). Laurent Mattiussi's argument corroborates Wessler's since he describes Molloy's double role here as both *narrator* and *author* of the 'lignes que le lecteur a sous les yeux' (Mattiussi 2004: 146). Note that both critics produce their readings based on the French text, thereby neglecting the novel's English counterpart. However, comparing both versions of *Molloy* reveals that Beckett's translation changes the assertion's grammar:

> *Voici mon commencement à moi.* Ils vont quand même le garder, si j'ai bien compris. Je me suis donné du mal. Le voici. Il m'a donné beaucoup de mal. C'était le commencement, vous comprenez. Tandis que c'est presque la fin, à présent. C'est mieux, ce que je fais à présent ? Je ne sais pas. La question n'est pas là. *Voici mon commencement à moi.* Ça doit signifier quelque chose, puisqu'ils le gardent. Le voici. (Beckett 1951b: 8)

> *Here's my beginning.* Because they're keeping it apparently. I took a lot of trouble with it. Here it is. It gave me a lot of trouble. It was the beginning, do you understand? Whereas now it's nearly the end. Is what I do now any better? I don't know. That's beside the point. *Here's my beginning.* It must mean something, or they wouldn't keep it. Here it is. (Beckett 1965: 4. My emphasis)

The italicised sentences portray a French Molloy emphasising identity and possession through pronominal repetition. The disjunctive pronoun in *à moi* works as a *complément prépositionnel* of 'commencement', which reinforces the idea that Molloy's beginning is very much his own self's, distinct from what others want him to write. Now, this example can be explained by linguistic constraint: an equivalent turn of phrase was not available to Beckett while translating. He could have, however, resorted to literary figures of insistence such as writing 'my own' or putting 'my' in italics. Instead, he toned down the protagonist's self-reflective discourse. The study of Beckett's translation process is far from being an exact science. There are, for instance, counterexamples to the phenomena observed above: some English texts contain added occurrences of first-person pronoun repetition absent from the French text.[5] These changes do not, however, have the same effect as 'Voici mon commencement à moi', in that they serve instead to underline the self-reflective nature of the narrator's utterance. Furthermore, translation shifts strengthening self-assertion in the French version occur more frequently than in the opposite direction. This phenomenon of greater emphasis in the French text compared to the English will be one of our focuses.

The chapter therefore explores the effects of Beckett's translations, in that it sets out to examine the differences in personal pronoun translation across the Trilogy. In particular, it analyses the repercussions of these differences on the representation of the mind. I argue that the author's translation choices account for major changes pertaining to the origin and nature of the narrative voice: they emphasise its fragmented self and its portrayal as a figure more inclusive of the narratee. The following pages will show how the use of pronouns in French contributes to a stronger assertiveness of the narratorial self and ultimately has an effect on reader inclusivity. Of course, the topic of the self in Beckett's prose has interested many scholars in the past, which is why a brief survey of the main concerns addressed by past critical debate on the subject can help to contextualise it.

The Beckettian Self

The scope of approaches employed in the study of the Beckettian self is as wide as it is varied. Yet they all revolve around one overarching issue which Maurice Blanchot coined in his review of *The Unnamable*: 'Qui parle dans les romans de Samuel Beckett?' (Blanchot 1959: 287). Blanchot's question points towards two essential areas of inquiry. First with the relative pronoun *qui*, which suggests that someone should be identifiable within the text. Second, this individual seems responsible for the *speech* which occurs in the novel. Exploring the self and exploring the narrative voice therefore seem to be two obvious points of departure. The first to approach them both together was Eric P. Levy, who focused on an enunciative approach to prove that the Beckettian narrator was trapped in his sole purpose: 'the endless experience of trying vainly to complete the narrative act' (Levy 1980: 5). However, Levy dipped in philosophical and psychological waters as well: in fact, his argument that Beckett deprived his narrators from both identity and experience shared the critical views of Frederick Hoffman, his main predecessor. Hoffman's monograph started off with an intertextual enquiry in order to 'locate Beckett within the modern history of the self's language', but ultimately shifted its focus to 'the elusive ego' in his prose (Hoffman 1962: 9). His final word on the trilogy is that it is 'quite simply and superficially stated, a portrayal of the loss of self': beginning with 'the impact of pain (and loss of members) upon self-confidence', proceeding with an exploration of 'the mind of a moribund' and ending 'upon the question of the total loss of name and of naming, of being and creativity' (Hoffman 1962: 128).

Following Hoffman and Levy, postmodern theories heavily influenced the debate which then relied on Derridean deconstruction, Lacanian psychoanalysis and Deleuzian post-structuralism. Paradox, for instance, was central to Jean Yamasaki Toyama, who explored the intersections of play and paradox through Derridean thought and persuasively demonstrated that Beckettian identity was paradoxical because it was both joined and separated in both space and time (Toyama 1991: 35–87). Proving the division of the Beckettian subject was also Michel Bernard's main goal, when he set out to investigate the strong echoes between Beckett's oeuvre and both Jacques Lacan and Gilles Deleuze's theories by drawing on the triad of real, imaginary and symbolic, along with the theory of disjunction between the subject of the enunciation (*le sujet de l'énonciation*) and the subject of the statement (*le sujet de l'énoncé*) (Bernard 1996: 16–9). Bernard examines the use of first and second-person pronouns and concludes in favour of a theory of self-generating and independent language (Bernard 1996: 53–83). There are, however, other potential interpretations as to where language may emanate from, other than the narrator or *no one*, as I will argue later in this chapter.

Llewellyn Brown also draws on the Lacanian concept of the real (one that is 'non-negotiable, unimaginable and unbearable') to approach 'the structure of the voice' of which 'the most salient difficulty resides in its localisation and its attribution'[6] (Brown 2011: 173–6). This voice, he says, seems to emanate from 'outside of any positive realization in utterances' (Brown 2011: 176). Brown adds that a 'dimension' of this voice 'is tied up to the question of pronouns', in particular the first-person singular 'which reveals the paradoxical quality of the voice' (Brown 2011: 180).

Indeed, the narrator's contradictory claims about himself can be confusing to the reader. This ambiguity, argues Brown, is further emphasised by the fact that 'the narrator's voice uses the pronoun I, but at the same time he denies being I, and creates an inextricable confusion between I and he' (Brown 2011: 185). After analysing the effect of the absence of the pronoun you (along with the 'structuring function' related to its being a 'deictic pronoun'), Brown concludes that 'the I becomes the vector of the impersonal thus although the I and the me are omnipresent in his work, they only translate the very real absence of I' (Brown 2011: 188).

This brief literature review highlights the importance of examining pronouns in Beckett's texts. The subject will be explored on two different axes: The Transformed 'I' and The Transformed 'Other'. The first section will start by considering the way narrators in both languages assert themselves through various pronouns. French narrators seem to have the upper hand here, while the English ones seem more reluctant to speak of themselves, at times reducing themselves to their physical characteristics. It will also examine the translation of the narratorial French *je* to the English pronouns 'you' and 'they', and how it serves to emphasise the fragmentation of the self and the representation of the narrative voice as a compound of voices. Then, it will show how Beckett's tendency to omit the first-person while translating into English contributes to a fuller and more complex portrayal of the French narrator. The second section will consider the way narrators in both languages offer general statements and how they address the reader. It will examine Beckett's translation of the French impersonal *on* into the English impersonal 'one' and the impersonal 'you'. It will also identify the effect of these pronominal translations on the relationship between the text and the reader.

The Transformed 'I'

The use of the first-person pronoun is a subject of internal debate for the narrator of *L'Innommable/The Unnamable*. When pondering the issue, he concludes that it should be resolved indifferently: 'Vous me direz, peu importe le pronom, qu'il n'y a que le résultat qui compte' (Beckett 1953: 96). I argue, however, that the use of a pronoun impacts on the narrator's characterisation. Linguists such as Émile Benveniste have dissected the role of pronouns in constituting the subject through language. He defined the pronoun *je*, for instance, as 'l'individu qui énonce la présente instance de discours contenant l'instance linguistique *je*' (Benveniste 1966: 252–9). The following section shows how translation changes made to passages in the first-person pronoun affect the readers' perception of the narrators. It will first consider examples of translations which objectify or anonymise the narrator. Then it will study pronominal slips from the first-person to the second or third before looking at translations which end up omitting the first-person pronominal voice entirely.

The Self Reduced

The French narrator seems more self-assertive, whereas the English seems more reluctant to speak of himself, often reduced to his characteristics or to elements associated to him. When the Unnamable relates his memories of life as a limbless being in a jar cared for by a woman named Marie, his interpretation of her behaviour differs in both languages. I indicate the pronominal differences in the quotations with italics:

Le premier regard . . . est pour *moi*.
(Beckett 1953: 75. My emphasis)

Her first look . . . is for the *jar*.
(Beckett 1965: 325. My emphasis)

By replacing the first-person pronoun with 'the jar', the text allows for two potential readings; both involve a metonymic process, namely the reduction of the Unnamable's identity to his recipient. Firstly, it could be the way he perceives himself, in which case the French Unnamable is the most self-assertive. Secondly, the designation could originate from Marie, the owner of the 'regard'. If so, in this sentence the narrator could point to two interpretations: he could be quoting her thoughts through free-speech or he could have come to internalise the idea that he projects onto her. In both cases, the readings point towards a self-effacement of the English Unnamable compared to the French.

Shifting Selves

The narrative voice is also affected by shifts to the second-person pronoun which emphasises the dialogic structure of mental discourse. When the Unnamable expresses discontent towards his situation, he states the following:

je me disais, Voilà le havre que *je* n'aurais jamais dû quitter, c'est là que *mes* chers absents *m*'attendent, patiemment, et *moi* aussi *je* dois être patient. (Beckett 1953: 311. My emphasis)

I kept saying to myself, Yonder is the nest *you* should never have left, there *your* dear absent ones are awaiting *your* return, patiently, *you* too must be patient. (Beckett 1965: 52. My emphasis)

In both languages, the first phrase indicates that the narrator is talking to himself, and that what follows can be considered as interior monologue. This implies that his thoughts are directly quoted by himself within the enunciative structure of a mental dialogue. By replacing the first-person pronoun with the second, however, the English injects a sense of otherness to the mental discourse, thereby suggesting a form of divided consciousness. A similar slip occurs towards the end of the novel, when the narrator claims that Mahood and Worm have become memories:

> je ne l'ai jamais vu, pourtant je m'en souviens, pour en avoir parlé, j'ai dû en parler, les mêmes mots reviennent, et ce sont *mes* souvenirs. (Beckett 1953: 134. My emphasis)

> I never saw him, and yet I remember, I remember having talked about him, I must have talked about him, the same words recur and they are *your* memories. (Beckett 1965: 395. My emphasis)

Here however, there is no indication of a self-address, and the shift only impacts the very last pronoun. The replacement of 'mes souvenirs' by 'your memories' accentuates the sense of otherness. Furthermore, its ambiguous referent requires considering three interpretative hypotheses. First, the narrator could be addressing a character within the story. Second, he could be talking to himself, as in the previous example. Third, the narrator could be addressing a narratee (a fictive reader), in which case the sentence functions as a metalepsis. Based on our knowledge of the book, it is safe to brush aside the third reading. However, the first two assumptions remain valuable keys for interpretation; favouring one over the other seems impossible. Both interpretations remain viable and, in any case, the self-represented is evidently fragmented, whether a narrator is transcribing a character's thought process through free indirect speech or whether his consciousness is divided, and he is speaking to himself.[7]

This sense of otherness is further emphasised by pronominal shifts to the plural. Describing the struggle to lead the narrative, the Unnamable says:

> Je me demande si mon histoire ne s'arrête pas là, si *Mahood* ne l'a pas arrêtée là. En me disant, qui sait, Voilà où tu en es, tu n'as plus besoin de *moi*. (Beckett 1953: 72. My emphasis)

> Perhaps it stops there, perhaps *they* stopped it there, saying, who knows, There you are now, you don't need *us* anymore. (Beckett 1965: 323. My emphasis)

The switch from *Mahood* (and the *moi* which refers to him later) to 'they' and 'us' suggests that the threat against the English Unnamable's narrative leadership is greater than the French one's. L'Innommable names only one opposer, whereas the Unnamable posits the presence of multiple writer figures involved in the potential interruption of the story.[8] Therefore, the English version emphasises the characterisation of the narrative voice as a compound of other voices. It struggles more intensely with a divided consciousness, thereby portraying a self more fragmented than the French narrators whose selves are more coherent. This has an effect on the intelligibility of the text, which can either distance or elicit the reader – an effect of particular interest when examining the changes involving the second-person pronoun.

The Self Omitted

Most often, Beckett's altering of the narrative self results in the omission of the first-person pronoun itself, in particular with regard to metadiscursive comments. In the midst of his description of Mrs Lambert's moving arms, Malone confesses a linguistic uncertainty:

> Puis elle leur imprimait, à chacun de son côté, des mouvements difficiles à décrire et dont la signification n'était pas très claire. *Elle les écartait de ses flancs, je dirais brandissais si j'ignorais encore mieux le génie de votre langue.* Ça tenait du geste étrange, à la fois coléreux et désarticulé, du bras secouant un torchon . . . (Beckett 1951a: 50. My emphasis)

> Then she began to toss them about in a way difficult to describe, and not easy to understand. [*] The movement resembled those, at once frantic and slack, of an arm shaking a duster . . . (Beckett 1965: 202)

The omission of the French italicised sentence indicated by an [*] in the English impacts the reader's understanding of Malone's linguistic competence. It is tempting here to draw a parallel between the character and Beckett himself. Linda Collinge, for instance, considers this aside as a clear allusion to the author's removal of autobiographical elements (Collinge 2000: 143). For now, however, our analysis is concerned with proving the effect of Beckett's translation choices and not the intention behind them. Malone's metalinguistic comment contributes to the portrayal of the narrator's relationship with language, by flaunting his linguistic mastery. He sarcastically explains that if only he 'ignorais encore mieux le génie' of the French language, he would have used the verb 'brandissais' instead of 'écartait' to accompany 'les flancs'. His knowledge of French is such that he cannot force himself to commit this linguistic mistake, however much his tendency to pun on genitalia might push him in that direction. Furthermore, this interpretation corroborates the idea of the blurring between Malone's identity and that of the characters from his stories. Together they explain the odd use of first-person ending instead of the third in 'brandissais'.

The Reader Included

This section has shown that Beckett's use of the first-person pronoun in French accounts for a more assertive self than in English. The English version often reduces the narrator to its constituents by objectifying or anonymising it. It also emphasises the fragmentation of the self by regularly shifting the French first-person pronoun to the English second- or third-person. These characteristics emphasise the fuller and more complex characters in the French version. Furthermore, the English narrator's struggle with a divided consciousness is tougher. The French puts less emphasis, for instance, on presenting the narrative voice as a compound of other voices. This affects the relationship between the reader and the text, as well, because the effort required to interpret the text and construct the same image of the narrative self in English makes it more inclusive.

The Transformed 'Other'

Let us now return to the opening pages of the Trilogy quoted earlier. The first paragraph explicitly adopted the focal perspective of Molloy himself, made clear by the use of the first-person pronoun. It did also contain second- and third-person pronouns as parts of reported speech; these, however, worked within the larger frame of a narrative lead in the first-person.[9] The second paragraph, however, operates unsettling pronominal shifts:

> Cette fois, puis encore une *je* pense . . . Tout s'estompe. Un peu plus et *on* sera aveugle . . . *On* devient muet aussi, et les bruits s'affaiblissent. (Beckett 1951b: 8. My emphasis)

> This time, then once more *I* think . . . All grows dim. A little more and *you*'ll go blind . . . *You* go dumb as well and sounds fade. (Beckett 1965: 3. My emphasis)

Here the French text slips from the first into the third-person indefinite (or impersonal) pronoun *on*, a pronoun the English version translates into the second-person pronoun 'you'. This 'you', however, can be read as a generic 'you' – also referred to as the indefinite or impersonal 'you' which is presented in more detail

later. Both these pronominal shifts follow the mention of a blurring phenomenon which could cause the blinding, muting and deafening described by the
narrator immediately after. In this case, the 'estompe[ment]' or the 'dim[ming]'
would relate to the senses and would target faculties of perception and speech.
Another possible reading, however, would be that the blurring phenomenon in
fact describes a metadiscursive process, that is the slip from a definite referent of
speech to an indefinite one, from a personal *je* and 'I' to an impersonal *on* and an
impersonal 'you'. One issue remains, however: that is to evaluate the semantic
and pragmatic differences between both of these pronouns' uses. And to do so
requires that we first review the grammar and stylistics of their uses.

The French pronoun *on* simultaneously requires and does not require identification (Herschberg–Pierrot 1993: 29). Its referent can be either definite or
indefinite – sometimes including interlocutors and/or within an identifiable or
unidentifiable group; and it can include or exclude the speaker (Landragin and
Tanguy 2014: 99). It can act both as a personal pronoun or an indefinite pronoun and can be read both specifically or generically (Landragin and Tanguy
2014: 100–1). When it acts as a substitute to *je*, it in fact does not refer directly
to the first-person, but rather to an indistinct group which can include both
the narrator and the reader (Landragin and Tanguy 2014: 105). The English
pronoun 'one' shares all of the French *on*'s features: they can both serve in
generic comments, and behave identically with regard to reference, inclusivity
and exclusivity. When it is used impersonally, 'one' can simultaneously express
a generalisation and include a reference to the speaker (Malamud 2012: 12).
The generalisation in the 'one'–sentence relies on 'speaker-simulation' and the
solicitation of the hearer's empathy (Malamud 2012: 13). The impersonal 'one'
shares these two linguistic features with the impersonal 'you' which is considered as its colloquial equivalent (Huddleston 1984: 288).[10] It has two different
types of uses: an impersonal 'one' which 'applies to anyone and/or everyone'
and a vague 'one' which 'applies to specific individuals' but who 'are not identified, or identifiable, by the speaker' (Kitagawa and Lehrer 1990: 742).

Therefore, all three pronouns are equivalent in their two main functions:
semantically they all serve to convey genericity, and pragmatically they all
behave similarly with regard to reference, inclusivity and exclusivity. One
main difference which has already been pointed out is the disparity in their
sociolinguistic occurrences. It may indeed be tempting to argue that 'you' is
the most direct translation available to Beckett while translating *on*, since 'one'
seems to be more commonly associated with formal registers or aristocratic
characters. There are, however, a few counter examples to this argument.
Beckett does in fact also use 'one' in his translations,[11] which further justifies
the requirement to examine his tendency in translating impersonal *on* into

impersonal 'you'. Harking back to the excerpt about Molloy's metadiscursive blurring, one may then wonder what the difference is, if it is not only sociolinguistic. The following section will attempt to answer that question, by examining in detail the use of the pronoun 'you' to translate generic comments and addresses to the reader.

Generic Selves

In the following example, described by Milcent-Lawson as a moment where Beckett 'défige' idiomatic expressions, (Milcent-Lawson 2013: 141) the Unnamable formulates the paradox which underlies his narrative experiment:

> Et si *je* parlais pour ne rien dire, mais vraiment rien? . . . Mais il semble impossible de parler pour ne rien dire, *on* croit y arriver, mais *on* oublie toujours quelque chose, un petit oui, un petit non, de quoi exterminer un régiment de dragons. (Beckett 1953: 27. My emphasis)

> If *I* could speak and yet say nothing, really nothing . . . But it seems impossible to speak and yet say nothing, *you* think you have succeeded, but *you* always overlook something, a little yes, a little no, enough to exterminate a regiment of dragoons. (Beckett 1965: 297. My emphasis)

The narrator initially uses the first-person pronoun to express his desire to say nothing. However, in the second sentence which undermines the feasibility of his project, the narrator uses the impersonal pronouns *on* and 'you'. The pronominal slips from personal to impersonal serves here to emphasise the generic value of the narrator's claim. Yet the choice of the third-person in French over the second-person in English has an effect on the reading of the text. Indeed, the main difference then seems to be that the impersonal 'you' is explicitly more inclusive of the reader. Kitagawa and Lehrer claim that it has a 'rhetorical force and pragmatic implications' which mirror its 'normative "personal" use (Kitagawa and Lehrer 1990: 752). 'Speech act participants' they say, 'can be viewed as *dramatis personae*': impersonal 'you' can generate a 'sense of informal camaraderie . . . because the speaker assigns a major 'actor' role to the addressee' and 'lets the hearer into the speaker's world view, implying that the hearer also shares the same perspective (Kitagawa and Lehrer 1990: 752). This is where the major difference lies in both pronouns' use within generalisations: they both rely on speaker-simulation and the solicitation of the hearer's empathy, but the impersonal 'you' also relies on hearer-simulation. For this reason, impersonal 'you' makes the sentence – and ultimately the narrator's discourse as well – more inclusive in the English version.

If the example used to support the argument of a more inclusive English narrator was an isolated occurrence, then it could indeed be considered as insignificant. This, however, is not the case; in fact, Beckett systematically operates translation shifts like these in the Trilogy. The following two excerpts from *Malone meurt/ Malone Dies* and *L'Innommable/The Unnamable* serve to illustrate this:

> Une petite ombre, en elle-même, sur le moment, ce n'est rien. *On* n'y pense plus, *on* continue, dans la clarté. (Beckett 1951: 28. My emphasis)

> A little darkness, in itself, at the time, is nothing. *You* think no more about it and *you* go on. (Beckett 1965: 19. My emphasis)

> *On* croit seulement se reposer, afin de mieux agir par la suite, et voilà qu'en très peu de temps *on* est dans l'impossibilité de plus jamais rien faire. (Beckett 1953: 190. My emphasis)

> *You* think you are simply resting, the better to act when the time comes, or for no reason, and *you* soon find yourself powerless ever to do anything again. (Beckett 1965: 334. My emphasis)

Both these sets of examples show Beckett translating generic *on*-sentences with an impersonal 'you', thereby pulling the reader in the text more efficiently in the English than in the French version. *Molloy* has occurrences of this phenomenon as well, with a few additional changes happening simultaneously. For instance, when Molloy generalises on the trajectory of life in French and in English, *on* is not the only pronoun which is altered:

> Le fait est, on dirait, que tout ce qu'*on* peut espérer à la fin c'est d'être un peu moins, à la fin, *celui* qu'*on* était au commencement, et par la suite. (Beckett 1951b: 50. My emphasis)

> The fact is, it seems, that the most *you* can hope is to be a little less, in the end, *the creature you* were in the beginning, and the middle. (Beckett 1965: 28. My emphasis)

Here the text substitutes the indefinite *celui* for 'the creature', which specifically indicates the group of individuals to whom the generic comment applies to. A tension between inclusivity and exclusivity of the reader does arise though. The term 'creature' is ambiguous enough to have connotative meanings across multiple reigns: the human, the animal and the fictive, all three of which will respectively tend towards implying inclusion or exclusion of the reader.

In fact, in the Trilogy there is only one example of *on* translated into a generic 'you' unlikely to behave inclusively towards the reader. It appears when Moran, unable to remember which 'country' or 'region' Molloy is in, explains the common way of referring to 'territorial divisions':

> Et pour les exprimer *nous* avons un autre système, d'une beauté et simplicité remarquables, et qui consiste à dire Bally (puisqu'il s'agit de Bally) lorsqu'*on* veut dire Bally et Ballyba lorsqu'*on* veut dire Bally plus les terres y afférentes et Ballybaba lorsqu'*on* veut dire terres de Bally exclusives de Bally lui-même. (Beckett 1951b: 182. My emphasis)

> And to express them *we* have another system, of singular beauty and simplic- ity, which consists in saying Bally (since we are talking of Bally) when *you* mean Bally and Ballyba when *you* mean Bally plus its domains and Ballybaba when *you* mean the domains exclusive of Bally itself. (Beckett 1965: 128. My emphasis)

Here the first personal plural pronoun *nous* is indeed used impersonally, yet in a way which includes only those who use the system, in the process excluding the reader. The pronouns *on* which follow are therefore co-referentially exclusive as well. The English version mimics this exclusivity but adds a strong tension with inclusivity because of the traditional referent of the pronoun 'you'. This phenomenon is called vague 'you' by Kitagawa and Lehrer: as with the imper- sonal 'you' 'the interlocutor assumes the status of representative in some sense of the intended referent' but the difference is that the impersonal 'you' does not allow exclusion of the reader, while the vague 'you' does allow it (Kitagawa and Lehrer 1990: 744). However, because this is the only example of exclusive 'you' in the English version, and because it serves to translate an impersonal 'one' which is itself relatively exclusive of the reader, it does not undermine the argument that Beckett, intentionally or otherwise, emphasises reader inclusivity while translating the French pronoun *on* into the English pronoun 'you'.

Similar pronominal shifts occur in the very first pages of the Molloy narrative, when the narrator rejoices over having found his next project:

> Maintenant qu'*on* sait où l'*on* va, allons-y. Il est si bon de savoir où l'*on* va, dans les premiers temps. Ça *vous* enlève presque l'envie d'y aller. (Beckett 1951b: 28. My emphasis)

> Now that *we* know where *we*'re going let's go there. It's so nice to know where *you*'re going in the early stages, it rids *you* of the wish to go there. (Beckett 1965: 15. My emphasis)

Here the first two impersonal pronouns *on* are translated into an impersonal plural *we*, and the third *on* is translated to the impersonal 'you'. Then the French text slips into the impersonal plural *vous*, which is rendered in English as another impersonal 'you'. What is notable then, is that the English portrays the speech act participants as dramatis personae in an even more significant way than the ones before. It seems as though Beckett is indeed trying to accentuate the explicitness of reader inclusivity in his translations by resorting to the inclusive 'we'. The impersonal *vous* in this example is not the only one to appear in *Molloy* within generic statements. Its occurrence in Molloy's narrative does require a close reading as well. After having calculated his daily flatulence rate, the narrator claims in excitement:

> Extraordinaire comme les mathématiques *vous* aident à *vous* connaître. (Beckett *ML*, 1951b: 47. My emphasis)

> Extraordinary how mathematics help *you* know *yourself*. (Beckett 1965: 26. My emphasis)

Once again, the translation into impersonal *you* along with its reflexive form 'yourself' serves to express the concept of generality all the while explicitly addressing the reader. This example prompts us to examine the appearances of other second-person plural pronouns in the Trilogy which are closer to addresses than generic statements.

Addressing Selves

Molloy's narrative contains many addresses to the reader which Beckett often translates very closely. For instance, 'Mes pieds, voyez-vous' is strictly rendered as 'My feet, you see' (Beckett 1951b: 45; Beckett 1965: 25) The same goes for the following excerpt:

> Il y avait si longtemps que je vivais loin des mots, *vous* comprenez, qu'il me suffisait de voir ma ville, pour ne pas pouvoir, *vous* comprenez. (Beckett 1951b: 33. My emphasis)

> I had been living so far from words, *you* understand, that it was enough for me to see my town since we're talking of my town, to be unable, *you* understand. (Beckett 1965: 60. My emphasis)

However, some translations alter the addresses from the original, either by changing the second-person pronoun, or by substituting it entirely all the while

emphasising reader inclusivity. To illustrate these, we will look at two examples
of Molloy talking about two relationships with women, one romantic and one
maternal. The first excerpt is from the incipit, when the narrator alludes to a
'petite boniche' whose name he cannot remember:

> Ce n'était pas le vrai amour. Le vrai amour était dans une autre. *Vous* allez
> voir. (Beckett 1951b: 8. My emphasis)

> It wasn't true love. The true love was in another. *We*'ll come to that.
> (Beckett 1965: 3. My emphasis)

The pronominal shift from second-person plural to the first has an effect on
reader inclusivity along with the choice of the verb which follows it. In the
French version the reader is treated as a spectator, as one who is meant to witness the narrator's thoughts unfold. Whereas in the English he is treated as a
companion in the narrative's journey. The second example operates differently
yet affects the reader in similar ways. Molloy speaks of his mother's inability to
count further than two:

> Il y avait trop loin pour elle, comprenez-vous . . . (Beckett 1951b: 26)

> It was too far for her, yes . . . (Beckett 1965: 14)

The direct address to the reader is replaced by the affirmative 'yes' which can also
be interpreted as Molloy engaging with the reader. Beckett thereby maintains an
enunciative dialogue structure, without resorting to the second-person pronoun.

The Reader Included

This section examined the grammatical and stylistic effects of translation shifts
from third-person pronouns into second-person ones. Its focus was first set
on the translation of the French impersonal *on* used while narrators made
generic comments. Even though Beckett sometimes uses the English impersonal *one* to translate it, his use of the impersonal 'you' is evidently more
characteristic across the Trilogy. All three behave very similarly, both on a
semantic and pragmatic level: speakers generalise all the while including their
interlocutors as referents. However, there are differences in their interpretations which go beyond those in register which are often associated to them.
Using the generic 'you' to translate them instead of 'one' explicitly increases
the text's inclusivity. Both of these pronouns' uses within generalisations rely

on speaker-simulation and the hearer-empathy solicitation, however 'you' also relies on hearer-simulation. Beckett's tendency to use it in the English version contributes to the portrayal of a narrator who is more inclusive of the reader in his discourse. His use of the second-person plural 'we' to translate *on* also confirms this. By doing so, he accentuates the explicitness of reader inclusivity even more. This section then examined the translation of the second-person plural pronoun *vous* which typically occurred in the context of explicit addresses to the reader. These translations either switched the pronoun for another or changed the phrase altogether. In both cases Beckett regularly makes choices which emphasise reader inclusivity, as he did when translating the generic statements.

Modification and Alteration

This chapter has shown that pronominal differences in both versions of the Trilogy have effects on the representation of the protagonists' minds and discourse. Beckett's translation of the first-person pronoun – *je* – accounts for a more fragmented and less assertive English self than its French counterpart. This forces the English reader to put more effort into constructing an image of the narrative self which is equivalent to the one presented in the French version. Furthermore, Beckett's translation of second- and third-person pronouns – *vous* and *on* – works identically; it portrays the narrator as a figure more inclusive of the reader in his discourse by being deictically less distinct. This does not, however, mean that the intention behind these choices was necessarily to increase reader inclusivity.

This section therefore seeks to open up the discussion by considering another possible reason the author may have made these choices: namely that they are determined by language difference. In his letter to Herbert Blau, Beckett attributed a 'weakening effect' with respect to the French language, which could be part of the explanation why his pronominal translations increase reader inclusivity (Blau 1960: 90–1). Our analysis has shown that the French narrator is portrayed in a manner which is more consistent and more assertive. Moreover, Beckett's tendency to cut passages while translating fits within the general progression of his oeuvre: a production which grew sparser and sparser over time. But what if Beckett's lengthier writing in the French language was constrained by language itself? What if it was a reaction to this 'weakening effect', which required him to be more explicit, which required him to write more in French? This could mean that his creation of a more inclusive English text is constrained by the language itself. It could mean that Beckett makes English characters more inclusive of their readers because

English itself is more inclusive than French, rather than because French is more inclusive than English.

In other words, at the heart of the issue might lie Beckett's relationship with language differences and their potential to represent a fictional self. Let us consider the narrator Molloy, for instance. Beckett wrote two texts in which Molloy's self is represented, one text in French and the other in English. This leaves the bilingual reader with two potential readings: the French Molloy and the English Molloy can either be the same character or two distinct ones. If they are indeed the same, then Beckett's project would consist of writing the concept of Molloy's self in both languages, a sort of bilingual transcription of a unique self. If they are different, the author's enterprise changes accordingly: he would be the creator of two characters with two different selves, the French Molloy and the English Molloy. The question therefore becomes: are both of these selves linguistically constrained versions of some sort of overarching Beckettian concept of Molloy's self? Or does the author believe that the concept of self exists within language itself, and that the English concept of the self differs essentially from the French one? If the first is true, then the shifts which have been analysed in this chapter account for a transformation of the self, not a recreation. If instead, the second is true, rather than submitting the self to a transformation, Beckett is altering it, that is, submitting the self to the presence of an other.

Notes

1. Gendron (2008) and Stewart (2006) wrote about the repetitiveness of its beginning.
2. Weisberg (2000) explained how it caricatured the modern writer.
3. Reid (2003: 89) unravelled the contradictory behaviour of the narrator.
4. Duffy (1998: 178) and Lüscher-Morata (2005: 225) dissected its narratological role: the first in spatial terms and the second in temporal ones.
5. A few pronominal differences between *Malone meurt* and *Malone Dies*, as well as between *L'Innommable* and *The Unnamable*:

> Le large n'est plus éclairé que par reflets, c'est sur *moi* que mes sens sont braqués. (Beckett 1951a: 19. My emphasis)

> All my senses are trained full on *me, me.* (Beckett 1965: 80. My emphasis)

> Où maintenant? Quand maintenant? Qui maintenant? Sans me le demander. *Dire je.* Sans le penser. (Beckett 1953: 7)

Where now? Who now? When now? Unquestioning. *I, say I.* Unbelieving. (Beckett 1965: 286. My emphasis)

Mais au fait, s'agit-il de *moi* en ce moment? But now, is it *I* now, *I* on *me*? (Beckett 1953: 46; Beckett 1965: 310. My emphasis)

Et dont c'est faire le jeu que de poser de telles questions. Pourtant. Dans ma jarre, est-ce que *je* m'en posais? Dans l'arène, souvent debout encore et en marche, est-ce que *je* m'interrogeais? (Beckett 1953: 90. My emphasis)

And into whose hands *I* play when *I* ask *myself* such questions? But do *I*, do *I*? In the jar did *I* ask *myself* questions? And in the arena? (Beckett 1965: 331. My emphasis)

6. Further references to this article are given after quotations in the text.
7. Uncertainty behind the origin of an utterance in *L'Innommable/The Unnamable* but adding layers of confusion to this enunciative conundrum. When casting doubt over the existence of other characters, the French narrator says that 'Je crois que Murphy parlait de temps en temps, les autres aussi peut-être, je ne me rappelle pas, mais c'était mal fait, je voyais le ventriloque', whereas the English narrator says 'I think Murphy spoke now and then, the others too perhaps, I don't remember, but it was clumsily done, you could see the ventriloquist' (Beckett 1953: 103; 1965: 342; My emphasis). The identification of a puppeteer figure, the ventriloquist, is claimed as the French narrator's own, while the English one seems to externalise this judgement. Indeed, the sentence now allows for two possible interpretations: it can emanate from the narrator himself, ironically commenting on the poor construction of the text; or it can correspond to a focal point effect allowing the reader to hear the narrator's voice agreeing with general consensus.
8. This moment echoes another with Worm at the heart of the problem, when Beckett translates 'Maintenant je *m'entends* dire que c'est la voix de Worm qui commence, je transmets la nouvelle, pour ce qu'elle vaut' into 'Now I seem to hear *them* say it is Worm's voice beginning, I pass on the news, for what it is worth' (Beckett 1953: 98; Beckett 1965: 339; My emphasis). Where the French narrator *s'entend dire*, the English hears *them* say that it is Worm's voice beginning. Of course, the French allows for both readings to co-exist: indeed, the narrator could just as much be relaying the voice of others than his own.

9. The numerous *il* and *ils*, of course, are pronouns used by Molloy to describe his surroundings. The *vous* in 'Vous ferez ça plus tard, dit-il', is part of the visitor's speech reported by the narrator. A noteworthy example is a *vous* in Molloy's address to the narratee: 'Vous allez voir' translated to 'We'll come to that' (Beckett 1951b: 8; Beckett 1965: 3). This last pronominal shift in translation will be examined more closely later in the chapter.

10. Huddleston describes the generic 'you' as 'a stylistically less formal variant of non-deictic *one*' which does not include the addressee or exclude the speaker in its reference.

11. In *Molloy*, for instance, when the narrator reflects upon his geographical surroundings: 'Que c'est agréable d'être confirmé, après une période plus ou moins longue de vacillation dans *ces* premières impressions' is translated into 'How agreeable it is to be confirmed, after a more or less long period of vacillation, in *one's* first impressions' (Beckett 1951b: 21; Beckett 1965: 11. My emphasis). This impersonal use of the pronoun *one* is also found in sentences translating the French *on*, such as the following excerpts from *L'Innommable/ The Unnamable*: 'Peut-*on* parler d'une voix, dans ces conditions? Sans doute que non' / 'May *one* speak of a voice, in these conditions? Probably not' (Beckett 1965: 100; Beckett 1965: 336. My emphasis).

Works Cited

Primary Sources

Beckett, Samuel (1951a), *Malone meurt*, Paris: Éditions de Minuit.
Beckett, Samuel (1951b), *Molloy*, Paris: Éditions de Minuit.
Beckett, Samuel (1953), *L'Innommable*, Paris: Éditions de Minuit.
Beckett, Samuel (1965), *Three Novels: Molloy, Malone Dies, and The Unnamable*, New York: Grove Press.

Secondary Sources

Benveniste, Émile (1966), *Problèmes de Linguistique Générale, Volume I & II*, Paris: Gallimard.
Bernard, Michel (1996), *Samuel Beckett et son sujet: une apparition épanouissante*, Paris: Éditions L'Harmattan.
Blanchot, Maurice (1959), *Le livre à venir*, Paris: Gallimard.
Blau, Herbert (1960), 'Meanwhile, Follow the Bright Angels', *The Tulane Drama Review*, 5.1, 89–101.
Brown, Llewellyn (2011), 'Voices and Pronouns in Samuel Beckett's *The Unnamable*', *Journal of Beckett Studies*, 20.2, 172–96.

Collinge, Linda (2000), *Beckett Traduit Beckett: De Malone Meurt à Malone Dies: L'imaginaire en traduction*, Genève: Droz.

Duffy, Brian (1998), '*Molloy*: As the Story was told. Or not', in Marius Buning (ed) *Beckett versus Beckett. Samuel Beckett Today/Aujourd'hui*, 7, New York: Rodopi, 173–93.

Gendron, Sarah (2008), *Repetition, Difference, and Knowledge in the Work of Samuel Beckett, Jacques Derrida, and Gilles Deleuze*, New York: Peter Lang.

Herschberg-Pierrot, Anne (1993), *Stylistique de la prose*, Paris: Belin.

Hoffman, Frederick (1962), *Samuel Beckett: Language of Self*, Carbondale: Southern Illinois University Press.

Huddleston, Rodney (1984), *Introduction to the Grammar of English*, New York: Cambridge University Press.

Kitagawa, Chisato and Adrienne Lehrer (1990), 'Impersonal Uses of Personal Pronouns', *Journal of Pragmatics*, 14.5, 739–59.

Landragin, Frédéric and Noalig Tanguy (2014), 'Référence et coréférence du pronom indéfini "on"', *Langages*, 195.3, 99–115.

Levy, Eric P. (1980), *Beckett and the Voice of Species*, Dublin: Gill and Macmillan.

Lüscher-Morata, Diane (2005), *La souffrance portée au langage dans la prose de Samuel Beckett*, New York: Rodopi.

Malamud, Sophia A. (2012), 'Impersonal indexicals: *one, you, man*, and *du*', in *Journal of Comparative German Linguistics*, 15, 1–48.

Mattiussi, Laurent (2004), 'Kafka, Hesse … Beckett: de l'appropriation à l'expropriation de soi', in Alain Montandon (dir.), *De soi à soi: l'écriture comme autohospitalité*, Clermont-Ferrand: Presses Universitaires Blaise Pascal, pp.143–59.

Milcent-Lawson, Sophie (2013), 'Poétiques du défigement chez Giono et Beckett', *Pratiques*, 127–46.

Reid, James H. (2003), *Proust, Beckett, and Narration*, Cambridge, UK: Cambridge University Press.

Stewart, Paul (2006), *Zone of Evaporation: Samuel Beckett's Disjunctions*, New York: Rodopi.

Toyama, Jean Yamasaki (1991), *Beckett's Games: Self and Language in the Trilogy*, New York and London: Peter Lang.

Weisberg, David (2000), *Chronicles of Disorder: Samuel Beckett and the Cultural Politics of the Modern Novel*, Albany: SUNY Press.

Wessler, Éric (2009), *La littérature face à elle-même: l'écriture spéculaire de Samuel Beckett*, New York: Rodopi.

4

Vagaries of Bilingualism. A Curious Case of Beckett's Translations of his Own Poems

Sławomir Studniarz

Among the bilingual writers and the literary productions made available by the authors themselves in two different languages, the works of the Irish writer occupy a special place. Discussing Beckett's bilingualism, Ann Beer emphasises that 'unlike almost all other major bilingual writers of the twentieth century, Beckett's bilingualism was entirely voluntary', for it was 'driven partly by aesthetic and partly by psychological needs' (Beer 1994: 214). Rainier Grutman, in turn, points out Beckett's unique status as 'the single auto-translator that has received the most critical attention' (Grutman 2005: 19). Interestingly, he argues that auto-translation is not really translation; as he puts it, it is more of a double writing process (Grutman 2005: 19). It is becoming more and more evident that the final product of self-translation frequently acquires the status of a second original. More and more translation scholars hold the opinion that self-translators are 'recreators producing a new original on the model of the old' (Hokenson and Munson 1994: 199). As Brian Fitch points out, in the order of time the original comes first, but its precedence becomes 'purely temporal in character' (Fitch 1988: 131). This means that the original loses its unique, privileged status; its authority is provisional. Both texts are treated as 'variants' or 'versions' that enjoy equal status (Fitch 1988: 132–3).

Beckett's translations of his own poems from French into English puzzle both his admirers and his devoted scholars. As early as 1970, Lawrence Harvey in his pioneering study *Samuel Beckett: Poet & Critic* drew attention to the disparity between the French originals and their subsequent rendering in English. As is the case of many works by Beckett first written in French and then translated by himself, the French original and the English version are very rarely close analogues of each other. Grutman observes in his article 'Beckett and Beyond: Putting Self-Translation in Perspective' that the Irish writer 'turned his manuscripts into bilingual laboratories of which the published, monolingual versions cannot even begin to give an idea' (Grutman 2013: 192). Furthermore, he adds that 'by 1969, when he was awarded the Nobel Prize in literature, his "translations" followed so closely on the heels of their "originals" that the distinction had all but collapsed'; as a result, 'the hierarchy between the two had been effectively abolished' (Grutman 2013: 192). Grutman goes on to conclude that 'Beckett was able to transform his entire oeuvre into a diptych, with parallel panels in each language', and 'the resulting "bilingual work" is his single most arresting achievement' (Grutman 2013: 196).

As Hokenson and Munson remark (2007: 192), most of the research on Beckett's bilingual work so far has focused on his prose and dramatic works. In order to fill the existing critical gap at least partially, the present article will take into account all of Beckett's poetic texts rendered in the two languages by the author himself. Examination will begin with the two short poems from *Poèmes 37–39*: 'Dieppe' and 'elles viennent'. However, the bulk of the article will deal with the three poems first published in *transition* 48.2, June 1946: 'je voudrais que mon amour meure', 'je suis ce cours de sable qui glisse', and 'que ferais-je sans ce monde sans visage sans questions', and their English counterparts, respectively 'my way is in the sand flowing', 'I would like my love to die', and 'what would I do without this world faceless incurious'.[1] The survey will be completed by a scrutiny of Beckett's last works, 'Comment dire' and 'what is the word'.

According to Lawlor and Pilling, 'Dieppe' 'was originally written in French, although it first appeared in a variant English five-line version' (Beckett 2012: 384). As they further state, it was inspired by Hölderlin's poem 'Der Spaziergang', and the German poet is one of the 'luminaries of the old' evoked in the French version. The scene is set at the shore and depicts the moment of turning away from the sea, from 'the last ebb' and 'the dead shingle', with their connotations of death and transience. Lawlor and Pilling provide an interesting gloss on the construction of the poem, revealing that whenever the Irish author discussed this poem, 'he emphasised that "puis" ("then") – the word which, as it were, "does" the turning – was the key word' (Beckett 2012: 386).

Even from a cursory inspection of the two linguistic versions it may be concluded that the French text is more allusive. The closing phrase 'les vieilles lumières' is semantically richer and more explicitly ambiguous than the English 'the lights of old'. The French expression points to the Western intellectual heritage, and more specifically to the Enlightenment, 'le siècle des Lumières'. In addition, the French 'lumières' means also 'wisdom, insight'. Owing to the allusions embedded in the French text, the presented vignette depicting the speaker positioned on the shore, observing the sea and then turning toward the land, is converted into a deeply evocative image. The idea of an end, suggested by 'the last ebb', of a termination of a cycle ('again'), is juxtaposed with the persistent presence of the past, of the cultural legacy that serves as a beacon, guiding the speaker, who takes his steps toward 'the lights of old'.

Furthermore, the French text is full of subtle sonic echoes. Thus, 'encore' is reflected in 'mort', giving rise to the disturbing rhyming pair 'encore – mort', 'again dead', emphasising the cycle of destruction rather than renewal. In the alliterated sequence 'puis les pas', the speaker's steps, 'pas', seem to follow from this pivotal moment, 'puis'. The French version is richly orchestrated with the sonorants /r/ and /l/ throughout its four lines – the former appears seven times, and the latter as many as eight. But it is the final line: 'vers les vieilles lumières', that displays the most intricate design, in which 'vieilles lumières', /v l.r/, emerges as the inversion of the 'vers les', /v.r l/. It is worth pointing out that the configuration featuring /v/, /l/, and /r/, comes across as the voiceless variant of /r.fl/, which occurs in 'reflux' in the opening line of the poem, with the French word carrying an additional meaning of 'backward surge'. Hence, the verbal texture of the poem itself suggests the idea of a return or a cycle, and this quality has apparently been lost in translation.

When it comes to 'elles viennent' and its English version 'they come', it can be easily noticed that the two texts display a surprising structural and syntactic convergence. The lexical items and the syntax employed in the French and English texts are equivalent, which is supported by a close correspondence in the arrangement of verses. Thus, a high degree of fidelity in the translation has been achieved, which is certainly not the case in the three *transition* poems that will be scrutinised next. As Lawlor and Pilling explain, these poems are 'unique' as 'the only example of the first publication of his work with English and French versions set out . . . on facing pages' (Beckett 2012: 402). The scholars state that 'No manuscript of the French originals survives, but there is an undated holograph of SB's first attempts to translate the poems into English' (Beckett 2012: 402). The two linguistic versions of the poems subsequently appeared in the volume *Poems in English* published in London in 1961 by John Calder, and then in New York in 1963 by Grove Press. From the start, the English versions aroused controversy. There is an interesting anecdote included by Lawlor and Pilling in the commentary section of Beckett's *Collected Poems*, coming from Kay Boyle, an American novelist and a friend of Beckett. Boyle 'explains that she sent the book [the 1963 Grove edition] back to Beckett asking him "to be more accurate in his translation of his own work from French into English" and he obeyed' (Beckett 2012: 404). Beckett's alteration written in his own hand involved the change from 'mourning the first and last to love me' to 'mourning her who thought she loved me' (Beckett 2012: 404).

A closer look at the first poem, 'je voudrais que mon amour meure', and its English version, 'I would like my love to die', reveals that the French poem displays a dense network of sound and sense relations, conspicuously missing in the English text. In line 1, 'mon amour meure', /m m.r m.r/, love, 'amour', and death, 'meure', are brought together in sound. Thus, the line establishes an oxymoronic, disturbing equation between love and death. In line 2 'cimetière', a cemetery, through /m.r/ sonically evokes both love and death, 'amour' and 'meure', while it shares /s.r/ with 'sur'. In effect, a crucial semantic bond is created between 'mon amour', 'meure' and 'sur le cimetière', which includes the speaker's feeling for his beloved, death and the cemetery as the destination of the loved one.

The sequence is completed by the final '[qui crut] m'aimer', the illusion or semblance of the beloved's love for the speaker. What is more, so as to strengthen the equivalence between the elements of the chain, the phrase 'celle . . . m'aimer', /s.l m m.r/, phonically echoes 'le cimetière', /l.s.m.r/. She who loved the speaker is thus identified with the graveyard, where her resting place should be. The identification is fastened by the verb 'pleure', which means 'to rain' and 'to weep', giving rise to a pathetic fallacy, with the rain falling on the graveyard as the reflection of the speaker shedding tears for the beloved. Furthermore, the striking sound parallel binds the rain falling on the cemetery in line 2: 'qu'il pleuve sur le cimetière', /k.l pl s.r l.s.m.t.r/, and the speaker weeping for her who thought she loved him, in line 4: 'pleurant celle qui crut m'aimer', /pl s.l k kr m.m.r/. In addition, the phonic echo ties 'je voudrais' of the opening line, the speaker's wishing for his love to die, with 'je vais [pleurant]', the act of mourning the beloved. The consistent orchestration of the poem with sonorants and sibilants: /m/, /n/, /l/, /r/, /s/, /v/, creates a dense sonic weave and weft in the texture of the French version, resulting in the even tighter semantic alignment of the elements of the presented lyrical situation.

In the English text 'my love' is sonically distant from 'to die', but there is an attempt at compensation in the patterning of the sound texture: 'I', 'my', 'like', and 'die' share the vocalic nucleus /aɪ/, with the effect of including the speaker in the action of dying and suggesting a death wish on his part. But no equivalence is established between the speaker's love, dying, the object of his love and the cemetery, which is so prominent in the French version. Somehow, 'mourning' in the English version inserted in the place of the more accurate 'weeping', echoes 'amour' and 'meure' across the divide of the languages. However, the chosen expression of the speaker's grief in no way parallels 'raining'. In the light of these findings, it is rather evident that as a poetic text the English version does seem impoverished when set beside the French original.

The next poem of the *transition* group, 'je suis ce cours de sable qui glisse', employs a series of *topoi* conveying impermanence and the fleeting phenomenal reality, with 'sand flowing' as a conventional metaphor of time passing inexorably. Ruby Cohn notes that the sand is 'a felicitous image for the transience' (Cohn 2005: 158). Furthermore, lack of punctuation is meaningful, conveying the flow, and the second stanza is 'one unbroken sentence of direct address to the passing moment' (Cohn 2005: 158). According to the critic, life is 'at once built on sand and immanent in sand', 'blinded by fog and protected by fog', and the repetitive long vowel /i:/ in the English version is the 'keening vowel, eliciting sadness' (Cohn 2005: 158).

Echoing Harvey, Marjorie Perloff points out the ambiguity of the opening phrase 'Je suis', which can be translated either as 'I follow' or as 'I am', the ambiguity that, as she and Harvey emphasise, is not resolved in the English version, where it is rendered as 'My way is' (Perloff 2010: 217). She enumerates the following differences between the two versions of the poem:

1. 'Beckett roughs it up a bit, archaicising its smooth flow' in the English version;
2. 'harrying fleeing/to its beginning to its end' disperses movement rather than completing the circle of the French 'et finira le jour de son commencement';
3. In the second stanza the first line, 'cher instant je te vois', is omitted completely, as 'too embarrassing' (Perloff 2010: 217).

According to Perloff, 'the epiphany (*cher instant je te vois*) found in the mist that recedes, is that there will be no more elusive thresholds to cross, and the poet will live *le temps d'une porte*, the brief time between the opening of a door and its closing' (Perloff 2010: 217). However, the question arises, why 'the brief time'? The door is indeed a threshold, but rather than one final opening and closing, the repetitive opening and closing of the door is suggested in the French version by the verb *referme*, to close again: 'qui s'ouvre et se referme'. Thus, the speaker will permanently inhabit the time of the threshold, will be stuck in the liminal zone. Also, the epiphany is not yet found. In the French text the future tense is employed: 'n'aurai', 'vivrai'. The receding mist promises some revelation, not yet grasped, so the epiphany is in the future. In order to account for the striking substitution of 'le temps d'une porte' with 'the space of a door', Perloff concludes that 'the French poem emphasises the fleeting moment, the English version is more concerned with framing' (Perloff 2010: 217). But she ignores the obvious linguistic fact that the French verb *referme* denotes a repetitive or cyclical action, so the theory of the fleeting moment is untenable.

Equivalence of time and space is in evidence in both versions of the poem. In the French text, 'cher instant' will become *the place where* the speaker will cease from treading, 'où je n'aurai plus à fouler', and will live the time of the door. In the English version, the speaker's 'peace' is wishfully located in the receding mist, *in the moment* that will free him from crossing the thresholds, '*when* I may cease from treading the long shifting thresholds', and he will inhabit the 'space of a door'.

Impermanence, the fluidity of the sand flowing, of 'sable qui glisse', is heightened by the shifting thresholds, 'seuils mouvants'. There is no foothold in this elusive, ever receding phenomenal world, no purchase, nothing to cling to. Instability is inscribed in the very nature of reality. The present moment ever eludes the subject, because once it is fixed, once it becomes a fact of consciousness, it has already slid into the past. Time in human experience means the continual trickling of the present into the past. The release, 'cher instant', is relegated to the future, imaged as the curtain of thick mist that recedes, 'ce rideau de brume qui recule'. The speaker longs to transcend the precarious nature of time, to escape the universal process of becoming. His dream is to be trapped in the liminal condition, in an alternative temporal zone, in a moment that repeats itself, like a door that opens and closes again, 'une porte qui s'ouvre et se referme'.

In the French version the semantic thrust of the poem is reflected in its sound texture. The opening line is orchestrated with the sibilant /s/ and the liquid /l/, in 'suis', 'sable' and 'glisse'. These gliding sounds can be protracted indefinitely in articulation, and as such are apt acoustic vehicles for conveying the idea of flow, of the passage of time. In line 2 'galet', /g.l/, echoes 'glisse', /gl/. The sequence 'la pluie d'été pleut' in line 3 sonically binds the agent and its action. In the English version this is achieved by the repetition, 'rain rains', which lacks the subtlety of the French counterpart. In the French version, the speaker's life, 'ma vie', typographically pursues or rather precedes the speaker, 'moi', and simultaneously escapes him, runs ahead: 'sur *ma vie*/sur moi *ma vie* qui me fuit me poursuit'. The English version preserves the typographic arrangement: 'on my life/on me my life harrying fleeing', but the idea of the subject simultaneously being pursued by his life and pursuing it is absent in the English text. Internal rhyme binds the two antithetical terms 'fuit' and 'poursuit' in the French version. The sonic correspondence is only roughly preserved in the English text in the grammatical rhyme binding 'harrying' with 'fleeing', but the semantic opposition is missing – 'my life harrying' is not equivalent to the French 'ma vie que me poursuit'. The pivotal position of the line 'où je n'aurai plus à fouler ces longs seuils mouvants' right in the middle of the stanza turns it into a graphic threshold, surrounded neatly by two almost symmetrical pairs of lines. Furthermore, it is by far the longest one in the whole poem, containing thirteen syllables, and thus it typographically renders the ordeal of treading these 'long shifting thresholds'. The second stanza of the

English version misses the opening line of the French original. As a result, the line 'when I may cease from treading these long shifting thresholds' loses its central position, and the original design of the stanza collapses.

In the French text in the closing line of stanza 1, 'et finira le jour de son commencement', the future verb, 'finira', is syntactically related to the noun 'ma vie', but also possibly to 'la pluie', which yields two readings: 'the speaker's life will end the day with its beginning' or 'the rain will end the day with its beginning'. Additional ambiguity inheres in the possessive 'son', which may refer to the speaker's life, the rain, or the day. Assuming that the subject of the verb 'finira' is 'ma vie', the final line of the stanza can be rendered in the English paraphrase in two ways: 'my life will end the day with my life's beginning' or 'my life will end the day with the day's beginning'. Furthermore, the syntactic indeterminacy of the French text gives rise to yet another interpretation of the line in question: 'the speaker's life will end *on* the day of its beginning'. Notwithstanding these syntactic intricacies, in each case the end is equated with the beginning. If so, then there is no progress, no becoming, no unfolding. Perhaps this absence, this indefinitely extended liminal condition is embodied equally in 'the space of a door' and 'le temps d'une porte'.

The orchestration of the whole stanza is consistent, relying on the protracted, gliding speech sounds: nasals /m/ and /ŋ/, fricatives /f/, /v/ and /s/, and liquids /l/ and /r/. Thus, on the phonemic level, the end of the stanza: 'et finira le jour de son commencement', very nearly reinstates the beginning, with 'cours' of the opening line and its rhyming partner 'jour' of the closing line in analogical positions in a verse, to fasten the sonic convergence. Because the semantic circularity, that is the identity of the beginning and the end, is matched by the phonetic repetition, the patterning of the verbal material in stanza 1 acquires the status of an iconic sign. The sense is mapped onto the sound – there is an iconic correspondence between the thematised meaning and the arrangement of the phonemes. This more abstract type of iconicity is called by Max Nänny and Olga Fischer diagrammatic because it is the structure of the mapped concept that is reflected in the sonic weave and waft (Nänny and Fischer 1999: 22). In Beckett's poem the stated equation of the opening with the closure is underscored by the phonological recurrence.

In stanza 2, the phonetic instrumentation relies on the same set of speech sounds, with the exception of line 2, 'ce rideau de brume qui recule', which is orchestrated with plosives /b/, /d/, and /k/, in combination with /r/: 'rideau', /r.d/, 'brume', /br/, 'recule', /r.k/. These consonantal patterns involve a different articulation, and the plosives, which are rapid and abrupt, hint at a sense of completion, of closure, tantalisingly promised to be grasped in the receding mist. On the other hand, in the final line of the French text, 'qui s'ouvre et se referme', the verbs denoting the action of the door, 's'ouvre', /s.vr/, and 'se referme', /s.r.f.r/, emerge as phonic echoes, suggesting the identity of the closing and the opening, which recalls the familiar equation of the beginning with the end in the conclusion of stanza one.

The sound texture of the English version reveals some patterning, too, although it is by no means equivalent to the phonetic design of the French original. The opening stanza is orchestrated with the sonorants: /w/, in 'way', 'flowing', 'between', /l/, in 'flowing', 'shingle', 'long', 'live', and the twice-repeated 'life', /m/, in 'summer' and the much repeated pronouns 'me' and 'my', and the fricative /s/, in 'sand', 'summer', 'peace', 'receding', 'mist', 'space'. Thanks to the common configuration of /l/ and /f/ a crucial sequence is established, characterising the speaker's 'life' as 'flowing' and 'fleeting', additionally equating 'sand flowing' with 'life fleeting'. Harvey argues that in the English version 'Beckett takes full advantage of present participles available in English to suggest indirectly the passing of time ('flowing', 'harrying', 'fleeing', 'receding', 'treading', 'shifting')', concluding somehow hastily that 'we perhaps have the right to prefer the English version in these instances' (Harvey 1970: 228). Unlike the French original, the speaker's 'peace', his relief, the elusive promise located in 'the receding mist', and the wished-for effect, 'cease [from treading]' are tightly brought together in sound by means of the recurrent combination of /s/ with /iː/ o r /ɪ/, in 'peace', 'cease', and 'receding mist': /iːs iːs siː ɪs/. The combination of /l/ and /ʃ/ in conjunction with the fricative /f/ or / θ/ binds 'thresholds', /θ.ʃ.l/, with the qualifying epithets 'long shifting', /l. ʃ.f/, naturalising the connection between them, turning the latter into inherent qualities of the former.

The third poem published alongside 'je voudrais que mon amour meure' and 'je suis ce cours de sable qui glisse' is 'que ferais-je sans ce monde', with its English counterpart 'what would I do without this world'. In the English version 'sans questions' is rendered as 'incurious' and 'sans visage' as 'faceless'. Thus, instead of the accumulation of 'sans', which appears three times in the opening line of the poem: 'sans ce monde sans visage sans questions', there is a single 'without' and a sequence of two negative epithets. Furthermore, the striking parallelism built in line 3 in the French text: 'dans le vide dans l'oubli', is lost in the English version, which features simply 'in the void the ignorance'. The parallel rhyming phrases in line 7: 'vers le secours vers l'amour', are rendered without a rhyme as 'towards succor towards love'. There are also instances of parallelism in the second part of the French version: 'comme hier comme aujourd'hui' and 'à errer et à virer', which have not been preserved in the English rendition.

The chief marker of absence, 'sans', appears as many as six times in the first part of the poem, and it is additionally echoed by 'dans'. The strong internal rhyme binding 'sans' and 'dans' expands to include 'instant', repeated twice in line 2, and 'ensemble s'engloutissent' in line 5, featuring an impressive chain of four /ɑ̃/. Phonic echoes reach across the lines, for instance 'onde' in line 4 ('wave') heavily recalls 'monde' ('world') in line 1, in consequence binding semantically the two and equating the world with 'the wave where in the end body and shadow together are engulfed'. The semantic network created by sonic correspondences in the French version grows even denser when 'onde', / ɔ̃d/, and 'corps', /kɔr/ ('body'), coalesce in 'ombre', /ɔ̃br/ ('shadow'). The phonetic blending reinforces the idea of the prophesied final engulfment of 'body and shadow together' by the 'wave/world'. Phonetic reduplication occurs in 'sans ce silence', /sɑ̃ sə silɑ̃s/, and the configuration /s s s l s/ antici- pates a conspicuous pattern of configurations built on /s/ and /l/ in the con- cluding two lines of the first part: 'ce ciel', /s s.l/ ('this sky'), 's'élève', /s l/ 'soars'), and 'ses lests', /s l.s/ ('ballast'). This design is partially compensated for in the English version by the alliteration that binds 'sky' and 'soars', and the impressive internal rhyme in 'ballast dust'. Also, the second part of the English version builds an impressive network of present participles, which is absent in the French text: 'peering', 'looking', 'wandering', 'eddying', complemented by 'living', which is a gerund. The final three lines: 'in a convulsive space / among the voices voiceless / that throng my hiddenness', feature an abundance of sibilants and fricatives, altogether fourteen in such a short textual span – /s/ appears seven times, /v/ four times, and there is also one /z/ in 'voices', one/ ð/ in 'that', and one /θ/ in 'throng'.

The different phonetic orchestration of the final three lines of the English version is matched by the accompanying modulations in semantics. In the English text a substantial shift occurs in the final line of the poem, where the image of the voices locked together with the speaker, 'les voix enfermées avec moi', is replaced with the suggestion of the voices filling the enclosed space occupied by the speaker: 'the voices . . . that throng my hiddenness'. Furthermore, the speaker's condition is clarified in the English version as 'my hiddenness', whereas in the French text it is only hinted at by his activity: 'regardant par mon hublot', rendered as 'peering out of my deadlight', as if the speaker dwelled alone in the confines of a ship. Commenting on the English term 'convulsive space' as a counterpart of the original 'espace pantin', Harvey states that the image of an 'espace pantin' is 'the clearest statement thus far in the poetry of a conviction of the unreality of life on the little stage where marionettes go through their motions' (Harvey 1970, 244), whereas 'convul- sive space' in the English translation, as he puts it, 'catches the basic idea of movement unwilled and uncontrolled by the individual' (Harvey 1970: 245).

The present inquiry into vagaries of Beckett's bilingualism, the inquiry whose scope is limited to his translations of his own poetry, is concluded by the consideration of 'Comment dire' and its English version titled 'what is the word', the final works of the Irish author. As Lawlor and Pilling note (Beckett 2012: 474), the original French holograph of 'Comment dire' is dated October 29, 1988, whereas 'what is the word' appeared posthumously in December 1989. These two texts merit special attention not only as Beckett's valedictory artistic statements. They are also the most radical examples of his linguistic and structural experimentation, particularly noticeable in the extensive deployment of repetition and ellipsis, the hallmarks of Beckett's late poetics of verbal minimalism. The study titled *The Making of Samuel Beckett's Stirrings Still/Soubresauts and Comment dire/What is the Word*, by Dirk Van Hulle, painstakingly documents the circumstances behind and the successive versions of Beckett's final texts. As many as seven existing drafts of 'Comment dire' indicate that the process of composition of the poem was long and painful, reflecting the writer's struggle to regain speech after the stroke. For Cohn, the lines of the French text seem 'to echo Beckett's actual aphasia – curt, abrupt, and repetitive', but she admits that 'the last revision is a musical structure retaining only the recollection of aphasia' (Cohn 2005: 382–3).

These final artistic utterances remain as challenging as ever. Yet, much can be gained from attending closely to the structural features and the verbal patterning of the two versions, which exhibit a tight structural correspondence, very rarely to be found in Beckett's major bilingual works. Even a cursory glance reveals their peculiar construction, the tension between extension of a line and its reduction, whereby the two processes, expansion and contraction, clash in the arrangement of the verses. In 'what is the word' the first peak, the first victory of articulation over paralysis occurs in line 19, featuring the record number of 6 words: 'folly seeing all this this here -' (in the French text, it is matched by line 20: 'folie vu tout ce ceci-ci que de -'). Line 26 features eight words: 'folly for to need to seem to glimpse -', in the French version: 'folie que de vouloir croire entrevoir quoi -'. By far the longest line is line 50, the apex of the poem, crowning the articulative efforts. With its fourteen words, it comes closest in the poem to expressing a single complete idea, but it ends with 'what', which undercuts its semantic thrust, since the cognitive impulse is frustrated: 'folly for to need to seem to glimpse afaint afar away over there what -', matched by line 49 in the French text: 'folie que d'y vouloir croire entrevoir quoi'.

In the English text the refrain-like 'what is the word' appears seven times and then it appears at the end to close it. The phrase divides the poem into smaller units, perhaps delineating stages of a process. Hence, it seems reasonable to approach the poem by examining the chunks of the verbal material punctuated by the line 'what is the word' in the English version and 'comment dire' in the French text. The first break occurs after the initial three lines, when the speaker comes to halt, unable to complete 'folly for to -'. The choice of 'folly/ folie' as the verbal leitmotif is significant, it already conveys a judgment, deeming all human efforts 'folly'. The noun appears twelve times, rivalling 'what', which occurs as many as fifteen times. This preponderance is unique to the English text, since in the French version 'what' is rendered as either 'comment' or 'quoi', hence its presence is less striking. Instances of repetition abound in both linguistic versions, while the syntax is bare and broken. The difficulty lies in connecting meaningfully the disjointed interjections. The lexicon is limited to a handful of nouns, pronouns, verbs, and demonstratives, deictic expressions such as 'this', 'here', 'there', 'away', or 'loin', 'là', 'là- bas', 'ce' or 'ceci-ci', which in themselves, divorced from the context, are semantically empty. The first two units bring in apposition 'folly for to' ('folie que de') with 'folly from this' ('folie depuis ce'), amplified as 'folly from all this'. These prepositions project different cognitive scenarios. 'For' implies the reason for a hypothetical action, not yet specified, with the missing verb: 'folly for to', whereas 'from' suggests the cause, the folly as the result of some state of affairs, a condition enigmatically described as 'all this'. The speaker at this stage is unable to name the impulse motivating the cognitive effort, which is later, in the fourth section, defined as 'to need to seem to glimpse'.

The second unit is based on the interplay between two key lines: 'folly given all this' and 'folly seeing all this' ('folie donné tout ce' and 'folie vu ce'). The most frequently repeated word in this section is 'this': 'this this – this this here – all this this here –'. Confronted with 'this', the speaker cannot move beyond it, he remains stuck. The section highlights the speaker's inability to specify 'all this', this which is given, and this which is seen, 'seeing all this'. Interpretation is further thwarted by the ambiguity of the English expression 'given all this', which can be taken to mean 'allowing for', as a logical concession, or literally, as 'endowed with all', or in a negative sense, 'burdened with all this'.

The subsequent section marks the first entry of verbs, which represents a huge semantic leap forward in the poem's action, counteracting stasis implied by the nouns, gerunds, and demonstratives. 'See' modulates into a more tentative and fleeting 'glimpse', and this verb is further attenuated by placing 'seem' in front of it: 'see - glimpse - seem to glimpse -'. The phonic similarity binding the sequence 'see', 'seem', and through the final /s/ 'glimpse' as well, is an attempt to reproduce the chain of the sonically related verbs of perception in the French version, in which 'voir' modulates into 'entrevoir', and the two verbs are bound by internal rhyme with 'croire' and 'vouloir'. However, the English text only partially renders the dense network formed by these four verbs in the French text.

Nuances of meaning differentiating 'glimpse' and 'see', and then 'glimpse' and 'seem to glimpse' underscore the uncertainty and fragmentariness of perception. A glimpse offering a quick and incomplete view suggests a merely momentary and partial insight. Thus, inescapably, any epistemological inquiry and cognition are fundamentally flawed, as rooted in faulty, inadequate perception. However, this does not disable human drive for attaining knowledge, the impulse behind the cognitive effort defined as search for a fleeting, imperfect vision: 'need to seem to glimpse', and the French 'vouloir croire entrevoir', the latter implying the willingness rather than the need. The section ends with the interrogative 'what/quoi', shrouding the object of the intellectual quest in mystery.

In the following fifth section, the enigma is extended to incorporate the zone of inquiry, denoted by the cryptic 'where'. Thus, the mystery of 'what to look for' is heightened by the additional conundrum of 'where to look': 'folly for to need to seem to glimpse what where -'. Thus, cognitive efforts, epistemological endeavours reveal their contingency and fallibility - they are of a nature of groping clumsily in the dark. Section 6 picks up on the idea of locality; 'where' as the site of the quest is translated into a chain of deictic expressions: 'there', 'over there', 'away over there'. The much-cherished goal emerges as distant, 'afar', dimly perceived, 'afaint', hence elusive, unreachable. In both versions the series of deictic expressions envelope the object of epistemological pursuit, 'what/quoi', and defer the completion of the quest: 'afaint afar away over there what -' ('loin là là-bas à peine quoi'). Ultimately, 'what/quoi' denotes the inscrutable mystery. The veil cannot be pierced but the cognitive impulse itself, 'need to seem to glimpse', is valid and perhaps even imperative.

In as much as the two texts display a close semantic and structural correspondence, their titles are radically divergent, and they seem to pose two fundamentally different questions. 'Comment dire' conveys a dilemma of an artist using words as his medium, who tries to overcome the resistance of verbal material, with the English 'how to phrase it' as its closest equivalent. It may also point to an attempt to master the language and reveal a painful and halting striving for eloquence and excellence. As Cohn notes, 'That question was already posed in his earliest French fiction, and although Beckett never felt that he discovered an answer, he cast the question as his final burden' (Cohn 2005: 382). The English rendition of the title as 'what is the word' shifts the focus away from the considerations of craftsmanship and a verbal artist's struggle to articulate. If we equate 'word' with literature, which it represents metonymically, then the English title and at the same time the leitmotif of the poem emerges as a self-reflexive gesture of the writer, anxious to provide the fitting conclusion to his writing career. Yet his farewell is enigmatic. The title foregrounds the epistemological dimension, where 'what is the word' presents an unresolvable ambiguity, for it is simultaneously the question and its own answer. 'What' can be treated as a pronoun, as a question word, and at the same time as a noun, as a linguistic sign that is the solution of the query. However, both these readings equally defer the hermeneutic closure. After all, in either case what persists is the mode of interrogation, not assertion, because 'what' asserts nothing. On the other hand, Beckett's final 'word' evokes Logos, and John's equivocal claim 'In the beginning was the word'. It appears, then, that 'what is the word' engages with the theological and metaphysical issues and in his final text Beckett returns to the intellectual problematics of his early plays. Humanity is left with the inexplicable mystery, waiting for God's Word. Perhaps, despite mankind's perennial yearning to elicit a response from God, His silence will never be broken.

The scrutiny of Beckett's bilingual poetic texts prompts a conclusion that the French originals and the English versions produced by the author himself, with the sole exception of 'elles viennent' and 'they come', are never exact counterparts of each other. Transposing the French poems into a different linguistic and cultural setting necessitated an extensive application of compensation, 'a technique which involves making up for the loss of a source text effect by recreating a similar effect in the target text through means that are specific to the target language' (Harvey 2005: 37). Peter Newmark, who is credited with establishing this term in translation studies, claims that it is 'the procedure which in the last resort ensures that translation is possible' (Newmark 1991: 144), but its heavy deployment may result in a divergence between the source text and the target text. For Beckett, who so meticulously orchestrated his French poems, compensating for their intricate sound and sense patterning without straying too far from the semantic core, undoubtedly represented a major challenge. When it comes to 'Dieppe' and the three *transition* poems, even though the English versions in the organisation of their verbal texture do not match the French texts and the relation between sonority and semantics is on the whole suppressed in them, 'I would like my love to die', 'my way is in the sand flowing' and 'what would I do without this world' cannot be treated as literal transpositions in which the beauty is sacrificed in the name of the fidelity to the sense. Yet, despite their individual merits, the English versions overall do not display the same level of artistic sophistication and word play as the French texts. However, this assessment cannot be extended to Beckett's final grapple with words, that is 'Comment dire' and 'what is the word', as the two texts exhibit a high degree of equivalence in their versification, sound texture, construction and semantics. This, however, does not apply to the titles and the pivotal lines of these two poems, with their widely diverse resonances and implications.

Furthermore, the presented findings indicate that Beckett's bilingual poetic creations exist in a relation of complementarity rather than equivalence. Never striving for close correspondence in his poetic translations, Beckett fostered a semantic interplay between the French originals and their English versions, setting up a dialogic tension between them. Beckett's translating practice goes to prove the thesis advanced in translation studies that self-translators usually take advantage of poetic license and rewrite their originals, which 'in turn, can lead to a reversal, or at least a downplaying, of the hierarchy that normally favours the original over the translation, with neither version taking precedence' (Grutman and Van Bolderen 2014: 324). José Francisco Fernández rightly observes that 'As the author of the text, Beckett was entitled to change and modify the original, whereas a translator – by definition, an anonymous, invisible vehicle for the transmission of a work into another language – must not, and cannot, do this' (Fernández 2018: 134). In a final analysis, in the light of the presented observations and conclusions, it becomes perfectly clear why the discussed poems, as many other examples of Beckett's bilingual creation, invite a study of structural and semantic reciprocation between the two linguistic versions rather than a straightforward examination of each text on its own.

Note

1. All the quotations from Beckett's poems come from *The Collected Poem of Samuel Beckett* (2012), Seán Lawlor and John Pilling (eds), London: Faber and Faber.

Works Cited

Beckett, Samuel (2012), *The Collected Poems*, Seán Lawlor and John Pilling (eds), London: Faber and Faber.

Beer, Ann (1994), 'Beckett's Bilingualism', in John Pilling (ed), *The Cambridge Companion to Beckett*, Cambridge, UK: Cambridge University Press, pp. 209–22.

Cohn, Ruby (2005), *A Beckett Canon*, Ann Arbor: University of Michigan Press.

Fernández, José Francisco (2018), 'Between "Little Latitude" and a "Discreet Liberty": Beckett's Bilingualism and the Translation of His Work into a Third Language', *Samuel Beckett Today/Aujourd'hui*, 30, 127–41.

Fitch, Brian T. (1988), *Beckett and Babel. An Investigation into the Status of the Bilingual Work*, Toronto: University of Toronto Press.

Grutman, Rainier (2005), 'Auto-translation', in Mona Baker (ed), *Routledge Encyclopedia of Translation Studies*, The Taylor & Francis e-library, pp. 7–20.

Grutman, Rainier (2013), 'Beckett and Beyond. Putting Self-Translation in Perspective', *Orbis Litterarum*, 68:3, 188–206.

Grutman, Rainier and Trish Van Bolderen (2014), 'Self-translation', in Sandra Bermann and Catherine Porter (eds), *A Companion to Translation Studies,* Chichester: Wiley Blackwell, pp. 323–32.

Harvey, Keith (2005), 'Compensation', in Mona Baker (ed), *Routledge Encyclopedia of Translation Studies,* The Taylor & Francis e-library, pp. 37–40.

Harvey, Lawrence (1970), *Samuel Beckett. Poet & Critic*, Princeton: Princeton University Press.

Hokenson, Jan Walsh and Marcella Munson (2007), *The Bilingual Text: History and Theory of Literary Self-Translation*, Manchester: St. Jerome Publishing.

Nänny, Max and Olga Fischer (1999), 'Introduction', in Max Nänny and Olga Fischer (eds), *Form Miming Meaning. Iconicity in Language and Literature,* Amsterdam: John Benjamins Publishing Company, pp. 15–32.

Newmark, Peter (1991), *About Translation,* Clevedon: Multilingual Matters Ltd.

Perloff, Marjorie (2010), 'Beckett the Poet', in S.E. Gontarski (ed), *A Companion to Samuel Beckett*, Chichester: Blackwell, pp. 211–28.

Van Hulle, Dirk (2011), *The Making of Samuel Beckett's Stirrings Still/Soubresauts and Comment dire/What is the Word*, Uitgeverij: UPA University Press Antwerp.

5

Literal Translation vs. Self-Translation: The Beckett–Pinget Collaboration on the Radio Play *Cendres* (*Embers*)

Pim Verhulst

Samuel Beckett is famous for the fact that he translated his own bilingual work from English into French and vice versa, fairly consistently throughout his career, from the late 1930s on. Less well known, and certainly less studied, is the fact that he sometimes rendered his work into other languages by enlisting the help of third parties, including native speaker friends, (aspiring) writers or poets, literary editors and professional translators.[1] One reason for this critical oversight is that Beckett's collaborative translations are not always properly credited in their various editions but, more importantly, few of the material traces that document them survive. The publication of Beckett's letters has brought renewed attention to these creative interactions, but they still require the support of additional archival material like manuscripts and typescripts.

In order to better understand the significance of collaborative translation for Beckett and its impact on his bilingual poetics of self-translation, this chapter will focus on one of the best-documented cases. In the late 1950s, Beckett translated two of his English radio plays, *All That Fall* and *Embers*, into French as *Tous ceux qui tombent* and *Cendres*, with the help of Swiss-born French writer Robert Pinget, who was one of his closest friends at the time, but not yet an established literary name (see Houppermans 2003; Salado 2006; Mégevand 2010). For each case, multiple drafts have been preserved, annotated in both hands, supplemented with correspondence and an unpublished memoir. This allows for a detailed study of the co-translation process, paying special attention to the respective roles that Beckett and Pinget fulfilled. For the purpose of this chapter, I shall limit myself to *Embers/Cendres*, which is the shortest radio play of the two, but at the same time represents the most complex case.[2]

The Beckett–Pinget Collaboration on *Cendres*

Before we can discuss some actual examples from the manuscripts, it is necessary to first understand the context in which the translation came to be.
Even before *Embers* aired on the BBC Third Programme (24 June 1959),
script editor Barbara Bray and producer Donald McWhinnie made plans to
enter the radio play for the Italia Prize. To this end, a bilingual script had
to be submitted to the jury, and so a French version was urgently needed.
When Bray asked Beckett if such a text was available, or perhaps in the making, he replied on 22 May 1959 explaining there was only a German version
to be had and that he did not have time to translate it himself on such short
notice (TCD-MS-10948-1-032). The BBC then commissioned a French
text from Pinget (Beckett 2014: 239n2), whose stage play *Lettre morte* had
just been translated by Bray into English as *Dead Letter*.[3] Pinget's unpublished
memoir entitled 'Notre ami Sam', part of his papers at the Bibliothèque
Littéraire Jacques Doucet (BLJD) in Paris, sets out precisely how he went
to work on *Cendres*. Beckett arranged to meet him on a late July morning
at the Gare des Invalides on his way to Ireland, where he was to receive an
honorary doctorate from his alma mater, Trinity College Dublin (Beckett
2014: 235n3). During their session, Beckett explained a few words, phrases
and references that were causing difficulties for his friend. The Pinget papers
contain the annotated BBC script of *Embers* that was used for this purpose,
which is heavily glossed in French, almost entirely in Pinget's handwriting
(*BDMP11*, ET5).[4] Some seventy-five per cent of the more than 200 notes
on this document found their way into the first typewritten draft of *Cendres*.

This preliminary typescript – the earliest surviving version in French –
exists in three near identical copies, all differently annotated: the first one
(FT1) is clean; the second (FT2) is lightly corrected in Pinget's hand, mostly
in black but also in blue ink; and the third one (FT3) reproduces the previous
corrections, while also introducing a few unique ones, sometimes overrul-
ing the older alterations. This genealogy indicates that Pinget had transferred
his emendations from FT1 to FT2 and FT3, perhaps making further changes
on the latter in blue ink with Beckett's assistance. His stay in Ireland, with
stopovers in Surrey and London, lasted about two weeks, which would have
been time enough for a quick glance at Pinget's work, either back in Paris or
when passing through London. Whatever the case may be, revisions were still
superficial at this point and did not yet amount to a complete overhaul of the
text. On to the title page of the bilingual Italia Prize script, Pinget's version of
Cendres was presented as a 'traduction littérale' [literal translation] (*BDMP11*,
IP, 03v). In his unpublished memoir, he minimises his effort as little more than

a 'sanding down' of the text (*BLJD*, PNG 354–4, 18r), with Beckett coming in later to do the heavy carpentry. Still, Pinget contributed more than his disparaging remark suggests, going well beyond producing a mere first draft. At the same time, this version is good quarter longer than the original, on almost every page of the bilingual script, which adds to the overall impression that it served the interim purpose of extensive paraphrase or summary, not yet as the official 'authorised' or 'literary' translation, which Beckett would now begin chopping away at.

That he had become more closely involved in the translation process by the autumn of 1959 is confirmed by his letter to Bray of 5 November, in which he complained of having 'so much work (including *Embers* in French)' (Beckett 2014: 250). By 14 November, he was hoping to get 'on with Embers translation' (Beckett 2014: 255), and some two weeks later, by 30 November, he had 'finished revising' *Cendres* and given it to Maurice Nadeau for pre-book publication in *Les Lettres Nouvelles*, as he informed Pinget (Beckett 2014: 257). This letter confirms that Beckett took matters into his own hands for the final version, but Pinget continued to play a part in the preceding stages. Beckett began by completely retyping Pinget's translation, making changes to the text in the process and then further revising the result, for which he set a generous margin on the left-hand side of the document. Judging from the many handwritten corrections on the fourth surviving typescript in French (*BDMP11*, FT4), kept at the Harry Ransom Humanities Research Centre in Austin, Texas, Beckett again enlisted the help of Pinget in this later phase. His handwriting also appears on the typescript, mostly in blue ink, alongside the red ballpoint and grey pencil annotations that are mostly Beckett's, even though some have been erased and are difficult or impossible to decipher. This version was then typed up again as the fifth and final typescript in French (*BDMP11*, FT5), held at the University of Reading, which in turn became the setting copy for both the journal publication and the first edition by Les Éditions de Minuit.

Comparing these documents offers a unique glimpse into the process of collaborative (self-)translation that shaped the French text. It is not always possible to assign a word or turn of phrase to either Beckett or Pinget conclusively, because the writing is hard to identify in places and Beckett's voice may be guiding Pinget's hand or vice versa. Nevertheless, the fact remains that the earliest drafts are mostly Pinget's responsibility, except for Beckett's glosses and perhaps some minor emendations, with the later typescripts and the published texts being largely the result of authorial revision, although Pinget was still marginally involved at this stage. Up to a point, the combined material traces that document this collaboration allow us to study the dynamics of Beckett's more 'literary' self-translation against the backdrop of Pinget's more 'literal' third-party rendition, thus elucidating the creative choices that shaped each of these activities. From this it appears that Pinget usually translated for sense, which often led to a wordier result, while Beckett was more attentive to matters of radiophonicity, intertextuality and style, taking several liberties that a third-party translator might not. These include administering cuts, but also making revisions and additions.

Translating Radiophonicity

When studying the collaborative translation process, it is important to take the specific genre of *Embers* into account. For Beckett, it was his second radio play after *All That Fall*, having previously written a reportage of sorts, *The Capital of the Ruins*, for the Irish radio station RTÉ in 1946 (see Davies 2017). Pinget, by contrast, lacked experience with writing for the medium. *Dead Letter* was an adaptation of a play, and although he had written *La manivelle* in 1959, which Beckett in turn transposed into English as *The Old Tune*, this was in essence a scene extracted from a new novel Pinget was working on, *Clope au dossier*, reconceptualised for radio as a dialogue between two old men with added sound effects. Compared to Pinget, Beckett would often create subtle variants in the French version of *Embers* that affected the interpretation of a passage in light of the medium for which the radio play was conceived.

When Henry is thinking of Addie's music lesson, temporarily ignoring his wife, Ada, she says to him: 'You are silent today' (Beckett 2009a: 41). On Pinget's early drafts, the sentence was rendered literally – 'Tu es silencieux aujourd'hui' (*BDMP11*, FT1–3, 10r) – but then it was rephrased as a question: 'Tu es dans la lune?' (FT4, 07r). Apart from being a more colloquial turn of phrase, it identifies the mental state of Henry as lunacy, which connects him to other literary characters such as Ludovico Ariosto's *Orlando Furioso* and Rudolf Erich Raspe's Baron Munchausen, who make outlandish trips to the moon in strokes of madness. When Henry is daydreaming about Addie's riding lesson, Ada demands to know: 'What are you thinking of?' (Beckett 2009a: 41). Once again, Pinget proposes a literal translation: 'A quoi penses-tu?' (*BDMP11*, FT1–3, 10r), which became the more conversational and also more fitting 'Tu rêves?' (*BDMP11*, FT4, 08r), a phrase that emphasises Henry's proneness to phantasmagoria. It seems that Beckett considered yet another translation variant. The front inside cover of the notebook containing the manuscript of *Embers* features a stray note below some doodles of floating heads reading: 'Où as-tu la tête?' [Where is your head at?] (*BDMP11*, EM). Again, the phrase is significant, radio being often regarded as a medium that disembodies (McCracken 2002: 184), unlike theatre, where a character's physical presence is usually visible. In the sightless domain of wireless broadcasting, the source of a sound remains unseen, so its substance can never really be affirmed – an effect commonly referred to as 'acousmatics' (see Morin 2014).

Ada is most strongly affected by the disembodying effect of radio. Her presence on the beach is highly ambiguous, an effect that Beckett continued refining in both the English and the French draft versions, thus creating a genetic rapport across language barriers. Her two previously mentioned responses to Henry's absent-mindedness – 'You are silent today' / 'What are you thinking of?' – suggest that she is not witnessing the two Addie lessons, and is thus not part of Henry's revery, but sitting at his side in person. These sentences were also sites of substantial revision in the typescripts of *Embers*. At one point, Beckett replaced them with the reaction 'Poor Addie!' (*BDMP11*, ET2, 05r), before changing his mind again and reinstating the original responses (*BDMP11*, ET3, 06r). Ada's sympathetic exclamation would have localised her inside Henry's mind, as yet another figment of his dwindling imagination, not out there with him in the real world. Other passages are altered in a similar vein. When Henry gets up and walks over to the sea, he claims it is to 'Stretch my old bones' (Beckett 2009a: 42). Pinget narrows the meaning to 'limbs' or 'legs': 'Me dégourdir les membres' (*BDMP11*, FT1–3, 11r), on which Beckett puts a more poetic as well as an alliterative spin: 'Remuer ma vielle viande' (*BDMP11*, FT4, 08r). The shift from 'bones' in English to 'flesh' in French is again worthy of note, as it contrasts Henry's carnal presence more sharply with Ada's alleged spectrality.

At this point in the first English typescript, she continues: 'Well why don't you? (Pause) Don't stand there thinking about it. (Pause.) Don't stand there looking at me' (*BDMP11*, ET1, 05r). This last sentence was altered in the second typescript to conceal the object of Henry's gaze, obscuring whether Ada is actually there: 'Don't stand there ~~looking at me~~ staring' (*BDMP11, * ET2, 05r). In this passage, the French translation is equally open-ended, but makes a few further changes, for example when Pinget's 'Eh bien, pourquoi ne le fais-tu pas? (un temps) Ne reste pas planté là à y penser. (un temps) Ne reste pas planté là à regarder' (*BDMP11*, ET1–3, 11r) is revised as: 'Eh bien, ~~fais-le~~ remue-la. (Un temps.) Ne reste pas là à cogitasser. (Un temps.) Ferme ~~t~~la bouche et vas-y' (*BDMP11,* FT4, 08r). The verb 'cogitasser' is rare in French, possibly gleaned from a dictionary, but it resembles the English verb 'to cogitate' and further characterises Henry as a cerebral daydreamer, which again betrays the mark of Beckett. A less subtle change occurs when Henry returns from the water's edge and resumes his place alongside Ada, who repeats her comment from before. In the first two typescripts of *Embers*, it still reads: 'Don't stand there looking at me' (*BDMP11,* ET1–ET2, 05r), which is again blurred, but this time to: 'Don't stand there gaping' (*BDMP11,* ET3, 07r). Despite the gloss 'regarder fixement' on Pinget's English typescript (*BDMP11,* ET5, 09r), his effort does not quite capture the meaning of 'to gape': 'Ne reste pas planté là à regarder' (*BDMP11,* FT1–3, 11r). Beckett's originally does, but then he replaces it with a remarkable deviation: 'Ne reste pas là, à ~~béer~~ voir des fantômes' (*BDMP11,* FT4, 08r), further changed to 'tes fantômes' [your ghosts] (Beckett 1960: 57) in the published text. As is more explicitly suggested here than in English, Ada may very well be one of those apparitions that Henry stands watching.

Also, the passage that follows is sensitive to variation. In the manuscript of *Embers,* Ada says to Henry: 'Sit down. (<u>Pause</u>.) On the rug' (*BDMP11,* EM, 15r). This 'rug' is first replaced by a 'shawl' (*BDMP11,* EM, 10r), then a 'scarf', about which Henry asks Ada: 'Is that the old scarf I brought you back that time from Lucerne?' (*BDMP11,* EM, 13r). This question is ultimately dropped from the text, but it would have provided a realistic background story for the object, in turn confirming Ada's physicality. The seemingly negligible item of clothing causes trouble in the French translation as well. It is encircled on Pinget's English typescript, but without a gloss, and he first translates it as 'le châle' (*BDMP11,* FT1–3, 11r). This is then crossed out and replaced with 'mon fichu' (*BDMP11,* FT4, 08r) in the next version, but reverted again to the original 'mon châle' (*BDMP11,* FT5, 07r) in the last typescript. Perhaps more than just trivial details, the rejected variants – 'rug' and 'scarf' – are unisex items, whereas 'shawl', 'châle' and 'fichu' can only be worn by women. This makes it less likely for Henry to have brought them, and so they must come from Ada, which again makes her presence on the beach more palpable and likely. Beckett, who was not a native speaker of French, may have been uncertain about 'châle', briefly replacing it with 'fichu', but perhaps Pinget assured him of its femininity, so it could be reinstated.

In the next sentence, however, Ada becomes ephemeral again. Seeing Henry hesitate, she asks him: 'Are you afraid we might touch?' (Beckett 2009a: 42). 'As-tu peur qu'on se touche?' (*BDMP11,* FT1–3, 11r), is Pinget's literal translation, but Beckett ambiguates their contact by using a verb that evokes a fleeting brush with the spiritual world instead, at a seance for example: 'On pourrait se ~~toucher~~ frôler, c'est ça que tu crains?' (*BDMP11,* FT4, 08r). As the examples above have shown, unlike his co-translator, the author continues to shape the radiophonicity of *Embers* in translation.

Translating Intertextuality

Another domain where Beckett takes considerable liberties over Pinget is intertextuality. A good example is the phrase 'naughty world' (Beckett 2009a: 47), uttered by Bolton while swaying a candle over his head and pleading with Holloway for help. On the typescript that Pinget used as the basis for his French translation, the phrase is encircled and annotated in grey pencil with the word 'Shakespeare', followed by the gloss 'mauvais' (*BDMP11*, ET5, 14r). This is indeed a Shakespearean quotation, namely of Portia's lines, 'How far that little candle throws his beams – / So shines a good deed in a naughty world' from *The Merchant of Venice* (V.1; Shakespeare 2008: 1171). It seems that Beckett did not disclose the title of the play, possibly because he could not recall the exact provenance of the quote, as otherwise Pinget might have looked up a French equivalent in *Le Marchand de Venise*, a common translator's practice. It appears as 'monde corrompu' in the translation by M. Francisque Michel (Shakespeare 1869: 626), and as 'monde méchant' in the more canonical or better-known version by François-Victor Hugo (Shakespeare 1872: 270). In all of Pinget's typescripts, the phrase appears as 'monde mauvais' (*BDMP11*, FT1–3, 18r), thus entirely in keeping with Beckett's gloss, but it was excised from the French text again when Beckett retyped Pinget's version for further revision, without any form of compensation (*BDMP11*, FT4, 13r). Whereas Shakespearean echoes would frequently find their way into the later stages of Beckett's English self-translations – e.g. 'oeil las' becoming 'weary eye' and then 'vile jelly' from *King Lear* (III.7; Shakespeare 2008, 2433) in the drafts of *Ill Seen Ill Said* (Van Hulle 2009: 9) – the opposite tendency can be observed in the French translations of his English texts, be it after considerable hesitation across versions.

Another example occurs at the very end of the radio play. When Henry consults his appointment book and notices that the plumber is coming tomorrow, he seems to relish in the prospect of conversation by saying 'Words' (Beckett 2009a: 47). 'Words, words, words' is Hamlet's famous reply to Polonius's enquiry, 'What do you read, my lord?' as the Prince walks about while holding a book and talking to himself, all part of his elaborate ruse to feign madness (II.2; Shakespeare 2008: 1723). The repetition of 'words' in Shakespeare's *Hamlet* strikingly contrasts with the paucity of its single occurrence in *Embers*, where Henry is also engaged in the act of reading, not from a heavy tome filled with words of wisdom, but from a near empty calendar, painfully confronting him with the fact that words and social contact are becoming ever more scarce, forcing him to come up with stories and imagined companions of his own. Pinget duly translates 'words' as 'D̶e̶s̶ ̶m̶Mots' in the early versions (*BDMP11*, FT1–3, 18r), revising the phrase on the third typescript, but Beckett again drops it later, briefly considering the exclamation 'H̶o̶p̶-̶l̶à' (*BDMP11*, FT4, 13r). The added connotation, still present in the English text, is thus lost on French readers: Henry, similar to Prince Hamlet – in a moment of 'to be, or not to be' introspection – is contemplating suicide, wavering back and forth, from the pebbled beach to the water's edge, unable to decide if he should drown himself or persist with life, not knowing which would be worse. In this case, Beckett seems to try and make up for the lost association, but then he crosses it out.

In French colloquial parlance, the expression 'Hop-là' is used, for example, to lift something up, but also, more importantly in this context, as a meaningless word or an empty interjection. In light of *Hamlet*, it is telling that Beckett considered using a conversational filler to stand in for the more Shakespearean 'words', since it enacts stylistically the verbal starvation that Henry is suffering from. Even the adjacent words in the text of the radio play seem to be affected by this choice. When Henry recalls the purpose of the plumber's visit, he states: 'Ah yes, the waste' (Beckett 2009a: 47). He is probably referring to wastewater in general and the pipes that carry it out of the house to the drains, which appear to be blocked. Confused by the word 'waste', Pinget encircled it in grey pencil on the BBC typescript, writing the word 'vidange' next to it (*BDMP11*, ET5, 14r). He then connected the word with a curvy line to three other variants listed at the bottom of the page: 'désert/gaspillage/écoulement' (*BDMP11*, ET5, 14r). Because only the latter was an adequate translation, meaning the same as 'runoff' in English, Pinget adopted it for his translation: 'Ah oui, l'écoulement' (*BDMP11*, FT1–3, 18r). But, again, Beckett amended Pinget, opting instead for: 'Ah oui, le trop-plein. (Un temps.) Le trop-plein' (*BDMP11*, FT4, 13r). The meaning of 'trop-plein' is roughly synonymous with 'overflow', i.e. the outlet for excess water in a bathtub or a sink, yet the connotation is significantly different. Beckett's reiteration of the phrase compensates for the loss of 'words', so that again we have a stylistic enactment of verbal deficiency, the doubling of 'trop-plein' – literally 'too full' – contrasting ironically with the contents of Henry's appointment book, which is all too empty.

Even Henry's calendar, or the way it is referred to in the text as his 'little book' (Beckett 2009a: 47), could be construed as an intertextual reference, with a remarkable history in more than one language. It was added by hand to the fourth typescript of *Embers* (*BDMP11*, ET4, 11r), which Beckett sent to the BBC with additional directions for broadcast. Because the phrase was such a late addition, it did not yet appear in the typewritten layer of the document that Pinget used for his preliminary translation, although it was added later in grey pencil (*BDMP11*, ET5, 16r). When this addition was made is unclear, but probably not when Beckett met his friend at the station, as it is still missing from the typewritten layer of the first three typescripts of *Cendres* (*BDMP11*, FT1–3, 18r). Only the last one has it as a holograph annotation: 'Petit livre' (*BDMP11*, FT3, 18r). In the next version, it is rephrased as a 'schedule' or 'timetable': 'Emplois du temps à venir. (Un temps.) ~~Voyons en~~ Regardons voir' (*BDMP11*, FT4, 13). The phrase underwent a similar fate in the German translation of *Embers*. On 17 July 1959, Beckett made a point of bringing it up when he told McWhinnie, who was invited to direct *Aschenglut* for Sudwestfunk: 'The translation is excellent, very close to the original. It is by my usual German translator, Elmar Tophoven, and we have gone over it together. As he lives here it will be easy to deal with such things as "little book'" (Beckett 2014: 239n2).

This remark confirms that the phrase had not yet been added to the German text either, although Beckett would see to it later. Surprisingly enough, it is not in Suhrkamp's trilingual edition of *Dramatische Dichtungen* (Beckett 1964: 145), but it does appear in Reclam's bilingual version of *Embers/Aschenglut* (Beckett 1970: 43) and in the second volume of Suhrkamp's single-language *Werke*: 'Das Notizbuch. Mal sehen' [The notebook. Let's see.] (Beckett 1976: 61). Instead of opting for a literal translation such as 'petit livre', Beckett eventually rephrases it as a more idiomatic alternative, not only normalising the French and German versions but also undoing the intertextual resonance of the original.

Similar to the Shakespeare examples we have seen before, the phrase only works as a potential allusion in English, this time to Geoffrey Chaucer (Jesson 2009: 63–4). Towards the end of *Troilus and Criseyde*, Chaucer addresses his poem in the following terms:

> Go, litel book, go, litel myn tragedye,
> Ther God thi makere yet, er that he dye,
> So sende myght to make in som comedye!
> But litel book, no makyng thou n'envie,
> But subgit be to alle poesye;
> And kis the steppes where as thow seest pace
> Virgile, Ovide, Omer, Lucan, and Stace. (Chaucer 2003: 344; ll. 1786–92)

Compared to Chaucer's masterpiece, *The Canterbury Tales*, with its more than 17,000 lines, *Troilus and Criseyde*, at barely 2,000, is indeed a 'litel book', but it is still a prime example of profusion when compared to the Henry's 'little book', in which he struggles to fill even a page. The fact that he uses the exact same phrase is ironic, heightened further by Chaucer's invocation of literary greats from antiquity, which Beckett's protagonist can hardly aspire to. Beckett knew his classics, including Chaucer, as Mark Nixon and Dirk Van Hulle remind us in their study of his personal library: 'Although an Honours student in French and Italian, with English as a subsidiary subject, Beckett over the next four years, until he graduated in November 1927, studied the "pillars" of English literature, with a focus on Chaucer, Milton and Shakespeare' (Nixon and Van Hulle 2017: 20). His copy of A. Hamilton Thompson's *A History of English Literature, and of the Chief English Writers* (1914) has an entire chapter on Chaucer with numerous references to *Troilus and Criseyde*, and the same holds true for E. Legouis and L. Cazamian's *Histoire de la Littérature Anglaise* (1929). Although Beckett did not leave any marks in them, the Chaucer section in A. J. Wyatt and W. H. Low's *Intermediate Text-Book of English Literature, Part I* (1920) does show traces of reading, and the loose-leaf notes he took from the English edition of Legouis and Cazamian also include a few pages on Chaucer (TCD MS 10970, 02v–05r; Frost and Maxwell 2006: 107).[5] The 'father of English poetry' is usually associated with Beckett's *Dream of Fair to Middling Women*, its title and epigraph being borrowed from *The Legend of Good Women* (Knowlson 1996: 55), with a few more entries at the end of the 'Dream' Notebook (Pilling 1999: 169–71). It thus seems that Beckett was only slightly exaggerating when he listed Chaucer as one of the 'major influences' on his work in a letter to Nuala Costello of 10 May 1934 (Beckett 2009b: 208). Judging from *Embers*, that influence is not restricted to the 1930s, but extends into the 1950s, and even into the 1970s, when Beckett was still excerpting Chaucer in the so-called 'Sottisier' Notebook (Knowlson 1996: 653).

The potential allusion to *Troilus and Criseyde* is relevant in the context of translation as well. In the lines that follow, Chaucer expresses his concern that, given the great regional varieties in the spelling of Middle English dialects, a scribe might tamper with his text or its metre and thereby create misunderstanding:

> And for ther is so gret diversite
> In Englissh and in writyng of oure tonge,
> So prey I God that non miswryte the,
> Ne the mysmetre for defaute of tonge;
> And red wherso thow be, or elles songe,
> That thow be understonde, God I biseche! –
> But yet to purpos of my rather speche (Chaucer 2003: 344; ll. 1793–99)

Like Chaucer's poem in its day, *Embers* as a modern radio play also has the double status of a text and an oral performance, be it in the form of a radio recording, not a bardic recitation. Through the act of collaborative (self-)translation, the text is (re-)transcribed, in a sense, not into English but into French, the translator being faithful to the original, while the author is the one tampering with it, significantly altering its hermeneutic potential. The phrase 'petit livre' does not quite trigger the same associations in French that it might in English as 'little book', so its subtext is lost on foreign audiences and therefore, perhaps, omitted or rephrased. Since most allusions suffer a similar fate in *Cendres*, as the direct consequence of Beckett's intervention in the translation process, there might be a stylistic reason for their removal.

Translating Style

Overall, the French translation of *Embers* shows a tendency towards stylistic weakening. This is related to a comment Beckett made on 26 December 1957

in a letter to Barney Rosset, his American publisher, after temporarily abandoning the first draft of his radio play: 'There is something in my English writing that infuriates me and I can't get rid of it. A kind of lack of brakes' (Beckett
2014: 98n4). If Beckett is referring to verbal exuberance, indeed, *Embers* is rife
with wordplay. Some puns hold up in French, for example the meta-reflexive
reminder that we are listening to sea waves coming over the airwaves, 'ondes'
being a common term to use in the context of both water and the wireless,
but others do not. In view of the fact that radio is often considered to be a
blind medium (see Crook 2005: 53–69), one of the most central puns in the
text is 'see'/'sea' when Henry tells his blind father, who also stands in for the
sightless listener:

> I say that sound you hear is the sea, we are sitting on the strand. [*Pause.*] I
> mention it because the sound is so strange, so unlike the sound of the sea,
> that if you didn't see what it was you wouldn't know what it was. (2009a: 35)

As usual, Pinget's translation is both faithful and expansive, be it less formal
after revision:

> Je dis ce bruit que vous entendez 'on entend est la mer. (un temps. Plus fort.)
> Je dis ce bruit que vous 'on entendez est la mer, nous sommes assis sur la grève.
> (Un temps) Je le mentionne parce que ce bruit est tellement étrange, tellement
> pas comme le bruit de la mer, que si vous on ne ne compreniezait pas ce qui le
> fait vous on ne sauriezait pas ce que c'est. (*BDMP11*, FT1–3, 01r)

While Beckett clearly builds on Pinget's translation, his version is more con-
cisely worded:

> Je dis ce bruit qu'on entend, c'est la mer, nous sommes assis sur la grève.
> (Un temps.) J'aime autant le dire parce que le bruit est si étrange, ça res-
> semble si peu au bruit de la mer, qu'à moins de voir d'où il vient ce que
> c'est on ne saurait pas ce que c'est. (*BDMP11*, FT4, 01r)

Despite also reintroducing the verb 'to see' ('voir'), he makes no attempt to
recreate the pun, repetition ('ce que c'est') being ultimately preferred over
alliteration ('voir'/'vient'), as the only revision illustrates. In English, this passage connects to a whole range of water-related words and expressions, spread
out across the text, but because the pun holding it all together at the centre is
lost, the French text shows more stylistic restraint as a result.

One such example is the term 'washout'. It is the last word Henry's father
spoke to his son, after he refused to join him for 'a dip' in the sea: 'a washout,

that's the last I heard from you, a washout. . . . Slam life shut like that! [*Pause.*] Washout. [*Pause.*] Wish to Christ she had' (Beckett 2009a, 38). Aside from the obvious connection with water, the term 'washout' means a 'failure' or 'disappointment', and it also has the connotation of 'abortion', as John and Beryl Fletcher note: 'Vulg.: "I wish to Christ my mother had washed me out [e.g., with a douche] before I was conceived"' (Fletcher and Fletcher 1978, 131). This extravagant play on words proved quite hard to replicate in French. On Pinget's copy of the English text 'washout' is encircled, with the word 'avorton' written next to it in grey pencil (*BDMP11,* ET5, 05r). It also resurfaces in Pinget's translation: 'c'est la dernière chose que j'ai entendue de toi, un avorton. . . . Claquer la vie comme ça derrière soi! (un temps) Avorton. (un temps) Si seulement je l'avais été' (*BDMP11,* FT1–3, 06r). The word means the same as 'little runt' or 'weakling', but it can also imply a 'miscarriage'. Beckett makes it more colloquial and compressed in his revision, but not after considerable hesitation between tenses:

> ~~la dernière chose que tu m'as dite~~ ~~les derniers mots que tu as eus pour moi~~
> ~~c'était tes derniers mots pour moi ce furent les derniers que tu m'adressas~~
> tes derniers mots pour moi, espèce ~~d'avoron~~ d'avorton. . . . Sortir de la vie
> comme ça! (Porte claquée.) Avorton. (Un temps.) Dommage que non.
> (*BDMP11,* FT4, 04r)

It still lacks the watery association of 'washout', which in English implied that by slamming shut the door on life and rushing out, Henry's father also decided to kill himself by jumping off the cliff. As the son reminds him, the remains 'washed out' to sea, never washing up on shore: 'We never found your body you know, that held up probate an inconscionable time' (Beckett 2009a: 36). While this association is lost, Beckett does make more explicit the suicide of the father, which in *Embers* is closely related to the sound of the sea that Henry constantly hears in his head. Ada, too, apparently drowned herself, since she asks Henry, 'why life?' and taunts him with the assurance: 'Underneath all is as quiet as the grave' (Beckett 2009a: 44).

The pun on 'drowning', as in death by submersion, and 'drown out', that is, to override and thereby cancel a noise or sound, is not always reproduced either. When Henry tells Ada that he sometimes talks aloud to 'drown' the noise of the sea (Beckett 2009a: 36), Pinget translates it as: 'oh juste assez fort pour noyer le bruit' (*BDMP11,* FT1–3, 02r). The verb 'noyer' is the idiomatic one to use and also means 'drowning', but Beckett eventually replaces it with 'hearing': 'oh juste assez fort pour ne plus l'entendre' (*BDMP11,* FT4, 02r). The second time, when Ada tells Henry '[t]here is no sense in trying to drown it' (Beckett 2009a: 44), Pinget uses a synonym of 'drowning out': 'Ca n'a pas de sens d'essayer de le couvrir' (*BDMP11,* FT1–3, 14r). However, in this case Beckett prefers to keep the more obvious link with 'drowning': 'Ca n'a pas de sens de vouloir le noyer' (*BDMP11,* FT4, 10). So, too, in the third case, when Holloway's eyes look 'drowned' (Beckett 2009a: 47), Beckett follows Pinget's lead – 'yeux noyés' (*BDMP11,* FT1–3, 18r) – and only adds a tiny variation of his own: 'le regard, noyé' (*BDMP11,* FT5, 12r). *Cendres* even uses the verb on one occasion where *Embers* does not, when 'swimming' (Beckett 2009a: 46) is the description used for Holloway's eye and Beckett adopts Pinget's suggestion: 'tout ça noyé' (*BDMP11,* FT1–3, 18r). As this last example illustrates, in addition to toning down the watery images in French, Beckett is also heightening stylistic repetition by using the same limited set of words, thereby reducing the verbal richness of *Embers.*

   This maximalist indulgence in wordplay clashed with Beckett's poetics of 'taking away' or 'subtracting', which he famously opposed to Joyce's constant 'adding' (Knowlson 1996: 352), and which apparently was harder to accomplish in English than in his adopted tongue. The 'weakening effect' of French, as Beckett called it in conversation with theatre director Herbert Blau (quoted in Mooney 2010: 196), finds an expression in *Cendres* not just through cuts and revisions, but also, unexpectedly perhaps, in the form of additions. When Ada advises Henry to go and see a specialist because his problem is getting 'worse', Beckett first lets him interrupt her with a question, absent from the English text: 'Qu'est-ce qui peut empirer?' [What could possibly get any worse?] (*BDMP11,* FT4, 08r) In the final version of the translation, Beckett substituted the sentence with an answer to the question: 'Rien ne peut empirer' [Nothing could possibly get any worse] (*BDMP11,* FT5, 07r). Having thus 'worsened' *Embers/ Cendres* as far as he could at this point, through the help of Pinget and the French language, Beckett would carry on with his project, cross-linguistically, all the way to *Worstward Ho.*

Conclusion

The line 'Vega in the Lyre very green' (Beckett 2009a: 37) is one of the few literary allusions that Beckett does not undo in the French translation of *Embers.* From Pinget's initial long-winded suggestion – 'Véga très vert dans la constellation de la Lyre' (*BDMP11,* FT1–3, 03r) – it is rephrased more succinctly, and with alliterations, as 'Véga dans la Lyre vert vif' (*BDMP11,* FT4, 03r). Its provenance is *Ulysses,* more precisely the scene in 'Ithaca' where Stephen Dedalus and Leopold Bloom are gazing into the firmament at the back of 7 Eccles Street, before saying their goodbyes. As the narrator informs us, they observe a falling star speeding past 'Vega in the Lyre above the zenith beyond the stargroup of the Tress of Berenice towards the zodiacal sign of Leo' (Joyce 1993: 577). Perhaps this allusion is left standing as a literary tombstone of sorts for Joyce, laying to rest while still honouring his legacy. Like the pseudo-father and son in *Ulysses*, the pseudo-master and his onetime apprentice also had to part ways.

Beckett's collaborative (self-)translation with Pinget may have served as a strategy to better defend himself against the danger of Joycean wordplay, still looming large whenever he returned to English.[6] In that sense, having a non-native speaker of that language at his side, co-translating the text with him, was actually an advantage, but Beckett had to learn to play that role himself. It seems his experience with *Embers/Cendres* was a valuable lesson in this respect. On 1 December 1959, having just corrected proofs for Faber and Faber and getting ready to do the same for Nadeau and Jérôme Lindon, Beckett wrote to Bray: 'Hate the sight of it in both languages. Understand it better' (Beckett 2014: 260). This understanding gradually took shape over the course of the radio play's successive draft versions, in English, French and German. These documents, and the material traces they record, offer valuable insight into the dynamics of Beckett's collaborative (self-)translations, in turn establishing them as a crucial but neglected component of his bilingual oeuvre and poetics.

Notes

1. For a detailed survey of these collaborations, also with respect to genetic translation studies, collaborative translation and the German versions of Beckett's texts, see Van Hulle and Verhulst (2018) and Beloborodova, Van Hulle and Verhulst (2021).

2. For a full genetic study of both *Tous ceux qui tombent* and *Cendres*, also in relation to the geneses of their English versions, see Verhulst (2022).

3. *Dead Letter* was originally aired by the BBC Third Programme on 21 July 1959, with repeats on 14 August 1959 and 15 January 1960. This information, as well as the date of the first *Embers* broadcast, was retrieved from the BBC's *Genome* website, an online database containing all *Radio Times* billings from 1923–2009, see https://genome.ch.bbc.co.uk

4. 'ET52' is a shorthand notation referring to the fifth English typescript of *Embers*, available online in the Radio Plays module (no. 11) of the Beckett Digital Manuscript Project (www.beckettarchive.org), co-edited by Pim Verhulst and Vincent Neyt (forthcoming). For a complete list of abbreviations, see the 'Catalogue' of the online genetic edition or the 'Abbreviations' section in Verhulst (2022).

5. These student books can all be consulted online as part of the *Beckett Digital Library* (*BDL*), see https://www.beckettarchive.org/library/WYA-INT-1.html; https://www.beckettarchive.org/library/THO-HIS.html and https://www.beckettarchive.org/library/LEG-HIS.html.

6. For a more detailed study of *Embers* in relation to Joyce, see Verhulst (2017).

Works Cited

Beckett, Samuel (1960), *La dernière bande suivi de Cendres*, Paris: Les Éditions de Minuit.

Beckett, Samuel (1964), *Dramatische Dichtungen in drei Sprachen*, Vol. 2, Frankfurt am Main: Suhrkamp.

Beckett, Samuel (1970), *Embers/Aschenglut*, Stuttgart: Reclam.

Beckett, Samuel (1976), *Hörspiele/Pantomime/Film/Fernsehspiel*, Frankfurt am Main: Suhrkamp.

Beckett, Samuel (2009a), *All That Fall and Other Plays for Radio and Screen*, preface by Everett C. Frost, London: Faber and Faber.

Beckett, Samuel (2009b), *The Letters of Samuel Beckett: 1929–1940*, Vol. 1, Martha Dow Fehsenfeld and Lois More Overbeck (eds), Cambridge, UK: Cambridge University Press.

Beckett, Samuel (2014), *The Letters of Samuel Beckett: 1957–1965*, Vol. 3, George Craig, Martha Dow Fehsenfeld, Dan Gunn and Lois More Overbeck (eds), Cambridge, UK: Cambridge University Press.

Beloborodova, Olga, Dirk Van Hulle and Pim Verhulst (2021), 'Reconstructing Collaborative (Self-)Translations from the Archive: The Case of Samuel Beckett', *META: Journal des traducteurs/Translators' Journal*, 66.1 (forthcoming).

Chaucer, Geoffrey (2003), *Troilus and Criseyde*, Barry Windeatt (ed), London: Penguin.

Crook, Tim (2005), *Radio Drama: Theory and Practice*, London and New York: Routledge.

Davies, William (2017), 'A Text Become Provisional: Revisiting *The Capital of the Ruins*', *Journal of Beckett Studies*, 26.2, 169–87.

Fletcher, John and Beryl S. Fletcher (1978), *A Student's Guide to the Plays of Samuel Beckett*, London: Faber and Faber.

Frost, Everett and Jane Maxwell (2006), 'TCD MS 10970: English Literature', *Samuel Beckett Today/Aujourd'hui*, 16, 105–12.

Houppermans, Sjef (2003), *Samuel Beckett & Compagnie*, Amsterdam: Brill.

Jesson, James (2009), '"White World: Not a Sound": Beckett's Radioactive Text in *Embers*', *Texas Studies in Literature and Language*, 51.1, 47–65.

Joyce, James (1993), *Ulysses*, Hans Walter Gabler (ed), New York: Vintage Books.

Knowlson, James (1996), *Damned to Fame: The Life of Samuel Beckett*, London: Bloomsbury.

McCracken, Allison (2002), 'Scary Women and Scarred Men: Suspense, Gender Trouble, and Postwar Change, 1942–1950', in Michele Hilmes and Jason Loviglio (eds), *Radio Reader: Essays in the Cultural History of Radio*, New York: Routledge, pp. 183-208.

Mégevand, Martin (2010), 'Pinget Seen by Beckett, Beckett According to Pinget: The Unpublishable', *Journal of Beckett Studies,* 19.1, 3–14.

Mooney, Sinéad (2010), 'Beckett in French and English', in S. E. Gontarski (ed), *A Companion to Samuel Beckett*, New Jersey: Wiley-Blackwell, pp. 196–208.

Morin, Emilie (2014), 'Beckett's Speaking Machines: Sound, Radiophonics and Acousmatics', *Modernism/modernity,* 21.1, 1–24.

Nixon, Mark and Dirk Van Hulle (2017), *Samuel Beckett's Library*, Cambridge, UK: Cambridge University Press.

Pilling, John (1999), *Beckett's 'Dream' Notebook*, Reading: Beckett International Foundation.

Salado, Régis (2006), 'Beckett et Pinget: l'échange des voix', *Études anglaises*, 59.1, 31–46.

Shakespeare, William (1869), *Œuvres complètes de Shakespeare*, Vol. 1, M. Francisque Michel (trans), Paris: Firmin Diderot.

Shakespeare, William (1872), *Œuvres complètes de Shakespeare*, Vol. 8, François-Victor Hugo (trans), Paris: Pagnerre.

Shakespeare, William (2008), *The Norton Shakespeare*, Stephen Greenblatt (ed), New York: Norton.

Van Hulle, Dirk (2009), 'The Dynamics of Incompletion: Multilingual Manuscript Genetics and Digital Philology', *Neohelicon*, 36.2, 451–61.

Van Hulle, Dirk and Pim Verhulst (2018), 'Beckett's Collaborative Translations in the 1950s', *Samuel Beckett Today/Aujourd'hui*, 30.1, 20–39.

Verhulst, Pim (2017), 'Getting over Joyce in English: "Proteus", *Portrait* and the Genesis of Samuel Beckett's Radio Play *Embers*', *Genetic Joyce Studies*, 17 (Spring), 1–20.

Verhulst, Pim (2022), *The Making of Samuel Beckett's Radio Plays*, Brussels and London: University Press Antwerp and Bloomsbury.

Part II
Beckett's Translations of Other Authors

6

Esperando a Goethe: Translation, Humanism and 'Message from Earth'

Patrick Bixby

Padre Goethe que estás sobre los cielos
entre los Tronos y Dominaciones
y duermes y vigilas con los ojos
por la cascada de tu luz rasgados.

Father Goethe who are above the heavens
Among the Dominations and the Thrones
and sleep and watch with eyes astare
sluices of your downpouring light.

Gabriela Mistral, 'Recado Terrestre' ('Message from Earth'),
translated by Samuel Beckett (1949: 75)

In the spring of 1949, the newly founded United Nations Educational, Scientific and Cultural Organisation published a volume titled *Goethe: UNESCO's Homage on the Occasion of the Two Hundredth Anniversary of his Birth*, which contained, among other tributes, a poem penned by Gabriela Mistral and translated by Samuel Beckett. To date, the translation of 'Recado Terrestre' ('Message from Earth') has received only scant critical attention, although it represents a rather remarkable encounter between two Nobel Prize winners, between Latin American and European literary traditions, and between the aspirations of a revived humanism and a profound scepticism about those aspirations after the catastrophe of the Second World War. Mistral's poem takes the form of an extended prayer to '*Padre Goethe*', who is implored to leave his perch '*sobre los cielos*' ('above the heavens'), descend to a world recently ravaged by warfare and announce his return '*al apercibido*' ('to the chosen') (Mistral 1949: 75). The original Spanish version exemplifies the poet's unique blend of Christian mysticism and liberal humanism, which lends a tentative optimism to the invocation of the great man of letters. But Beckett's translation of the poem forms a more critical response to Goethe's humanist ideals and those of his fellow Weimar Classicists – as well as a largely unexamined contribution to Beckett's own literary production during this crucial period of his career. At a moment when Goethe's legacy was being re-evaluated around the world, Beckett's choices as a translator suggest an interrogation of the German author and his presumed 'timelessness', which would somehow transcend both the limitations of faith and the trials of history (Mistral 1949: 77). Beckett's renewed engagement with this legacy, via Mistral's poem, is thus demonstrative of his ambivalence toward not just the *Neuhumanismus* of the Weimar Classicists and the secular significance of Goethe's second coming, but the resurgence of humanist ideals in the postwar years.

I

Goethe was a useful figure for UNESCO in the late 1940s. In anticipation of the 200th anniversary of his birth, the newly appointed Director-General of the organisation, Jaime Torres Bodet, sent letters to a number of eminent writers and intellectuals, including Thomas Mann, Alfonso Reyes and Stephen Spender, soliciting contributions to a type of belated *Gedenkschrift* recognising the occasion. The UNESCO charter had been ratified just two years earlier and Bodet saw the anniversary as an opportunity to honour Goethe as a benevolent exemplar of German culture, as well as to define the mission of the recently-established organisation: as the Director-General said in his letters, he sought to salute in the German author 'an imperishable testimony to what the human mind can accomplish when its desire for knowledge, that is for analysis and awareness, is combined with the power of understanding, that is to say, harmonising and reconciling. That, exactly, is the spirit which animates Unesco' (Bodet 1949: ix). Emerging from the upheaval of the war, the organisation was founded with the express purpose of promoting peace through international collaboration in education, the sciences and culture; underpinning the UNESCO mission, as Maren Elfert has highlighted, was an enduring Enlightenment belief in the possibility of progress 'under the condition that human beings follow their capacity for rational agency' (Elfert 2017: 6). As the Goethe bicentenary neared, Bodet called on his addressees to honour the celebrated author of *Die Leiden des jungen Werthers*, *Faust* and *Wilhelm Meisters Lehrjahre*, 'whose whole existence was a heroic effort to achieve that inner balance, at the same time noble and constructive, which men and nations only attain by vigilant insistence upon clear thinking and by seeking a culture that shall free them from their prejudices' (Bodet 1949: x).

Yet the significance of this achievement was far more contested than Bodet acknowledged in his invitations. Nazi leaders had tried, but struggled, to accommodate Goethe and his fellow Weimar Classicists to their propagandistic aims, though in his 1936 novel, *Mephisto*, Klaus Mann (son of Thomas Mann) had linked the moral downfall of his protagonist to performances of *Faust*, produced by the State Theatre under the protection of the Ministerpräsident. To be sure, during the Nazi era, state-subsidised theatre companies often alternated the staging of National Socialist dramas with more traditional fare from writers such as Goethe and Schiller. After the war, as the German Democratic Republic sought to break from the legacy of National Socialism, it also turned to the Weimar Classicists as a source of cultural renewal: the poet and Socialist Unity Party leader Johannes R. Becher praised Goethe in 1949 as the 'liberator' of Germany after the war and claimed that Hitler's barbarism would not have been possible if the writer's legacy had remained alive in the 1930s (Lepenies 2009: 160). But, with the labour of moral restoration getting underway in both East and West Germany, a number of intellectuals were critical of the ease with which Goethe was evoked to absolve the national spirit of its sins. For instance, when the philosopher and theologian Karl Jaspers was presented with the prestigious Goethe Prize in 1947, he took the opportunity to decry the evocation of the German author as a distraction from the horrors of National Socialism: 'Our real happiness about his greatness, the fact that we are deeply moved by the force of his love, should not prevent us from doing exactly what he himself tried to avoid: to behold the abyss . . . He is like a representative of humanity, but without offering us a path we can follow' (quoted in Boemer 2015: 181).

The same year, Thomas Mann published his *Doktor Faustus*, a novel that revises the Faust legend as an allegory for the damnation of the German soul on entering into an accord with Hitler and the Nazi regime. Goethe had been an important influence throughout Mann's career and would remain for the novelist an emblem of humanist ideals, transcending German chauvinism and all manner of parochialism. After sixteen years of exile in Switzerland and the United States, Mann finally returned to Germany in the summer of 1949 to present his lecture '*Goethe und die Demokratie*' (previously delivered as 'Goethe and Democracy' at the Library of Congress in May of that year) in Frankfurt and Munich before receiving the Goethe prize in Weimar. In the lecture, after demurring that he had 'nothing new' to tell his audience, the novelist went on to claim, much like Bodet, that 'there is in Goethe a foundation of unshakably great humanity and of a reliable goodness which reconciles all contradictions in a lofty, almost godlike fashion. And I think you will find even the political contradictions evident in his *Weltanschauung* to

be dissolved in this unfailing humanity' (Mann 1950: 3, 9). Even if he demonstrated an antagonism toward democracy, Goethe could be counted as a
deeply democratic figure because he put his talents to work in 'the best interests of humanity', rather than remaining aloof in an 'artistic-poetic' pessimism
(Mann 1950: 8). Mann's contribution to the UNESCO volume, 'Goethe's
Werther', makes much of the *Zeitgeist* that attended the composition of the
writer's first novel – 'the disgust with civilisation, the emancipation of emotions, the agitated yearning for a return to elemental nature, the struggle
against the chains of a torpid culture' (Mann 1949: 64) – but the essay steers
well clear of any implications for contemporary moral or political questions,
focusing instead on Goethe's romantic interests and youthful psychology, as
revealed by 'a masterpiece in which devastating feeling and precocious artistic
understanding achieve an almost unique combination' (Mann 1950: 74).

For many of those championing his legacy, Goethe was nonetheless a peda-
gogical figure whose example could teach the postwar world sorely needed
lessons. Bodet argued that the German writer was a great 'educator', as well as
a 'great European' and 'great universalist', whose humanist faith had convinced
him that cultural and scientific inquiries were valuable precisely insofar as they
could profit others: 'Man, having reached the culmination of his individual
growth, turns to the multitude of his fellowmen and appraises his message in
terms of the benefit which they are able to derive from its meaning' (Bodet
1949: xi). After the war, Goethe's legacy was also enjoying something of a
revival in Latin America, with the publication of popular editions of his work,
including *Las penas del joven Werther* and *Faust*, as well as biographical essays
and anthologies, some of them intended for school children (Rukser 1961).
In Mistral's poem, the *Geist* of the 'great European' is linked with a multi-
cultural, cosmopolitan view of the world, which acquires the names not just
of 'Tierra', but 'Deméter, y Gea y Prakriti', and thus takes on associations
with Greek mythology, Hinduism and Buddhism (Mistral 1949: 76). That
is to say, the German writer is enlisted to serve the internationalist agenda of
Chilean poet: Mistral had begun her working life as a teacher in the rural south
of Chile, before promoting educational reform in Mexico, working closely
with the League of Nations to develop their Committee of Arts and Letters
and then contributing to its Institute for Intellectual Cooperation. Now, after
receiving the Nobel Prize for Literature in 1945 and serving briefly on the
United Nations Subcommittee on the Status of Women, she took up Bodet's
invitation to address Goethe's legacy – though perhaps not in the way the
Director-General had intended.

Mistral's 'message' begins with a salutation imitating the Lord's Prayer and
then goes on to speak to the spirit of the German writer in an imploring

voice (Mistral 1949). In this regard, the poem is a petition, or rather a series of petitions, that evokes the Gospels and their eschatological teachings regarding the coming Kingdom of God, our 'Father'. But the '*recado*' also draws on a genre of epistolary verse from the Latin American poetic tradition, here addressed to Goethe with the request that he descend from on high and return to the world of men below, bringing a spirit that the human realm now lacks. The Goethean spirit is found manifest in the natural world, which is rendered sacred and numinous by his poetic imagination, as well as by the ecstatic vision of the poetic speaker. The speaker goes on to imagine the movements of the German writer's mind, animated by both the memory of his days on earth and his consciousness of the ordeals that now plague human history. In his seeming omniscience, Goethe had anticipated the turbulence of the twentieth century in the terrifying images of his famous *Walpurgisnacht* scene in *Faust*, images that the speaker now adopts to depict the dehumanisation of her contemporaries: '*la gente de la boca retorcida por lengua bífida, la casta ebria del "sí" y el "no"*' ('the people with twisted mouth and cloven tongue, the race inebriate with yes and no') (Mistral 1949: 78). With these images, the speaker acknowledges the persistent malevolence of a benighted and grotesque world, inhabited by monstrous creatures whose forms distort the beauties of the natural world. Directing the *recado* at Goethe, the speaker invites him to look down from his heavenly perch onto the fallen world, where he will discover that a subterranean and nocturnal evil prevails. But already, at the very moment to this petition to the great man of letters, the first signs of a transformation, of a new dawn, are sweeping across the earth: his influence, his voice, his poetry begins to revive the stricken planet and breathe new life into it. A new stirring of love and plenitude, a Goethean sacred, emerges from the natural world and starts to wipe away the bloody vision of a divided humanity that has reigned in the twentieth century. It is yet only a slight *siseo* ('hiss') or *silbo* ('whistle'), but it is at last discernible.

II

For many years, very little scholarly attention was directed toward Beckett's efforts as a translator of Latin American poetry for UNESCO in the late 1940s and early 1950s, including both 'Message from Earth' and the far more extensive *Mexican Poetry: An Anthology*; but, whenever the subject was broached, commentators never failed to note that the writer undertook the work as what he called 'a purely alimentary job' – that is, as nothing more than a means to put food on the table during his lean postwar years in Paris. These same commentators usually remarked that the Irishman had only a passing knowledge of the Spanish language and had to rely on 'the help of a scholar specialised in Spanish, and some friends' to complete the work (quoted in Ackerley and Gontarski 2007: 319). Recent scholarship, including the important archival work of María José Carrera, has begun to provide a much fuller picture of the work Beckett did as a translator for UNESCO and the significance it had for him as a writer. Carrera has suggested that, rather than an 'irrelevant sideline' to his literary output, these translations should be included as an 'unexpected presence' in the canon of his work (Carrera 2019: 63). Darren Gribben has extended this line of argument further to claim that during these years 'translation provided Beckett with the opportunity to find something important about his own voice, in English [and French]' (Gribben 2011: 326). Meanwhile, Emilie Morin has drawn attention to just how out of place Beckett felt at UNESCO: 'the liberal humanism sponsored by the organisation and its internal politics were deeply alien to him, and he had nothing positive to say about its internationalist ambitions' (Morin 2017: 122). She has also pointed out the delicate issues associated with the Goethe volume, given the competing political implications gathering around the German writer as Beckett undertook his translation of 'Recado Terrestre'.

Goethe had been an important, if also rather ambivalent, point of reference for Beckett before the war, and the German writer now appeared before him during his celebrated 'siege in the room', as he moved on from the composition of *En attendant Godot* and commenced work on *L'Innommable*. To be sure, at this critical moment in his career, Beckett took on the job not just of translating Mistral's poem but of revising the entire English version of *Goethe: UNESCO's Homage on the Occasion of the Two Hundredth Anniversary of his Birth* – meaning that, whether he wished it or not, he was obliged to spend an extended period of time poring over writings dedicated to the Weimar Classicist.

Earlier in his writing life, Beckett had responded rather sardonically to the *Neuhumanismus* of Goethe and his coterie. In *Dream of Fair to Middling Women* (1932), for instance, the narrator reflects on his own developing abilities as a storyteller by quipping: 'We live and learn, we draw breath from our heels now, like a pure man, and we honour our Father, our Mother, and Goethe' (Beckett 1993: 193). With this jest, which nods to both Daoist wisdom and the Weimar Classicists, Beckett positions his narrative – and, as I have argued elsewhere, his entire oeuvre – in a parodic relationship with Schiller's educational ideal of the 'pure man' and Goethe's narrativization of that ideal in his archetypal Bildungsroman, *Wilhelm Meisters Lehrjahre* (Bixby 2009: 22–8). For these German writers, grounded firmly in a humanist tradition stretching back to ancient Greece, *Bildung* represented an enduring *Humanitätsideal* of individual cultivation, of the capacity to achieve coherence and wholeness through identification with an archetypal humanity. In this regard, *Bildung* draws directly on its root meaning (*Bild* as 'picture' or 'image'), with the implication that education, especially aesthetic education, promotes human perfection through an ethical association with the balanced unity of the aesthetic object. This ideal is also comically undercut in 'Gnome', a brief verse from the same period, which Beckett wrote in response to Goethe's *Bildungsroman* but, as Mark Nixon has noted, after the style of Goethe and Schiller's *Xenien* poems (Nixon 2011: 67):

> Spend the years of learning squandering
> Courage for the years of wandering
> Through the world politely turning
> From the loutishness of learning (Beckett 1977: 7)

Beckett read a great deal of Goethe in the mid-1930s, as evinced in the extensive notes that he took from *Dichtung und Wahrheit* in the spring of 1935 and *Faust* in the summer of 1936, while he prepared for his own abortive *Wanderjahr* in Germany. The notetaking was primarily a means to improve his command of the German language, though Beckett gave up before finishing the play, because he found the 'determined optimism' – 'all the on & up' – that it expressed 'so tiresome'. As he wrote to Thomas MacGreevy in September 1936, he finally grew too weary to go on when he encountered the phantasmagoric depictions near the end of Part I of *Faust*: 'The Classical Walpurgisnacht was too much for me, and I feel no inclination to go on, though I am told it improves in Acts 3 and 5' (quoted in Van Hulle 2006: 284). After the war, as Dirk Van Hulle points out, Beckett did make use of his notes from Goethe in *Molloy*, though in a manner that once again seems to question the authority of Goethe as a great educator: Moran, wanting to prevent his son from ruining his cherished stamps by putting them into his pockets, attempts to 'impress' the lesson on him, albeit unsuccessfully, by evoking Faust's sacrificial motto: '*Sollst entbehren*' ('Thou shalt forego; shalt do without') (Van Hulle 2006: 292).

Perhaps more than anything, Beckett's translation of Mistral's poem should be viewed as a resumption of his long engagement with Goethe's writing – and especially his strained dialogue with Goethe's brand of humanism. This is borne out in a number of significant, if sometimes slightly odd, choices he made in reworking of 'Recado Terrestre' into his own poetic idiom. The first of these choices, in line seven of the poem, is the rather puzzling substitution of '*and, though the finger of opprobrium points*' (Mistral 1949: 77) for '*y, aunque te den como piedra de escándalo*', (Mistral 1949: 76) which translates more literally as 'and, even if they hit you like a scandal stone'. Mistral's phrase, *'piedra de escándalo'*, is one that appears several times in the Bible, first in Isaiah 8:14, but perhaps most famously in Peter 2:8, rendered in the King James version as 'and a stone of stumbling, and a rock of offense, even to them which stumble at the word, being disobedient'. The etymology of the Greek *'skandalon'* suggests something like the 'obstacle that hinders the march' or 'stumbling block' and in Peter it is the ruin of those who reject the Saviour. Figured as the cornerstone of the church, He is a 'stumbling block', and the manner of their stumbling is disobedience to the word of the Gospel, especially in the mode of evil speaking. In Mistral's poem, then, *'piedra de escándalo'* suggests that Goethe's descent to earth and the sacralised natural world is also a kind of fall from grace, which can only be remedied only through his words, his speech. Beckett's translation, 'and, though the finger of opprobrium points', loses these Biblical associations and substitutes for them a different sort of accusation: a secular form of public indictment arising from shameful, perhaps even illicit, conduct.

Before drawing any larger conclusions from this single line of verse, we should join it with the opening of the next stanza – '*Parece que te cruza, el Memorioso, / la vieja red de todas nuestras rutas*' (Mistral 1949: 76) – which Beckett's translation renders as 'It seems that in your timelessness is spread / the immemorial net of all our ways' (Mistral 1949: 77). Mistral's lines, which could be translated more literally as 'It seems to cross you, the Memorious, the old network of all our routes', suggest that Goethe, above in heaven, has a deep memory of human history, including its many trials and tribulations. Perhaps, as Cedomil Goic has suggested, the lines also evoke the notion of Platonic remembering – that is, the Greek philosopher's reminiscence theory of knowledge based on the transmigration of souls that retain experience garnered from past lives (Goic 2012: 98). Beckett's translation, abandoning the classical reference, offers instead an implicit criticism of Goethe and Weimar Classicism insofar as their collective project represents a flight from the pressures of historical change into the utopian embrace of art and antiquity. This is apparently the case despite the fact that the movement emerged at the time of the French Revolution and the Reign of Terror and that it is now summoned in the aftermath of the Second World War and amidst the developing tensions of the Cold War. For all its earnest promotion of an autonomous and universalising aesthetic of wholeness and harmony it could not, of course, escape the dreadful details of human history. As we have seen, in his contribution to the UNESCO volume, Mann had located Goethe's first novel within a social, cultural, political milieu on the brink of the French Revolution, but the essay had nonetheless highlighted the romantic and psychological aspects of the Werther's story as most significant to readers in both the late eighteenth century and the mid-twentieth century.

For Beckett, 'it seems' that the present circumstances have compromised Goethe's 'timelessness' - and, along with it, any presumption that the humanist tradition of Western literature and culture might somehow transcend the exigencies and emergencies of the age in order to speak to something constant in human nature.

In the next two stanzas, which Beckett's translation renders with greater fidelity to the original, the poem shifts its focus to Goethe's contemporary, postwar audience – those who await his return - as the poetic speaker identifies with a collective 'us', who crouch like ensnared animals 'stricken with fear'. But, as the German writer foresaw in the *Walpurgisnacht* scene of *Faust*, these men and women have become a grotesque menagerie of monstrous creatures, extending his nightmarish vision into the current century because they are unable to agree on even the most basic values:

Somos, como en tu burla visionaria,
la gente de la boca retorcida
por lengua bífida, la casta ebria
del "sí" y el "no", la unidad y el divorcio,
aun con el Fraudulento mascullando
miembros tiznados de palabras tuyas. (Mistral 1949: 78)

We are, as in your visionary jest,
the people with twisted mouth and cloven tongue,
the race inebriate with yes and no,
with oneness and divorce,
and muttering with the Falsifier still
darkly a broken smatter of your words. (Mistral 1949: 79)

In the mid-1930s, as we have seen, Beckett had given up reading *Faust* when he reached the Walpurgisnacht scene because he found the 'determined optimism' exhausting: 'I can understand the 'keep on keeping on', he explained to MacGreevy, 'as a social prophylactic, but not at all as the light in the autological darkness, or the theological' (quoted in Van Hulle 2006: 295). Evidently, despite the tragic elements of Faust's story, Beckett's attention was fixed on what he perceived to be Goethe's insistence on the notion that human life can find fulfilment, a kind of secular salvation, in the pursuit of earnest endeavours combined with an acceptance of the natural order of things. If this kind of wishful thinking promises a salutary effect on the social body, providing it a kind of integrity and coherence, it could not be justified, for Beckett, on any other grounds.

Mistral's emphasis in this stanza is precisely on the darkness of Goethe's vision, as she links the gathering of witches and demons – those deformed and bestial images of humanity depicted in the *Walpurgisnacht* episode – with the evils of the recent war. Here Beckett's addition of 'still' stresses the persistence of such infernal scenes through the course of the twentieth century, while his evocative 'darkly a broken smatter' for '*miembros tiznados*' (more literally, 'smudged' or 'blackened' 'limbs') suggests the fragmented and superficial version of Goethe's writings put to nefarious propagandistic uses by the Mephistophelian political leaders of recent history. The darkness only deepens in the next stanza, which finds the poetic speaker and her contemporaries, 'still living in the cave . . . where the larva bloodless breeds . . . / And bat-grease and owl's sullen down / shed still a night that fain would be eternal / and feed for ever on its black bitumen' (Mistral 1949: 79). But, even in the midst of this terrifying gloom, there is still a glimmer of hope that humanity will leave behind a malevolent past (a night that would only 'fain' be eternal) and enter a future of enlightened beneficence and harmonious coexistence. For, following on earlier classical echoes, this 'cave' or 'grotto' evokes Plato's famous cave and the benighted experience of its inmates, though in doing so, it also foretells the discovery of the sun and a transformation of the human condition – freed from the chains of our illusions, including the internecine ideologies of the nation state.

That promise is finally uttered, if only with hushed tones, in the final stanza of the poem, though just when the promise might be fulfilled remains open to question. In Mistral's original, the stanza begins with the tentative '*Pero será por gracia de este día*' (Mistral 1949: 78) indicating not so much an action that will transpire in the times to come as a degree of uncertainty regarding whether it will come pass at all – could it be? – and exactly when 'this day' ('*este día*') might be. Should the day transpire at some point in the future, it will be the time '*que en el percal de los aires se hace / paro de viento, quiebro de marea*' (Mistral 1949: 80). Beckett's translation renders these lines as 'Yet it will even be by this day's grace / that in the cambric of the skies the wind is lulled, and hushed the wave' (Mistral 1949: 81) and in doing so enacts several subtle, but significant, alterations to the import of the original. First, his addition of 'even' brings the syllable count to the required pentameter, matching the other lines in the poem (just as Mistral employs a repetitive twelve-syllable line), but it also suggests a kind of surprise that the grace of this day-to-come will bring the actions described in the lines that follow. That sense of surprise then carries over into Beckett's use of the simple present passive tense, formed with the present of 'to be' and the past participles 'lulled' and 'hushed', which nonetheless remain suspended in the indeterminate time of 'this day'. Mistral's phrases, the compound nouns 'paro de viento' (more literally, a 'stop in the wind') and *quiebro de marea* (a 'break in the tide'), on the other hand, provide more certainty and solidity to these events.

These subtle shifts in connotation are emphasised by the more pronounced changes in denotation that Beckett's translation deploys in the lines that follow:

Como que quieres permear la Tierra,
sajada en res, con tu río de vida,
que desalteras al calenturiento
y echas señales al apercibido. (Mistral 1949: 80)

What time you seek to permeate the earth,
stricken like a beast, with your river of life,
and slake the fevered's thirst
and signal to the chosen. (Mistral 1949: 81)

Rather strangely, Beckett's translation renders '*Como que quieres permear*' ('*As if* you want to permeate') as '*What time* you seek to permeate' and in so doing throws the temporality of Goethe's return into radical doubt. Mistral's original, drawing on a Christian mysticism that finds illumination in the workings of the natural world, offers a provocative simile comparing Goethe's second coming and his renewed spiritual vitality to a kind of natural disaster – a upheaval that will, nonetheless, bring relief to those who suffer from the evils of contemporary history and eagerly await the beneficence of his return. Beckett's translation, however, turns this comparison into a question of just when the return will occur. Moreover, his choice of 'to the chosen' for '*al apercibido*' speaks to those special few who, as in the Bible, have been selected to receive the blessings of the returning Saviour, whenever he might descend to meet them. But '*apercibido*', especially as it is used in translations of the New Testament, is more often rendered as the 'prepared' or the 'ready', suggesting that the time of the return is already at hand – that the second coming of Goethe is impending, even if its exact moment cannot be predicted. An example of this usage can be found in the crucial lines of Matthew 24:44: '*Por tanto, también vosotros estad apercibidos; porque el Hijo del hombre ha de venir a la hora que no pensáis*' ('Be ready then; for at a time which you have no thought of the Son of man will come') (English–Spanish Bible 2018).

At this point in the poem, parallels not just with the Gospels, but with Beckett's own recently complete play, *Waiting for Godot*, become too evident to ignore. Yet while his protagonists, Vladimir and Estragon, remain in a perpetual cycle of anticipation and disappointment, as they await some meaningful communication from or contact with Godot, the speaker of 'Message from Earth' finally receives an answer, however faint, to her persistent entreaties:

Y vuela el aire un guiño de respuesta
un sí-es no-es de albricias, un villano,
y no hay en lo que llega a nuestra carne
tacto ni sacudida que conturben

sino un siseo de labio amoroso
más delgado que silbo: apenas habla. (Mistral 1949: 80)

And in the air a stir of answer trembles,
a quiver of good news, a thistle-down,
and never a hint in what assails our flesh
of roughness or of hurt,
nought but a w[h]ispering of loving lips
less than a hiss: scarce a breath. (Mistral 1949: 81)

Again, Beckett's translation, composed in the immediate aftermath of his work on *Godot*, makes a few slight, though significant, alterations to the import of Mistral's original. The answer received by the speaker is artfully rendered as 'a quiver of good news, a thistle-down', alluding directly to the Gospels with their 'good news' of the coming of the Kingdom of God: 'a quiver' captures the attenuated quality of this answer, which comes only '*un sí-es no-es*' or 'somewhat' in the form of '*albricias*'. But here Beckett's translation is perhaps too precise in its evocation of the Gospels, since '*albricias*', a term seldom used in Spanish translations of the Bible, is more properly a gift given to a messenger who brings good news or an expression of joy made when one receives good news, whereas the 'good news' or 'gospel' itself (from the Greek, 'εὐαγγέλιον' or '*euangélion*') is usually rendered '*las buenas noticias*', '*las buenas nuevas*', or '*el evangelio*'. No doubt there is a certain expediency in Beckett's use of 'good news', since English has no direct equivalent to 'albricias', but the translation enacts an important shift in the relationship between the poetic speaker and the spirit of Goethe: rather than sharing in the joy of the good news, they become passive recipient and rather indifferent messenger.

The lines that follow make it clear that the 'good news' will not be accompanied by the eternal judgment of the men and women of every nation, resulting in harsh punishment for some – but the news is, at least as yet, merely a whisper. In this regard, the trembling answer recalls '*toutes les voix mortes*' ('all the dead voices') that '*chuchotent*' ('whisper'), '*murmurent*' ('murmur') and '*bruissent*' ('rustle') to Vladimir and Estragon whenever the two fall silent and – along with other social, psychological and existential impulses – thus compel them to keep speaking throughout the play (Beckett 1966: 54). The requirements of iambic pentameter may help to explain Beckett's choice of 'whispering' for '*siseo*' ('hissing') and then 'a hiss' for '*silbo*' ('whistle'). In any case, the poem holds out the promise that Goethe's resuscitated humanism will overcome evil, much like the Gospels tell the Christian faithful that the Second Coming will bring salvation. Commentators have long suggested that Beckett's play presumes the demise of timeless certainties, which previous generations had turned to in their hours of need, but which had finally crumbled in the face of a second global conflict in the twentieth century. If a general decline in religious belief had been compensated for by the rise of other faiths – Humanism or Progress or Capitalism or Revolution or Nationalism or some other modern ideology – then, for Beckett, the Holocaust and the horrors of mass warfare had finally put an end to such delusions, even if the echoes of their poets, preachers and propagandists continued to reverberate. While the promise of a return is muted to '*apenas habla*' ('barely speaks') in 'Recado Terrestre' it is 'scarce a breath' in 'Message from Earth'.

What I am claiming finally is that, as Goethe's spirit is summoned to return to a world devastated by the evils of National Socialism, Beckett's 'Message from Earth' casts a far more sceptical light on the value of his humanist legacy than does Mistral's 'Recado Terrestre'. To be sure, the dead voices of previous generations murmur in the work of both writers: *En attendant Godot* is strewn with reminders of the Western tradition, cacophonous echoes of the Greeks, the Bible, Shakespeare, Descartes, Berkeley and many others. Although these voices fail to speak to a world devastated by war, the possibility of breaking with tradition in order to forge something radically new seems negated by the incessant repetitions in the play, just as by the insistent return to figures like Goethe. Recently, Jean-Michel Rabaté has demonstrated vividly the 'determined animus against postwar humanism' to be found in Beckett as early as his 1945 essay 'La Peinture des van Velde ou le monde et le pantalon', which concludes with a series of reflections on the 'human': 'Here is a word, no doubt a concept too, that has to be reserved for times of huge slaughters . . . This is a word that is being bandied around today with an unrivalled fury. Just like dum-dum bullets' (quoted in Rabaté 2016: 19). Weaponising the humanist tradition for their ideological purposes, his contemporaries have deflected attention from the 'relentless slaughter that we call "progress"' and its association with 'the triumphant march of humanity' (Rabaté 2016: 20). But, for Beckett, the courage to go on should not, cannot, come from the delusions of the past; better to accept our status as ensnared animals 'stricken with fear', and go on, nonetheless. In his translation of 'Message from Earth' we can locate another version of this judgment: it is less a panegyric, praising the spirit of Goethe and commemorating his legacy, than an extended, if rather ironic, lament directed toward a tradition whose return is hardly to be celebrated.

Works Cited

Ackerley, C. J. and S. E. Gontarski (2007), *The Grove Companion to Samuel Beckett: A Reader's Guide to his Works, Life, and Thought*, New York: Grove.

Beckett, Samuel (1966), *En attendant Godot*, Paris: Minuit.

Beckett, Samuel (1977), 'Gnome', *Collected Poems in English and French*, New York: Grove, p. 7.

Beckett, Samuel (1993), *Dream of Fair to Middling Women*, New York: Arcade.

Bixby, Patrick (2009), *Samuel Beckett and the Postcolonial Novel*, Cambridge, UK: Cambridge University Press.

Bodet, Jaime Torres (1949), 'Foreword', *Goethe: UNESCO's Homage on the Occasion of the Two Hundredth Anniversary of his Birth*, Paris: UNESCO, pp. ix-x.

Boemer, Peter (2015), *Goethe* (trans. Nancy Sanden Boerner), London: Haus.

Carrera, María José (2019), 'Samuel Beckett's Translations of Latin American Poets for UNESCO', *Samuel Beckett Today/Aujourd'hui*, 31.1, 53–65.

Elfert, Maren (2017), *UNESCO's Utopia of Lifelong Learning: An Intellectual History*, New York: Routledge.

English-Spanish Bible – The Gospels IX – Matthew, Mark, Luke & John (2018) (Basic English, 1949; Reina Valera, 1909), Truthbetold Ministry.

Goic, Cedomil (2012), *Estudios de poesía: Cartas poéticas, otros poemas largos y poesía breve*, Santiago: LOM Ediciones.

Gribben, Darren (2011), 'Translating Others, Discovering Himself: Beckett as Translator', *Studi Irlandesi: A Journal of Irish Studies*, 1.1, 325–40.

Lepenies, Wolf (2009), *The Seduction of Culture in German History*, Princeton: Princeton University Press.

Mann, Thomas (1949), 'Goethe's *Werther*', *Goethe: UNESCO's Homage on the Occasion of the Two Hundredth Anniversary of his Birth*, Paris: UNESCO, pp. 64–74.

Mann, Thomas (1950), *Goethe and Democracy*, Washington, D. C.: Library of Congress.

Mistral, Gabriela (1949), 'Message from Earth', *Goethe: UNESCO's Homage on the Occasion of the Two Hundredth Anniversary of his Birth*, Paris: UNESCO, pp. 75–81.

Morin, Emilie (2017), *Beckett's Political Imagination*, Cambridge, UK: Cambridge University Press.

Nixon, Mark (2011), *Samuel Beckett's German Diaries, 1936–1937*, London: Continuum.

Rabaté, Jean-Michel (2016), *Think, Pig!: Beckett and the Limit of the Human*, New York: Fordham University Press.

Rukser, Udo (1961), 'Goethe en el mundo hispánico', *Los anales de la Universidad de Chile*, 123, 26–37.

Van Hulle, Dirk (2006), 'Samuel Beckett's *Faust* Notes', *Samuel Beckett Today/ Aujourd'hui*, 16.1, 283-97.

7

'A stone of sun': José Juan Tablada's Poems in Samuel Beckett's Translation

María José Carrera

In her book on *Beckett's Political Imagination* (2017), Emilie Morin analyses the cultural politics of the 1949 UNESCO commission to translate into French and English an anthology of Mexican poetry. There she takes issue with Eliot Wein-berger's claim that Samuel Beckett, the designated English translator, made a number of questionable choices in his translations because he was completely unfamiliar with the indigenous Mexican cultures; Morin claims instead that it is precisely with those same choices that he purposefully introduces coded hints at 'colonial conquest and imperialist custom' (Morin 2017: 127), thus strength-ening the original poems' subtext. This debate, far from being inconsequential, touches upon some of the key issues that confront Beckett scholars when tackling the study of this sideline in his career. How aware Beckett was of the speci-ficities of the foreign culture he was translating and how aware of each of the poets' idiosyncrasies we may never get to know. But it is undeniable that the Mexican anthology produces a few interesting close encounters with poets that do not generally occupy the Beckett scholarly community. Nineteen titles of the 103 in the published anthology have been insightfully annotated in Seán Lawlor and John Pilling's edition of *The Collected Poems of Samuel Beckett* (Beckett 2012: 152–81, 420–32). We can also avail ourselves of the original Spanish and English typescripts and a personal notebook containing the translator's manuscript notes for information (if only partial) on the translation processes involved (see Carrera 2012; 2015; 2019). With a combination of both types of procedures - annotated commentary and use of manuscript sources – this essay aims at illustrating and contextualising the specific challenges posed by the poems of one of the authors included in the anthology, challenges which go beyond their Mexican-ness or lack of it. It is our contention that this sort of two-sided close reading, especially if applied to as many poets in the anthology as possible, will enhance our overall perspective on Beckett's contribution to the UNESCO commission.

My choice of José Juan Tablada (1871–1945), the poet who embodies the transition from modernism to avant-garde in Mexican poetry, is justified on account of his poetic merits, but also because he belongs to the exclusive group of four poets with more than one title selected by Octavio Paz, the translations of which make it to the final anthology in full. The other three are the Baroque poets Miguel de Guevara and Luis de Sandoval y Zapata, and the twentieth-century poet Alfonso Reyes.[1]

Tablada wrote haikus, ideographic, and 'Mexican' poems, the three types being represented in the translated anthology. The transcriptions that Beckett was given either lacked the title of the original, or did not reproduce its physical layout, or had (in one case only) disarranged lines. In spite of these shortcomings, we will see Beckett making choices when rendering these poems into English that may be less anecdotal and dismissible than we might expect.

José Juan Tablada (1871–1945)

José Juan Tablada was a diplomat, novelist, journalist, essayist, literary and art critic, and painter who only wrote poetry in a very specific moment of his life: between 1891 and 1928. A supporter of the dictatorship of Victoriano Huerta, when the revolutionary triumph was about to take place (1910) he moved to Paris, where he lived for a couple of years, when the avant-garde was in full swing. In 1914, with the end of Huerta's short term as President of Mexico, Tablada had to go into exile in New York, where he died shortly after his appointment as Vice-Consul in 1945, having spent a couple of years in Colombia and Venezuela and almost a decade back in Mexico.

As a poet, Tablada was responsible for the start of Modernism in Mexico. Like his contemporaries, he embraced Modernism's penchant for the exotic; but unlike the others he based his work on the culture of Japan, which he knew directly from his first visit to that country in 1900, when he was sent by the *Revista Moderna* on an editorial commission. His acquaintance with the workings and essence of the Japanese haiku joined forces with his familiarity with the work of the Imagist French poets whose works he knew before he moved to Paris in 1910, after his second trip to Japan, and both turned him into the initiator of the Mexican avant-garde. Recognised as the poet who brought the haiku to the Spanish-speaking world (Litvak de Kravzov 1966: 303), he also stands out for having written ideographic and simultaneous texts only a few years after Apollinaire's. His experimental phase is summed up in a sort of trilogy conformed by two books of haikai – *Un día . . . Poemas sintéticos* (1919) and *El jarro de flores (Disociaciones líricas)* (1922) – and a volume of visual poems, *Li-Po y otros poemas* (1920), published in between. Eventually, led by an enthusiasm for the poetry of Ramón López Velarde and by the rediscovery of Mexico after the Revolution, his poetry enters a final stage of nationalist colourism: his collection *La feria (Poemas mexicanos)* (1928), published in New York, brings Tablada's poetic endeavours to an end.

Samuel Beckett was given twenty-six poems from Tablada's experimental and Mexican phases, twenty-two of which are haikai. The first eleven haikus are from the 1919 collection, and the second set of eleven haikus are from the 1922 publication. The visual poem 'Nocturno alterno' that Beckett has to translate belongs originally to *Li-Po y otros poemas* (1920). The three remaining poems selected by Paz – 'El alba en la gallera', 'El loro' and 'El ídolo en el atrio' – were originally published in *La feria* (1928) and thus belong to Tablada's Mexican phase. The different types of demands made on the translator by the three types of compositions – haikus, ideographic verses and Mexican poems – will be the substance of the remaining part of this essay.

Haikais: 'Los sapos', 'La luna', 'Peces voladores'

Tablada learnt the art of haiku directly from the Japanese professor Okada Asataro during his first stay in Japan in 1900, and soon started creating his own compositions, which he preferred to refer to as 'haikai'.[2] This was also the term preferred by the French poets, among them Paul-Louis Couchoud, a lesser poet who introduced the haiku into French in 1905. Like him, Tablada is credited with having introduced the haiku into a Western poetry, in his case that written in Spanish, with many others following suit on both sides of the Atlantic Ocean: Jorge Luis Borges, Ramón Gómez de la Serna, Juan Ramón Jiménez, Jorge Guillén, etc. The Mexican soil proves fruitful for Tablada's haikus and sees the genre evolving into three different directions which are already present in Tablada's compositions: the folklorist, characterised by the use of a simple vocabulary and vivid colours painting Mexican landscapes and tropical flowers and fruit; the impressionistic that favours the sea landscapes, twilights and dawns painted in lilac, golden and white colours; and the *greguería*, a humoristic or ironic type, based on an unexpected personification or syntactical twist (Litvak de Kravzov 1966: 304–9).

Tablada's haikai, most of which are about animals, favour the folklorist and the impressionistic, and both types are present in the selection that Samuel Beckett was given by Octavio Paz. This puts him in a position which is unique in his career: that of having to translate a Japanese poetic form. We must be aware, however, that the Mexican haiku that Tablada inaugurates gets rid of the syllabic and thematic constraints of the original – the syllabic count of five–seven–five is not always respected; alliteration and end-rhymes may appear – but preserves its power to suggest by means of an evanescent image.

What Beckett's working copy of the poems calls 'Jaikais de "un día"' are twelve of the thirty-seven haikus in Tablada's collection *Un día . . . Poemas sintéticos* (1919). The transcript shows that (most probably) Octavio Paz, the editor of the anthology, had second thoughts on his selection, crossed out the ninth haiku, and excluded it from Beckett's translation lot. It immediately becomes evident to those familiar with Tablada's carefully crafted book that the transcribed haikus lack important information from the original which might have been very helpful for the translator. In Tablada's book, the haikai (or synthetic poems, as he calls them in this publication)[3] are thematically linked through their organisation into four different sections – Morning, Afternoon, Twilight, Night – with a Prologue and an Epilogue; moreover, unlike the traditional Japanese compositions, all of Tablada's haikus bear an individual title: 'Las abejas', 'El murciélago', and so on; and, in true Japanese fashion, each one of them is accompanied by a watercolour illustration made by the poet himself. In Beckett's working copy, the poems have no individual titles and lack the context provided by the section division in the original. The translator numbers the poems by hand, and that is how they will be published by Indiana University Press: with Beckett's numbers.

I have chosen the fourth poem in the Twilight section to illustrate the challenges the translator ran into and how he faced them. The haiku, which is called 'Los sapos' (the toads), becomes haiku number six in the anthology. Seiko Ota discusses this poem in the context of what she considers to be Tablada's contributions to the genre: in this case, his treatment of the toad, a recurrent motif in Japanese haikus, from a perspective which is more visual than aural (Ota 2014, Chapter 3, Section 8).

LOS SAPOS
Trozos de barro,
Por la senda en penumbra
Saltan los sapos.

Unaware of the poem's presentation in the original publication – with title and watercolour making the reader aware, from the beginning, of what should come as a final revelation; that is, that the 'trozos de barro' are actually 'sapos' – Samuel Beckett coincides with Tablada in running counter to this trademark of the Japanese form by having, in his translation, the toads make their appearance in the first line:

VI
Lumps of mud, the toads
along the shady path
hop . . .
(Paz 1969: 151)

Interestingly, and in spite of the softening effect of the final three dots that close Beckett's translation because they are there in the transcription of the poem that he is handling, Beckett's last line still comes as a twist, a disruption to the flow of the poem so far. His version closes with a brisk and sonorous

Figure 7.1 'Los sapos' (Tablada 1919: 71)

'hop' that, as expected in a haiku, comes as a surprise to the reader, not because it discloses anything but on account of its terseness.

To set off the quality of Beckett's rendition, we can put it side by side with that of A. Scott Britton – who, incidentally, does not mention Beckett's translations in his introduction or bibliography. In Britton's 2016 version, Tablada's 'barro' becomes clay as well as mud, and 'la senda en penumbra' is just a road.

Preserving the original poem's distribution of content in the three lines does not turn his translation into a more adequate rendering than Beckett's, as we see it:

TOADS
Clumps of mud and clay
on the road,
toads hopping.
(Tablada 2016: 57)

Among the seven haikus in the section entitled Night, the fourth compartment into which the poems of *Un día . . .* are organised, Paz selects 'La luna', eventually haiku number eleven in the Mexican anthology:

LA LUNA
Es mar la noche negra;
La nube es una concha;
La luna es una perla . . .

Tablada's three dots and semicolons do not appear in the transcript that Beckett was given and will not appear in the published anthology. More importantly, the verbal form which is used in the three lines of the poem – 'es' (is) – will be absent from Beckett's translation; by getting rid of the only verb in the original, he enhances the imagistic effect of the poem:

XI
Sea the black night,
the cloud a shell,
the moon a pearl.
(Paz 1969: 152)

Interestingly, with his economy of means Beckett succeeds in giving us a much more literal version than that of A. Scott Britton, with the added quality that Tablada's synthetic poem is much more condensed in his translation: while Beckett reduces Tablada's 'la luna es una perla' to 'the moon a pearl', Britton feels the need to clarify to the reader that 'the moon is the pearl within'; within the shell of the clouds, that is:

THE MOON
The dark night is the sea,
the clouds, a shell,
and the moon is the pearl within.
(Tablada 2016: 59)

The second set of eleven haikus that Beckett translates – thirteen were initially selected but two were then discarded by the editor – is taken from Tablada's 1922

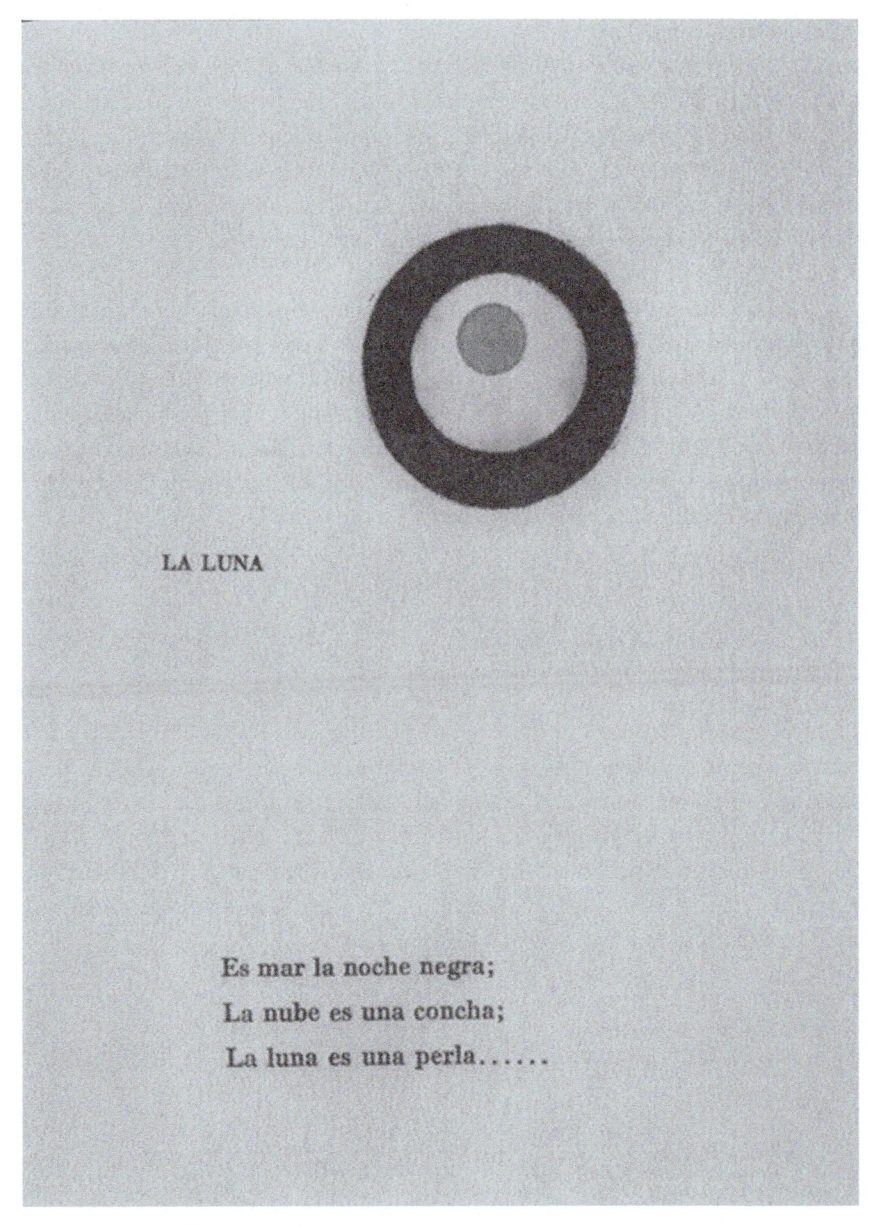

Figure 7.2 'La luna' (Tablada 1919: 97)

collection *El jarro de flores (Disociaciones líricas)*. In the collection's prologue, Tablada specifies that these 'disociaciones líricas', like the previous 'poemas sintéticos', are composed 'al modo de los *hokku* or *haikai* japoneses' (in the manner of the Japanese *hokku* or *haikai*) that he claims to have introduced into the Spanish poetry as a revolt against 'la zarrapastrosa retórica' (the seedy rhetorics) and as being the most suitable vehicle for modern thought in its pure lyricism and its capacity for surprise and irony (Tablada 1922, 'Hokku', 5).[4] Unlike the haikai in *Un día* . . . Tablada's lyrical dissociations are not accompanied by an illustration; but, like their predecessors, they are organised into different sections, nine in this case ('Bestiary', 'Landscapes', 'Seascapes', 'Trees', 'Fruits', among others), and they also have individual titles, none of which is given in the selection prepared for the translator of the anthology; neither is any allusion to the section they belong to.

This puts the translator clearly at a disadvantage when rendering into English haiku number nine, for instance, which is titled 'Peces voladores' (flying fish) and is the fourth and last haikai in the book's fifth section, called Seascapes. Indeed, the section title is illustrated with an engraving of flying fish made by the Mexican artist Adolfo Best-Maugard. With the lack of the important contextual information provided by the poem's title, the two-line piece is much more difficult to interpret:

PECES VOLADORES
Al golpe del oro solar
estalla en astillas el vidrio del mar.
(Tablada 1922, 52)

The bangs and explosions in the original poem have a strong visual and aural component. It is in the translation of the latter that Beckett excels. He renders the exploding sounds in the original with equal, if not greater, strength: 'smitten' and 'breaks' convey the shattering violence of the original, which becomes more evident if we compare his version with that of A. Scott Britton who, for instance, turns 'al golpe de' into a 'kiss' and leaves out the visual and aural blast transmitted by 'estalla':

IX
Smitten by the solar sun
the glass sea breaks to shivers.
(Paz 1969: 153)

FLYING FISH
Shards of glass in the
sun-kissed water.
(Tablada 2016: 75)

Beckett, moreover, contributes the tautological 'solar sun', reinforcing the 's' alliteration that he seems to be playing with, perhaps in imitation of the original's cacophonic 'estalla en astillas' (bursts into slivers). As a result, it is much easier to hear the noise made by the flying fish in his translation, in spite of his being in the dark about its provenance.

Ideographic Poems: 'Nocturno alterno'

Published in between his two books of haikai, Tablada's *Li-Po y otros poemas* (1920) testifies to the poet's love for the Orient in general. 'Li-Po', the first half of the book, is a string of twenty-five thematically linked visual poems devoted to the life of the eighth-century Chinese poet Li-Po or Li Bai (701–62) in a form reminiscent of Apollinaire's calligrams but indebted to Chinese influences, as Adriana García de Aldridge has proved (1983). The second part of the book presents sixteen ideographic poems, some of which Tablada describes as being not only graphic but architectonic, and with a capacity to synthesise which allows him to capture modern life in all its multiplicity (quoted in Meyer-Minnemann 1988: 434, 437). The 'thinnest sonnet in Spanish' (Weinberger 1992: 28) and a poem that must be held to a mirror to be read are among the experiments here included.

Standing as the lone representative of this Apollinarian phase in the translated Mexican anthology is 'Nocturno alterno', the fifth poem from this second part of *Li-Po y otros poemas*. It is a simultaneist poem whose composition relies on the juxtaposition of two independent textual units (independent, but semantically linked), which take turns in the odd and even lines of the poem and are printed with two different font types and sizes before they finally converge into the same text, printed in a single type, at the tail end of the poem. In 'Nocturno alterno', the different nocturnal ambiences of New York (the odd lines) and Bogotá (the even lines) are contraposed and then brought together under the same moon.

Nocturno Alterno

Neoyorquina noche dorada
     Fríos muros de cal moruna
Rector's champaña fox-trot
     Casas mudas y fuertes rejas
Y volviendo la mirada
     Sobre las silenciosas tejas
El alma petrificada
     Los gatos blancos de la luna
Como la mujer de Loth

       Y sin embargo
         es una
           misma
             en New York
               y en Bogotá
                 LA LUNA..!

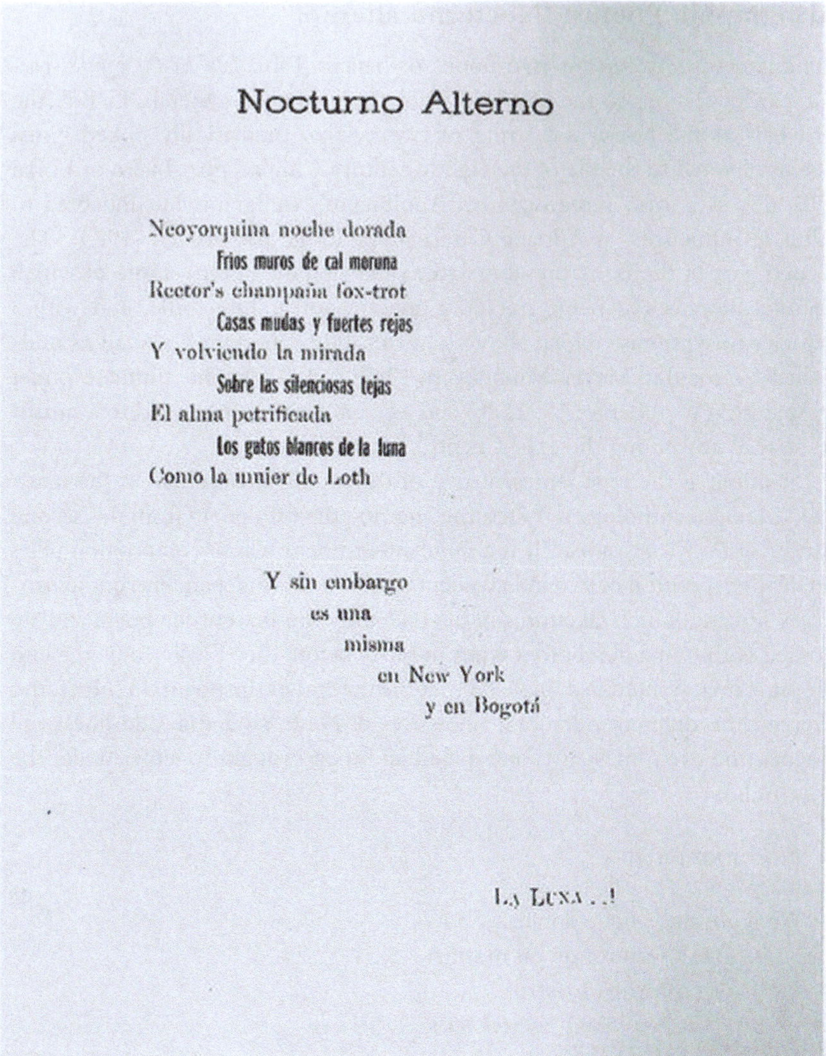

Nocturno Alterno

Neoyorquina noche dorada
  Frios muros de cal moruna
Rector's champaña fox-trot
  Casas mudas y fuertes rejas
Y volviendo la mirada
  Sobre las silenciosas tejas
El alma petrificada
  Los gatos blancos de la luna
Como la mujer de Loth

  Y sin embargo
   es una
    misma
     en New York
      y en Bogotá

    La Luna..!

Figure 7.3 'Nocturno alterno' (Tablada 1920: n.p.)

Samuel Beckett cannot have been initially aware of the fact that this was an ideographic poem, given the plain transcription that he was given: fifteen lines without any sort of indentation and punctuated with eight commas and a period,
none of which is meant to be there. Perhaps made in one of his meetings with
Octavio Paz, the manuscript notes on the typescript with the original poem that
he was given – indicating that alternating lines are to be indented and also that
they form two separate sequences (with numbers before each of the first nine lines

marking the two simultaneous textual units: 1 1 2 2 3 3 4 4 5) – result in Beckett replicating in his translation the indentation of the lines in the original. But the different font types, or the initial capitalisation of all lines – which emphasises their separateness – are lost in Beckett's version and in the published anthology, where fifteen punctuation marks appear. By sticking closely to the grammar of the original, Beckett succeeds in making the alternating lines readable both as a single sequence and separately, but nothing leads the reader in that second direction:

Alternating Nocturne

Golden New York night,
    cold limedark walls,
Rector's, foxtrot, champagne,
    still houses, strong bars,
and looking back,
    above the silent roofs,
the spirit petrified,
    the white cats of the moon,
like Lot's wife.

And yet
        it is one,
                at New York,
                    at Bogota,
                        and the same
                        moon!
                                    (Paz 1969: 159–60)

These typographic shortcomings, of which Beckett is not responsible, but which are especially unfortunate in a graphic poem, make this his least satisfactory translation of Tablada's poems so far.[5]

Mexican Poems: 'El ídolo en el atrio'

Although Tablada's last poetic effort, the book *La feria: Poemas mexicanos* (1928), still contains five haikus – 'Jaikais de la feria' and 'Jaikais del circo' – and an ideogram – 'Ex Voto a López Velarde' – this collection of thirty-eight poems marks a significant change with his previous production. Brimming with recollections of Mexican folklore and local colour, with an inclination for the pre-Columbian, the poems in *La feria* are strongly indebted to the work of his friend Rafael López Velarde, a younger poet who is also represented in the UNESCO anthology with eleven poems, and whose untimely death gave origin to the last poem before the Epilogue in Tablada's book. It is Velarde's Americanism in particular that Tablada imitates, but the youthful poet's intimate approach gives way to the older poet's preference for the external: cocks, parrots, and toads abound in a landscape of *feria* and *fiesta*, with circus, clown, and roulette included; a fair that is tainted by the twilight of its appoaching end, where the senses are still active but no longer deceive us, as Tablada claims in the book's Preface (Tablada 1928, 'La feria': 9). In spite of his debt to López Velarde, it is the national, religious, and cultural syncretism that pervades these poems that ultimately makes them Tablada's own: the Aztec goddess of sustenance coexists with San Benito; Cuauhtémoc and Don Pelayo are cheered in the same line at the sound of the *teponatzle* (an Aztec musical instrument) and the Spanish *pandereta* (tambourine), while Criole heads sport Spanish *mantillas y peinetas* (traditional lace veils and high combs). This syncretism lies also at the core of the poem I have chosen to focus on, 'El ídolo en el atrio' (Tablada 1928: 103), the second of the three long poems selected by Octavio Paz for the Mexican anthology – the other two being 'El alba en la gallera' and 'El loro'.

The title of 'El ídolo en el atrio' already hints at the fusion of religions and cultures that informs the whole collection by referring simultaneously to the fifteenth-century monolith known as the Aztec Calendar Stone (the *ídolo* in the title) and to its placement on one side of the Western tower of the Cathedral of Mexico City for most of the nineteenth century, the cathedral being preceded by an open atrium or forecourt (the *atrio* in the title). It takes Tablada just a few lines to start delving into the associations between the sun stone – which may have been an altar – and the human sacrifices inherent to the pre-Columbian culture, religion and mythologies. The blood-thirsty sun god in the centre is encircled by the still images of the glyphs representing the twenty days in the Aztec month (alligator, wind, house, lizard, serpent, and so on); in the middle section of his poem, Tablada sets in motion the animals in those symbolic figures (and others), making a noisy incursion into a tropical forest populated by jaguars, boas, bisons, iguanas, quetzals, maccaws, tapirs, and others.

The bewilderment of the translator who has little to no acquaintance with the subtleties of the Aztec culture (spanning the first thirty-two lines of the poem) nor with the local fauna (thirty-four more lines) is reflected in a colourful number of notes of all types besetting the Spanish version that he was given to translate. Pens and pencils; blues, reds and blacks; asterisks; French translations; all sorts of clarifications are sought after in what seems to be a process of returning to the poem once and again. Furthermore, some of the words there annotated by Beckett are also annotated in the two loose pages that accompany the original Spanish and English typescripts, and in a personal notebook that he kept; such is Beckett's need of information about their meaning.

Beckett's final solutions for the numerous Mexicanisms and words in Nahuatl
in the poem are varied in type. They range from the last-minute adaptation
of *zempazúchiles* (marigold; a flower that symbolises the offerings to the dead)
with the generic 'helianthi' – after toying with 'sunflower' as a translation – to
the straight borrowing of the original term in *zompantli* (the place in the Aztec
temples where the skulls of the victims were arranged in rows) and in *nemontemi*
(the last five days of the year which were considered to be ominous and when
people were advised to remain indoors to avoid all evil). He felt less certain about
borrowing the Mexicanism *chalchihuite* (emerald, precious stone) which recurs
in his notes and provokes the second afterthought once the translation has been
prepared for UNESCO. The Nahuatl *Teocali* (a pagan temple) is rendered with
the adjectiveless 'temple': this choice reinforces the abovementioned religious
syncretism of the poem, an indistinction between the two religions which is also
evident in the stanzas where the sun stone is referred to as 'the Table of the Law'
and Mexico as 'the Promised Land' (Paz 1969: 156, 158).[6]

After all this noise and movement, Tablada's poem comes to an unexpected
end with a surprising vignette where the humble armadillo (a symbol of the
underworld, of the dead, and of Mexican warriors) fools the powerful eagle
(a symbol of the sun and the foundation of the Aztec empire) and escapes,
only to reappear in the shape of a guitar. In the Mexican culture, armadillos
are associated with music and dance, and musical instruments made with the
shells of the armadillos are not uncommon. Tablada's guitar is being played by
a Zapatista patriot while he stands by the idol in the atrium with a hand swol-
len with love for the promised land.[7] The Zapatistas, incidentally, had burnt
down Tablada's home and manuscripts in 1914 on account of his support of
the dictatorship of Victoriano Huerta and his satires against the revolutionaries,
which had led him into exile in New York. Knowing this, I believe, makes us
see the poem in a completely new light.

Does this unexpected and ironic ending – with the eagle being outdone by
the armadillo, and the Aztec empire being reduced to the status of a song evoked
by a melancholic revolutionary – give a political overtone to the rest of the poem?
And what is more important for us, is Beckett enhancing the political reading
of the poem when he translates 'el pertinaz espanto / de las viejas mitologías'
(*pertinaz* meaning 'enduring') as 'the unconquerable dread / of old mythologies'
(Paz 1969: 156), thus supporting the colonial reading that Emilie Morin proposes
for the whole Anthology? (Morin 2017: 124–9). I certainly think he is; and that
poem and translation merit a second reading in this post-colonial light only.

Next to this political reading of an apparently exotic and folkloric poem stands
what I consider to be one of the translator's main achievements in his rendering
of 'El ídolo en el atrio' into English: his way of dealing with the first line, 'Una
piedra del sol'. Beckett's phrase 'stone of sun' (Paz 1969: 155) was proof for

Eliot Weinberger of his unsuccessful tackling with the Mexican lot (Weinberger 2007: 618); as I see it, Beckett has given a new meaning to the phrase and may have sparked one of the best-known Mexican poems in the twentieth century. The standard way of referring to the monolith in Spanish is *piedra del sol* (that is, 'belonging to the sun', or 'with a sun on it'), that is, a 'sun stone'; Beckett's rendering of this as 'stone of sun' (as if it was a 'stone made of sun') may be conjectured to have made an impression on Octavio Paz, who would have translated it back into Spanish in his landmark 1957 poem 'Piedra de sol'.

Conclusion

This essay has shown that the task that Beckett faced when he undertook the 1949 UNESCO commission to translate an anthology of Mexican poetry was daunting, but also that the sources of Beckett's difficulties are not always related to the Mexican origins of the poets or the Mexican content of the poems. Indeed, as our selection has shown, poems with an Oriental slant and poems with an avant-garde flair proved as challenging as the most Mexican, if not for the choice of culturally-loaded terms in the original poem – the vocabulary of those experimental poems being quite simple – certainly for the lack of important contextual information (missing titles and illustrations, standardised formal outline) that plays an essential role in the poetic experience that the originals convey. And yet, in spite of these shortcomings, Beckett's English versions prove not only adequate renderings, but are occasionally extremely successful ones. The English version of 'El ídolo en el atrio' may lack some of the cultural specificities of the original – can the *zempazúchiles* be translated into any other culture? – but succeeds in grasping the overall ironic combination of the images of death introduced with the sun stone at the beginning of the poem and the patriotic fervour of the Zapatista standing by that same stone at the end.

Even though the poetic merits of José Juan Tablada are superseded by those of the bigger names in the Mexican tradition, I believe that Beckett's encounter with his work deserves more attention than it has got so far, and perhaps he and the other Mexican poets in the *Anthology* should not be so easily taken for granted when we discuss Samuel Beckett.

Notes

1. With only one poem selected by Paz, the following nine poets also make it to the published anthology in full: Matías de Bocanegra (1612–88), Ignacio Manuel Altamirano (1834–93), Manuel M. Flores (1840–85), José Peón y Contreras (1843–1907), Justo Sierra (1848–1912), Rafael López (1875?–1943), Efrén Rebolledo (1877–1929), Manuel de la Parra (1878–1930), and Francisco González León (1868?–1945). As for the work of the remaining

twenty-three poets selected by Paz, they are translated and published selectively, or (in one case) neither translated nor published at all.

2. Originally a kind of linked verse (one person would begin the haikai, and others would follow), the haikai opens with a three-line verse that contains the name of one of the four seasons of the year. The word 'haiku' was invented in the 1890s to name this opening verse once it becomes an independent poem (Ota 2005: 133n1; Litvak de Kravzov 1966: 301).

3. Tablada's use of the word 'synthetic' to refer to his poetry can be traced to various sources, some of them pictorial (Ota 2014, '*Un día* . . . (1919) La primera colección en español de haikús'). In a letter to his friend Ramón López Velarde (13 November 1919) Tablada defends his recent poetry as being synthetic, dynamic, without any explicative or rhetorical elements; a simultaneously lyrical and graphic expression; pure poetry (quoted in Meyer-Minnemann 1988: 435); a poetry that marks a strong contrast with the excesses of the prevalent Modernist poetry, we could add.

4. For the name 'disociaciones líricas' Ota claims the direct influence of the French poet Couchoud, who claims that the Japanese brain dissociates whereas the Western brain constructs. A process of selection to suggest a natural scene with just a brushstroke is what underlies Tablada's concept of dissociation (Ota 2014, 'La segunda colección de haikús: *El jarro de flores*').

5. A. Scott Britton's extremely free rendering of the original does not prove a suitable alternative English translation (Tablada 2016: 123) but Eliot Weinberger's – included in his essay on Octavio Paz in Asia (Weinberger 1992: 28) – does:

> New York night gold
> *Cold walls of Moorish lime*
> Rector's foxtrot champagne
> *Mute houses and heavy gates*
> And looking back
> *On the silent roofs*
> The sould petrified
> *The white cats of the moon*
> Like Lot's wife
> And nevertheless
> It is always
> the same
> in New York
> or Bogota
> MOON . . .

6. For transcriptions of Samuel Beckett's notes on the Mexican Anthology typescripts preserved at the University of Texas at Austin and on the 'Sam Francis' Notebook kept at the University of Reading, see Carrera 2012 (100, 102–3, 106–7) and 2015 (161, 165).

7. A disarranged line in the transcription of this section of the Spanish original (line seventy-six appears as line seventy-eight) must have caused Beckett some confusion, but he eventually solved the riddle.

Works Cited

Beckett, Samuel (n.d.), 'Sam Francis' Notebook. Beckett International Foundation, University of Reading, UoR MS 2926.

Beckett, Samuel (1950), 'Anthology of Mexican Poetry, typescript with author emendations and notes'. Harry Ransom Humanities Research Center, The University of Texas at Austin, Beckett Collection, HRC SB MS 1/5.

Beckett, Samuel (2012), *The Collected Poems of Samuel Beckett: A Critical Edition*, Seán Lawlor and John Pilling (eds), London: Faber and Faber.

Carrera, María José (2012), '"handicapped by my ignorance of Spanish": Samuel Beckett's Translations of Mexican Poetry', in Tomasz Wiśniewski (ed), *Back to the Beckett Text*, Gdańsk/Sopot: Uniwersytet Gdański, pp. 93–107.

Carrera, María José (2015), '"And then the Mexicans": Samuel Beckett's Notes toward *An Anthology of Mexican Poetry*', in Conor Carville and Mark Nixon (eds), *'Beginning of the Murmur': Archival Pre-texts and Other Sources*, Samuel Beckett Today/Aujourd'hui, 27, Leiden: Rodopi, pp. 156–70.

Carrera, María José (2019), 'Samuel Beckett's Translations of Latin American Poets for UNESCO: Gabriela Mistral and Miguel de Guevara', in J. Little, G. Nugent-Folan, E. Morin and M. Nixon (eds), *Draff/Résidu, Samuel Beckett Today/Aujourd'hui*, 31.1, Leiden/Boston: Brill, pp. 53–65.

García de Aldridge, Adriana (1983), 'Las fuentes chinas de José Juan Tablada', *Bulletin of Hispanic Studies*, 60.2, 109–19.

Litvak de Kravzov, Lily (1966), 'El *haikai* mexicano', *Comparative Literature*, 18.4 (Autumn), 300–11.

Meyer-Minnemann, Klaus (1988), 'Formas de escritura ideográfica en *Li-Po y otros poemas* de José Juan Tablada', *Nueva Revista de Filología Hispánica*, 36.1, 433–53.

Morin, Emilie (2017), *Beckett's Political Imagination*, Cambridge, UK: Cambridge University Press.

Ota, Seiko (2005), 'José Juan Tablada: La infuencia del haikú japonés en *Un día . . .*', *Literatura mexicana*, 16.1, 133–44.

Ota, Seiko (2014), *José Juan Tablada: Su haikú y su japonismo*, México D. F.: Fondo de Cultura Económica, Ebook.

Paz, Octavio (ed) (1969) [1958], *An Anthology of Mexican Poetry*, translated by Samuel Beckett, Bloomington and London: Indiana University Press.

Tablada, José Juan (1919), *Un día . . . Poemas sintéticos*, Caracas: Imprenta Bolívar.

Tablada, José Juan (1920), *Li-Po y otros poemas*. Caracas: Imprenta Bolívar.

Tablada, José Juan (1922), *El jarro de flores (Disociaciones líricas)*, Nueva York: 'Escritores Sindicados'.

Tablada, José Juan (1928), *La feria (Poemas mexicanos)*, Nueva York: F. Mayans, Impresor.

Tablada, José Juan (2016), *The Experimental Poetry of José Juan Tablada: A Collection in Spanish and English*, translated by A. Scott Britton. Jefferson, NC: McFarland & Co.

Weinberger, Eliot (1992), 'Paz in Asia', in *Outside Stories, 1987–1991*, New York: New Directions Books, pp. 17–45.

Weinberger, Eliot (2007), 'Beckett/Paz', *Fulcrum: An Annual of Poetry and Aesthetics*, 6, 616–21.

8

Translation's Challenge to Lyric's Immediacy: Beckett's Rimbaud

Amanda Dennis

avec des rythmes instinctifs, je me flattai d'inventer un verbe poétique accessible, un jour ou l'autre, à tous les sens. Je réservais la traduction.

Rimbaud, *Une saison en enfer* (*Délires* II)

The lyric 'I' of Rimbaud's 'Délires II' invents a language accessible to all the senses, and then withholds the translation. Such withholding (*réserver*) may hint that the sense-language in question does not lend itself to equivalency; it is direct, unmediated, untranslatable. It is true that the difficulty of balancing fidelity and fluency in literary translation may make it an exercise in loss, an art of failure. Style, sound, meaning, polysemy, resonance, and rhythm cannot all carry over, and for the incommensurability of languages, the translator takes the blame: *traduttore, traditore.* (In the English, 'translator, traitor', alliteration is all that remains of the Italian's playful paranomasis). In spite of, or because of such losses, translation plays a role in the renewal of language, stretching the target language with the task of accommodating new meanings'.[1] In Beckett's case, self-translation becomes a technique of revision, if not a principle of his poetics, if his works can be thought to exist doubly, in two languages. Sinéad Mooney, arguing for the importance of translation to Beckett's work, cites the first edition book jacket of *Company,* 'Written in English, has already been translated into French by the author and revised in the light of the French text' (Mooney 2011: 15). The English *Company* came into existence in a highly mediated fashion, its final version taking shape in 'conversation' with its French translation. This mode of composition-through-mediation distinguishes Beckett's writing; it is also intrinsic to translation.

In the pages that follow, I will draw on one of Beckett's early translations – of Rimbaud's 'Le Bateau ivre' – to examine how it complicates the lyric poem's claim to subjective immediacy, revealing the highly mediated nature

of what passes itself off as immediate and developing Beckett's sense of language
as material and self-referential, which informs his later poetics of self-translation.
I will look at how Beckett's translation activates networks of cultural memory and sonic resonance by replicating and replacing the dense intertexts of
Rimbaud's poem, revealing, among other effects of translation, the lyric as
indebted to the society from which it claims separation.

In *Dickinson's Misery: A Theory of Lyric Reading* (2005), Virginia Jackson
argues that lyric poetry – a form that claims for itself subjective immediacy –
is in fact highly mediated and has been carefully constructed as a genre in
the nineteenth and twentieth centuries. She describes the personal, material
circumstances surrounding the composition of Emily Dickinson's poetry, noting that addressees of private correspondence, writing materials, and news
items are obscured when the poems are edited for publication, creating an
illusion of a lyric 'I' cut off from society.[2] As Jonathan Culler points out,
the connection between the lyric and subjective immediacy dates from the
Romantic period and finds its fullest expression in Hegel, for whom the distinguishing feature of the lyric was subjectivity coming to consciousness of
itself through experience and reflection (Culler 2015: 2). Though other theories of the lyric, including Culler's own, have updated this Hegelian view, an
association between the lyric, self-presence and immediacy persists, such that
the lyric 'I' can appear as if it were somehow free of temporality and society.
The twentieth-century lyric persona is '[a] fictional persona of all times and all
places, the first-person speaker of the lyric could speak to no one in particular
and thus to all of us' (Jackson and Prins 2014: 5). Both Culler and the editors of *The Lyric Theory Reader* (2014) describe how the lyric 'I' was replaced,
primarily in Anglo-American pedagogy, by making the speaker of the poem
into a fictional persona. But this narrativizing of lyric eliminates a tension that
makes it interesting: the tension between the poem's pretence of escaping
mediation and its embeddedness within society and culture.[3] The work of
translation, I suggest, is relevant here because it calls attention to the ways in
which literary texts are mediated by mnemonic, cultural, temporal, generic
and linguistic conditions and conventions. Taking Beckett's spirited translation
of 'Le Bateau ivre' as a case study, I will show how 'Drunken Boat' expresses
Beckett's scepticism about the immediacy and spontaneity associated with the
lyric by foregrounding, in his translation, the associative networks that create the poem's effect, even as the poem's theme is one of being unmoored.
(Indeed the 'poem's extraordinary combination of imaginative boldness and
technical control' drew a more recent translator, Alan Jenkins, to spend fifteen
years translating the work into English alexandrines that would suggest the
'sea-shanty's rollicking rhythms') (Jenkins 2007). Beckett's translation of 'Le

Bateau ivre', insofar as it reveals the layers of mediation behind the illusion of immediacy, may have inspired his later style of self-translation, and I will look at a brief passage of *Molloy,* translated in collaboration with Patrick Bowles, to frame this question.

Beckett's translation of 'Le Bateau ivre' did not appear in print until almost thirty years after it was made. The manuscript was discovered by chance by one of Beckett's editors, Felix Leakey, who, on a foxhunting holiday in Ireland, met Nuala Costello, a friend to whom Beckett had given a copy of 'Drunken Boat' in the mid-1930s. The typescript of 'Drunken Boat' survived a fire in Nuala Costello's home only because it was tucked inside her copy of *The Oxford Book of French Verse* next to a printing of Rimbaud's 'Le Bateau ivre'.[4] Beckett translated 'Le Bateau ivre' in 1932 on commission from the literary review *This Quarter.* He needed money in order to leave Paris when authorities began checking foreigners' papers after the assassination of the French president, Paul Doumer (Beckett did not possess a valid *carte de séjour).* The translation earned Beckett 700 Francs, which allowed him to settle for a short time in London, but it was never published in the review, which was discontinued at the end of 1932. Lest these facts detract from the importance of Rimbaud to Beckett, it is worth emphasising that Beckett himself proposed the project to the editor of *This Quarter,* because he had already begun work translating 'Le bateau ivre' (Beckett 1977: 144). Beckett's interest in Rimbaud is clear also from the lectures he gave at Trinity College in 1930 and 1931; he emphasised the theme of dislocation between poet and audience, with particular reference to Rimbaud and the Symbolists:

> *Fin de siècle* poetry may be explained by the withdrawal of these poets from the general life of that period. Neither *room* nor *place* for the poet in the utili-tarian society produced by the revolution . . . The *cult of the unique personal point of view* is symptomatic of the extent to which they [the Symbolists] found themselves out of touch with their fellows and thrown inward upon the selves of their own imagination: *Rimbaud.*[5]

Rimbaud's influence on Beckett's early work was considerable, and Damian Love has carefully documented the extent to which not only Rimbaud, but the Symbolist movement more generally (with its sense of crisis at the disruption of communicative axes (linking sender to message to receiver) influenced Beckett, a writer 'at home in the domain of failed communication' (Love 2005: 478–81). Both Sinéad Mooney and Marjorie Perloff, in their readings of 'Drunken Boat', have remarked upon Rimbaud's influence on Beckett. Mooney discusses how the poet inspires Beckett's 'aesthetic of incoherence' in *Dream of Fair to*

Middling Women (Mooney 2011: 47), and Marjorie Perloff traces a line of continuity between Beckett's translation of 'Le Bateau ivre' and his work on *Comment C'est* nearly three decades later (comparing the journey toward Pim to the 'journey of Rimbaud's 'Bateau ivre', a paradigm of the descent into the self) (Perloff 1981: 230).

Translators and translation theorists might agree that successful literary translation not only discovers a text's way of situating itself relative to linguistic, literary, and cultural contexts, but it also recreates comparable relations in the target language. In 'The Task of the Translator', Walter Benjamin claims that the process of translation demands sensitivity to how a text's effects are achieved, through sonority, allusion, linguistic memory, literary tradition, etc.; the translation must use this sensitivity to find its 'echo' (to use Benjamin's terminology) in the target language.[6] Clive Scott's excellent meditation on translating Rimbaud's *Illuminations* explores what this reinvention may entail in its most experimental, creative forms (he uses different spatial configurations of poems on the page to accentuate Rimbaud's way of layering images to divert purely linear readings) (Scott 2006). The translator must work with a different palette of possibilities, associations, verbal connotations and sonorities to create effects analogous to that of the original.

The thematic content of 'Le Bateau ivre' makes it a particularly interesting literary object with which to explore how linguistic and social structures mediate our experience of lyric 'immediacy'. Rimbaud's poem valorises a coming unmoored from social restrictions, an unmooring he associates with intoxication and with the dissolution of boundaries between self and world; the poem dramatises saturation in a fluid element. 'Les fleuves m'ont laissé descendre ou je voulais' (the rivers let me go where I wanted), Rimbaud writes, positioning his lyric subject '[d]ans les clapotements furieux des marées' (in the furious lashings of the tides), where, 'les Péninsules démarrées/N'ont pas subi tohu-bohu plus triomphants' (the peninsulas, unmoored, didn't suffer commotion more triomphant).[7] Rimbaud's triumphant delight in disorder is underscored by the fusion of two linguistic units, *des* + *marées* (tides), into the word *démarré* (to become unmoored). Rimbaud uses word play based on sound to evoke the severing of liaisons that anchor and position a subject of experience within its social context. Beckett's translation reproduces this emphasis on unmooring: 'Then, delivered from my straining boatmen, / . . . I made my own course down the passive rivers'. Beckett's version – 'I made my own course' – gives the lyric subject more agency in distinguishing itself from the social fabric. And though 'tides', in English, cannot fuse together into the word, 'unmoored', Beckett captures the sense of this wordplay in a slightly more narrative fashion:

Blanker than the brain of a child I fled
Through winter, I scoured the furious jolts of the tides,
In an uproar, and a chaos of Peninsulas,
Exultant, from their moorings in triumph torn. (Beckett 1977: 95)

The fleeing through winter, the scouring of tides, gives us the boat's intentional detachment from social context – a loosening mirrored by a chaotic seascape; 'les Péninsules démarrées', becomes 'a chaos of Peninsulas, / Exultant, from their moorings in triumph torn'.

Commentators of Rimbaud have noticed how curious it is that a poem so dedicated to unmooring (from social tradition) should be stitched from such a dense weave of intertextual allusions, primarily to Baudelaire's poem, 'Le Voyage'. The poem's radical unmooring derives, paradoxically, from its ties to a literary tradition – primarily one of French lyricism, though allusions to more varied sources have been noted also: Jules Verne's *Vingt mille lieues sous les mers,* Chateaubriand's *Voyage en Amérique*, children's encyclopedias and travel magazines (Shields 1995: 149–64; 151).[8]

If Beckett's translation recreates the rich effects of the 'Le Bateau ivre', it is at least in part because Beckett anchors his poem wholly in another linguistic milieu, submitting his translation to the possibilities and limitations – sonority, patterns of association, and linguistic-literary history – particular to English. Beckett chooses not to follow Rimbaud's rhyme scheme and strict metrical regularity, but he reproduces all twenty-five quatrains in (predominantly) five- or six-beat lines (Jenkins 2007: 7). Alan Jenkins calls Beckett's translation 'buoyant, magniloquent, oddly literal-minded and plain odd', and he cites a review of Beckett's translation by Christopher Ricks, who describes it as revealing an 'early Beckett of smouldering fantastication' and 'passionate idiosyncrasy' (Ricks as quoted in Jenkins 2007: 7). Such impressions notwithstanding, I will begin by looking at the meticulousness with which Beckett handles the poem's complex temporality in translation. Time, like the lyric, is sometimes associated with immediacy, but experiences of temporality are, of course, socially and especially linguistically mediated (Beckett's representation of time in 'Drunken Boat' necessarily responds to the tense structure of English).

Beckett plunges his reader midstream into his poem, which moves, like Rimbaud's, at a bracing allegro. But Rimbaud eases his readers into the pace of his poem by means of his use of the French imperfect tense (*je descendais*) and his placement of the word *comme*. Rimbaud's use of *comme* as the first word of his poem has the effect of qualifying what follows. It creates space, distances the reader from the events of the poem and allows her to regard them, if she chooses, as imaginative occurrences.[9] Beckett forgoes the English imperfect – 'I was drifting' or 'I was descending' – as well as any mediating niceties (he might have used the word 'as', which Alan Jenkins uses in his 2007 translation: 'As I nosed down the placid river I could feel/The towropes slacken') (Jenkins 2007: 17). He begins with an adjectival description. His beginning creates for the reader the sense that she is suddenly in the midst of a fast-flowing current: 'Downstream on impassive rivers suddenly/I felt the towline of the boatmen slacken'. Where Rimbaud uses the *imparfait* to create temporal depth and texture, Beckett resorts to an adjective. But the overall complexity of time in Rimbaud's poem is not easy to reproduce in English. In the first stanza, for example, four events occur at four different times and for differing durations.

Comme (1) *je descendais* des Fleuves impassibles,
(2) *Je ne me sentis plus* guidé par les haleurs:
Des Peaux-Rouges criards les (3) *avaient pris* pour cibles,
Les (4) *ayant cloués* nus aux poteaux de couleurs. (Quoted in Beckett
      1977: 92. My emphasis)

Beckett's adjectival 'downstream' and his addition of 'suddenly' may be attempts to recreate variation between the background of the boat's continual movement downriver and the one-time *event* of its severance from the towlines that had been guiding it (in the French *passé simple*).

More generally, Rimbaud's poem uses the French *imparfait* as a background against which events are recounted in different tenses. It is not that Beckett ignores the rich temporal layers in the original – on the contrary, he follows its shifts, such as when the speaker remembers Europe in the present tense: 'I weaving for ever voids of spellbound blue,/Now remember Europe and her ancient ramparts'.[10] Beckett's attention to tense, combined with his inability to follow Rimbaud's meanderings between tenses with the same effortless fluidity, is evident in his decision to use the English present perfect in stanzas 9–13. Here, Rimbaud sets the *passé composé* against the general background of the *imparfait*: *J'ai vu, J'ai rêvé, J'ai suivi, J'ai heurté,* and *J'ai vu.* Beckett's use of the past perfect – *I have seen, I have dreamt, I have followed, I have fouled, I have seen* – is a faithful translation of the *passé composé* in French, but has a grander, more totalising feel – an effect that overwhelms the background tense (the boat's motion downstream, in the *imparfait*).[11] French easily accommodates the simultaneous perception of foreground and background tenses (and Rimbaud's poem moves between these). In Beckett's translation, however, time feels more sequenced than layered. Beckett adds the word coiled at one stage – 'I coiled through deeps of cloudless green' – perhaps as a gesture to this motion and depth for which the English tense structure is ill-suited. English cannot achieve the same effect of free, elated, vertical motion through layers of time and possibility, and the lyric 'I', with its claim to immediacy – to speaking directly, impervious to time – is constrained more neatly within a linear sequence of time in Beckett's translation.

The structure of tenses in English is not the only reason Beckett's poem feels sparser. Rimbaud achieves an unmooring effect by layering and proliferating colours and sensations (as well as tenses), where Beckett's translation's approach to imagery is more stringent. Marjorie Perloff aptly compares Beckett's 'Drunken Boat' to 'a black-and-white print of a colour film called 'Bateau Ivre' (Perloff 1981: 229). The superfluity of images in Rimbaud's poem, in addition to its quick rhythm, creates a blending effect; the protean sea is at once a poem, (metonymically) waves, swells, sobs or tears, a martyr, milky, green, and blue. The boat is figured as lighter than a cork, a carcass, a sacrifice, and sweeter than the sour flesh of an apple ('Plus douce qu'aux enfants la chair des pommes sures').[12] In Rimbaud's poem, water imagery works to collapse structures that separate self from other and distinguish far from near, an effect particularly marked in the poem's middle stanza: 'Des écroulements d'eaux au milieu des bonaces/Et les lointains vers les gouffres cataractant!' Beckett renders this: 'The calm sea disembowelled in waterslides/ And the cataracting of the doomed horizons'. Rimbaud's exuberant blending gives way, in Beckett's translation, to a more arrestingly precise, even violent description. Mooney remarks on the affective difference between Rimbaud's poem and Beckett's translation, noting how many terms in the English evoke illness and bodily injury (haemorrhage, fever, weals, disembowelling), such that Beckett's translation conveys 'an experience of nightmare more than ecstasy' (Mooney 2011: 53). In general, Rimbaud creates the poem's effect of dissolving time and borders between things (paradoxically) by adding qualifiers (if the poem were divested of these structuring particles, there would be mere semantic confusion and not the blend of tight control and imaginative daring for which the poem is famous). Rimbaud's use of temporal or comparative qualifiers has the effect of 'harmonising' each image with its predecessor and successor, marking it off as one among many possible realities. Aside from *comme*, which marks the beginning of the poem and recurs in stanzas 12 and 19, we find *plus . . . que* (3,4,5,7), *ainsi que* (8,16), *pareils à* (9,11) *qu'on appelle* (4) *par instants* (15), *quelquefois* (8), *parfois* (16), *Or* (18) and *presque* (17). Though Beckett finds translations for some of these qualifying particles, for the most part his images are more starkly metaphoric. They contradict each other in a drier, more arid (rather than fluid) Beckettian space. The contrast between Rimbaud's colourful mosaics of images and Beckett's sharper, more penetratingly direct and controlled use of language comes across as early in the first stanza: 'Des Peaux-Rouges criards les avaient pris pour cibles,/Les ayant cloués nus aux poteaux de couleurs' and 'Redskins had taken them in a scream and stripped them and/Skewered them to the glaring stakes for targets'. While Rimbaud's 'haleurs' have been artfully tacked upon coloured posts, taken out of their functional roles and pinned up (naked) for our view-ing pleasure, Beckett's boatmen have been stripped and skewered to glaring stakes. The severity of Beckett's images gives us a sense of time that is imme-diate, pressing, and urgent, which is different from the expanding sequences of metaphors arrayed in Rimbaud's poem.

While Beckett's poem strips away some semantic-sensory confusions that swell the hexameter quatrains of 'Le Bateau ivre', it also subtracts a literal unit of time. In the fourth stanza, Rimbaud's boat danced for, '[d]ix nuits, sans regretter l'oeil niais des falots'. In Beckett's translation, we find: 'Nine nights I danced like a cork on the billows, I danced'. Beckett renders 'dix nuits' as 'nine nights' in part perhaps to transpose the internal rhyme of the French; one might argue that the sonority lost by his decision not to carry over the ABAB rhyme scheme is made up for by his alliterative lines (for instance): 'freights of Flemish grain', 'Blanker than the brain of a child', 'in triumph torn'. But his sonorous nine nights (instead of ten), may also allude the Hindi festival of Navaratri, during which boundaries are challenged and expanded.[13] The subtraction of a single night may also hint, subtly of course, at how the layers of tenses, variations in duration, ambiguities and coils of time give way in Beckett's translation to a more pressured and forward-racing temporality. In other words, time is *felt,* in Beckett's translation, insofar as its vocabulary foregrounds the vulnerability of a *body* whose time is not infinite, and its use of English tenses gives it a more sequential organisation. This treatment of time in translation undermines an exuberant premise of Rimbaud's lyric poem: to have slipped free of time into an ecstasy of more flexible temporalities.

Rimbaud's poetic allusions also shape his readers' experience, stimulating a collective cultural memory by awakening a network of linguistic associations. Words, symbols, images, and themes in 'Le Bateau ivre' echo, for instance, lines from Baudelaire's 'Le Voyage': 'le cerveau plein de flamme, /Le coeur gros de rancune et de désires amers, /Et nous allons, suivant le rythme de la lame, / Berçant notre infini sur le fini des mers', 'nous n'avons vu des astres/Et des flots', and the cry: 'Ô cerveuax enfantins!' (Baudelaire 1975: 33). Rimbaud's poem recalls not only 'Le Voyage', but also Baudelaire's 'Le Cygne' and Victor Hugo's 'Oceano nox', part of the tradition of poetry that to educated French readers in the nineteenth century would have been second nature. As a translator, Beckett has the almost insurmountable task of rooting his poem within an analogous tradition so that the particularity of its own language might find comparable resonance for Anglophone readers. Beckett does this, I argue, in part by drawing upon religious language, which, as the fodder of rote memorisation in protestant grammar schools, would be familiar to many English-speaking readers. Consider the fourth stanza of 'Drunken Boat':

> I started awake to tempestuous hallowings.
> Nine nights I danced like a cork on the billows, I danced
> On the breakers, sacrificial, *for ever and ever*,
> And the crass eye of the lanterns was expunged. (Beckett 1977: 95)

Beckett's use of 'for ever and ever' will echo in the minds of protestant English readers as 'forever and ever, Amen', and Beckett's use of the word 'hallowings' may reinforce our association with the closing to the Lord's Prayer. Beckett uses similarly religious vocabulary later in the poem, when he translates '– Des écumes de fleurs ont bercé mes dérades/Et d'ineffables vents m'ont ailé par instants', as 'In spumes of flowers I have risen from my anchors/And canticles of wind have blessed my wings'.[14]

But the most pronounced way Beckett achieves an effect comparable to that created in 'Le Bateau ivre' is by means of repetition.[15] Beckett's recycling of the word 'passive' at the end of the second stanza, which echoes 'impassive' in the poem's first line, is a good example of this repetition of whole words, which occurs throughout the poem, texturing Beckett's translation not through intertextual allusion but through self-reference: 'Downstream on im*passive* rivers suddenly' is followed seven lines later by 'I made my own course down the *passive* rivers' (My emphasis).[16] Consider also the repetition in stanza 11 of the word 'feet': 'Storming the reefs, mindless of the *feet*, /The radiant *feet* of the Marys' (My emphasis). In Rimbaud's poem, *pieds* appears only once. The tendency to repeat whole words in close proximity runs throughout Beckett's translation. Rather than extravagant metaphors, Beckett tends towards repetition of certain words, which creates an 'echo' effect throughout the poem. Excesses like 'jam' for poets, 'confiture exquise aux bon poètes', are excised from Beckett's version, which translates the line in question as: '[I] Have pierced the skies that flame as a wall would flame/For a chosen poet's rapture, and stream and flame'. Here (and in general) 'Drunken Boat' uses verbal repetition rather than overlapping images and sensations. 'O que ma quille éclate! O que j'aille à la mer!' becomes 'May I split from stem to stern and *founder, ah founder!*' (My emphasis). Kathleen Shields discusses this tendency to repeat whole words as well as prepositions in Beckett's 'Drunken Boat'; she counts four '*of*'s in stanza 12 ('tangle *of* / The flowers *of* the eyes *of* panthers in the skins *of* men'). For Shields, this diminishes the poem's fluency in English. She links it to a foreignising tendency in Beckett's translation, an attempt to rigidify English by injecting into it foreign material (Shields 1995: 154–5). But these 'oddly echoing sound effects' that Shields notices also create texture within the poem in translation, emphasising its existence in *relation* (to a poetic tradition and to language) (Shields 1995: 155). The translation *performs* its own work of repetition, creating *literal* as well as cultural resonance. Readers are viscerally aware of the materiality of language through its effects on the body as we encounter these echoic, lulling repetitions.

These techniques of allusion to linguistic-cultural tradition and sonic texturing by means of the repetitions of words become part of Beckett's aesthetic of self-translation, in particular in his work with Patrick Bowles on the English *Molloy*. I have imagined a 'straight' translation of *Molloy* to illustrate a general tendency of the French texts to be somewhat quirky-sounding and to lose some of this in Beckett's translation, which avails itself of his keen ear. Where a line in the French might translate plainly as 'I'm rather fond of old sayings' ('J'aime assez les formules'), Beckett renders this: 'I am no enemy of the commonplace', which sounds not only more sonorous but more colloquial (addressing itself perhaps to a Hiberno-English sensibility) (Beckett 1982; Beckett 2009: 34).[17] More generally, in *Molloy's* passage to English a rounding out occurs, such that the text becomes more sonorous and less staccato. Where the French can sound abrupt, fast-paced, and (as I have said) quirky, the English becomes full and elegant in its more poetic passages. Consider, for instance:

> voilà qu'une énorme lune s'encadrait dans la fenêtre. Deux barreaux la partageaient en trois parties, dont la médiane restait constante tandis que peu à peu la droite gagnait ce que perdait la gauche. Car la lune allait de gauche à droite ou la chambre allait de droit à gauche, ou les deux à la fois peut-être, ou elles allaient toutes les deux de gauche à droite, seulement la chambre moins vite que la lune, ou de droite à gauche, seulement la lune moins vite que la chambre.

> all of a sudden there was the *moon*, a huge *moon* framed in the window. Two bars divided it in three segments, of which the middle remained constant, while little by little the right attained what the left lost. For the *moon* was moving from left to right, or the *room* was moving from right to left, *or both* together perhaps, *or both* were moving from left to right, but the *room* not so fast as the *moon*, or from right to left, but the *moon* not so fast as the *room*. (My emphasis)

A 'straight' translation of this passage would not include so many repetitions of 'moon' and 'room', but Beckett as translator exploits the sound possibilities present in the English language, creating sound patterns in the English text. My argument is that this draws attention to the materiality of language (through sound), undermining a lyric I's claim to speak outside of temporal, linguistic, and social contexts.

To explore the idea of how translation unmasks the lyric's pretensions to immediacy, I have focused on the difficulty of translating the complex temporality in 'Le Bateau ivre' and how this is handled in Beckett's translation. I have remarked on the ways in which temporality and intertextuality get rendered in Beckett's translation through a privileging of repetition and self-reference. The larger question opened by such a close look at this early project is one of how Beckett's translation, understood as a laying bare of allusions and networks of reference, informs Beckett's positioning of his work vis-à-vis language as a medium that makes use of sound, rhythm and literary tradition, creating an aesthetic dedicated to exacerbating and making visible (rather than hiding) our inextricability, as speaking and writing subjects, within these material and social contexts.

Notes

1. Walter Benjamin writes: 'Translation . . . of all literary forms it is the one charged with the special mission of watching over the maturing process of the original language and the birth pangs of its own' (Benjamin 1996: 256).
2. Jackson distinguishes her project from that of Paul de Man, who, in 'Anthropomorphism and Trope in the Lyric', calls the lyric a 'modern critical fiction'. While Jackson agrees that the lyric subject is not what it pretends to be, she does not proclaim the disappearance of the 'phenomenal or experiential subject of the lyric utterance'. Rather, she seeks to show that 'genres are not born but imperfectly made' and encourages meta-criticism of the lyric as a genre. She finds Dickinson's work helpful because it 'resists substituting the alienated lyric image of the human – the very image the modern reading of the lyric has created – for the exchange between historical persons . . .'. As a strategy for lyric reading, Jackson recommends keeping 'both their material and contingent as well as their abstract and transcendent aspects in view at the same time' (Jackson 2005: 100–17).
3. Theodor Adorno makes a version of this claim in 'Lyric Poetry and Society', arguing that modern poetry is not *distanced* from modern life so much as it makes visible the condition of alienation of modern life. He writes: 'the universality of the lyric's substance . . . is social in nature' and suggests that because the work of the lyric is the expression of social antagonism, modern poetry is in accord with the experience of its readers (Adorno 1957: 37–54).

4. For a more detailed account of the recovery of Beckett's 'Drunken Boat', see the notes appended to *Collected Poems in English and French: Samuel Beckett* (1977).

5. Leslie Daiken, notes on lectures by Samuel Beckett, 1930–31, unaccessioned holding of the Beckett International Foundation, Reading University Library, as quoted in Love (2005: 480).

6. Benjamin posits a 'kinship' between languages that is beyond 'words, sentences and associations'. This kinship, which allows for the possibility of translation, is the fact that 'in every one of them as a whole, one and the same thing is meant' (Benjamin 1996: 253–63).

7. Beckett, *Collected Poems* (1977: 92–105). All future quotations from Beckett's 'Drunken Boat' and Rimbaud's 'Le Bateau ivre' are from this edition.

8. For further discussion of the sources of 'Le Bateau ivre', see Noulet (1953: 189–280), Cohn (2015: 161), Rimbaud (1960: 424–25), Delahaye (1923: 92–93) and Starkie (1973: 132).

9. For a very different account of the function of the word 'comme', specifically in Baudelaire, see 'Anthropomorphism and Trope in the Lyric', where de Man explicates 'Correspondances' and the later sonnet 'Obsession' (de Man 1984: 239–363).

10. A study of the occurrences of the present tense in the poem would be interesting in and of itself. The present tense occurs, in both poems, in stanzas 6, 7, 8, 14, 21, 22, 23, 24, and in formal form in stanza 25 ('je ne puis plus/Enlever' and 'I may/Absorb no more'). When it is not being used to express knowledge, regret/remembrance, or desire on the part of the subject, the present tense is used descriptively after the word 'where' (*où*). Two examples: 'Où les serpents géants dévorés des punaises/*Choient* des arbres tordus avec de noirs parfums!'; 'Where giant reptiles, pullulant with lice, /*Lapse* with dark perfumes from writhing trees'. And 'où, flottaison blême/Et ravie, un noyé pensif, parfois, *descend* . . .'; 'Where, dimly, they *come* swaying down, /Rapt and sad, singly, the drowned . . .'. If this point seems trivial, consider the fact that the word 'who' (*qui*) ('moi' in stanza 18) are followed by the *imparfait* in Rimbaud's poem and by either the past or the present perfect tense in Beckett's. (See stanzas 18–21.) *Person* is put in a background tense, where *place* is elevated to the present, to the everlasting.

11. Wallace Fowlie's translation, by contrast, mixes present perfect and simple past ('I have seen', 'I have dreamed', but 'I followed', and 'I struck against'). (Rimbaud 2005: 131).

12. Beckett's translation of this line, 'More firmly bland than to children apples' firm pulp', is an example of the awkward sentence construction

and tendency towards repetition that has led one reader of his translation to write that Beckett 'foreignises'. Shields argues that Beckett's translation 'injects the English language with foreign substance in order to immobilise it' (Shields 1995: 156). Sinéad Mooney expands upon this point to discuss how Beckett's 'curiously deconstructive piece of translation' uses repetition to draw attention to the nuts and bolts of sentence structure, foreshadowing Beckett's later experimental prose (Mooney 2011: 52).

13. This reading is supported by the allusion that nine nights makes to an ancient Hindu festival known as *Navaratri* (literally 'Nine Nights' in Sanskrit: *Nava* – Nine and *Ratri* – Nights). During this festival, nine forms (or metaphoric) incarnations of a goddess (Shakti or Durga) are worshiped and there is general attention directed to the idea of expanding one's boundaries. There are other references made to Hinduism in Beckett's poem 'Echo's Bones', which indicates his general interest in the subject. See the *Collected Poems in English and French* (Beckett 1977: 9–28).

14. Instead of the word, *bercé* (which appears in Wallace Fowlie's edition), *béni* appeared in the version from which Beckett was working: 'Des écumes de fleurs ont *béni* mes dérades'. James Knowlson and Felix Leakey note in the introduction to their 1976 edition of Beckett's 'Drunken Boat' that Beckett had taken account of the erroneous *béni* in a felicitous way (Knowlson and Leakey 1976: 13).

15. It is also possible that the lines 'Where, dimly, they come swaying down, /Rapt and sad, singly, the drowned' (stanza 6) are subtle allusions to Ezra Pound's 'Portrait d'une Femme', a poem which begins: 'Your mind and you are our Sargasso Sea, /London has swept about you this score years/ And bright ships left you this or that in fee/ 'Ideas, old gossip, oddments of all things, /Strange spars of knowledge and dimmed wares of price'. Beckett's use of the word 'dimly' suggests this connection, as there is nothing in Rimbaud's poem that would have inspired his choice of the word.

16. Gerald Macklin notes how Beckett's translation of 'Et j'ai vu quelquefois ce que l'homme a cru voir' as 'my eyes have fixed phantasmagoria' alters the text to refer to Rimbaud's *Une saison en enfer* in which the poet refers to himself as 'maître en fantasmagories' (this term also appears in 'Métropolitain' in the *Illuminations*). Macklin writes: 'the successful translator of an author must immerse himself in the language of that author's entire *oeuvre*'. The use of 'phantasmagoria' makes an allusion to Rimbaud's larger corpus, embedding 'Drunken Boat' within a larger textual field (Macklin 2003: 147-8).

17. Subsequent references are to these French and English editions.

Works Cited

Adorno, Theodor (1991) [1957], 'On Lyric Poetry and Society' in Rolf Tiedman (ed), *Notes to Literature Vol. I*, translated by Shierry Weber Nicholson, New York: Columbia University Press, pp. 37–54.

Baudelaire, Charles (1975), *Oeuvres complètes*, Claude Pichois (ed), Paris: Gallimard.

Beckett, Samuel (1982) [1951], *Molloy*, Paris: Les Éditions de Minuit.

Beckett, Samuel (1960), *Company*, London: Calder.

Beckett, Samuel (1977), *Collected Poems in English and French: Samuel Beckett*, New York: Grove Press.

Beckett, Samuel (2009), *Three Novels: Molloy/Malone Dies/The Unnamable*, New York: Grove Press.

Benjamin, Walter (1996), 'The Task of the Translator', in Marcus Bullock and Michael W. Jennings (eds), *Walter Benjamin: Selected Writings*, Vol. I, 1913–1926, translated by Harry Zohn, Cambridge, MA: Harvard University Press, pp. 253–63.

Cohn, Robert Greer (2015) [1974], *The Poetry of Rimbaud*, Princeton: Princeton University Press.

Culler, Jonathan (2015), *Theory of the Lyric*, Boston: Harvard University Press.

Delahaye, Ernest (1923), *Rimbaud*, Paris: Albert Messein.

De Man, Paul (1984), 'Anthropomorphism and Trope in the Lyric', in *The Rhetoric of Romanticism*, New York: Columbia University Press, pp. 239–363.

Jackson, Virginia (2005), *Dickinson's Misery: A Theory of Lyric Reading*, Princeton: Princeton University Press.

Jackson, Virginia and Yopie Prins (eds) (2014), *The Lyric Theory Reader: A Critical Anthology*, Baltimore: Johns Hopkins University Press.

Jenkins, Alan. *Drunken Boats* (2007), *The Cahier Series* no. 4, Dan Gunn (ed), Lewes: Sylph Editions.

Knowlson, James and Felix Leakey (eds) (1976), *'Drunken Boat': A Translation of Arthur Rimbaud's Poem 'Le Bateau ivre'*, Reading: Whiteknights Press.

Love, Damian (2005), 'Doing Him into the Eye: Samuel Beckett's Rimbaud' *Modern Language Quarterly*, 66, 4.

Macklin, Gerald (2003), '"Drunken Boat": Samuel Beckett's Translation of Arthur Rimbaud's "Le Bateau ivre"', *Studies in 20th Century Literature*, 27.1, 140–61.

Mooney, Sinéad (2011), *A Tongue Not Mine: Beckett and Translation*, Oxford: Oxford University Press.

Noulet, Emile (1953), *Le Premier Visage de Rimbaud*, Brussels: Académie Royale.

Perloff, Marjorie (1981), *The Poetics of Indeterminacy: Rimbaud to Cage*, Evanston, IL: Northwestern University Press.

Rimbaud, Arthur (1960), *Oeuvres*, Suzanne Bernard (ed), Paris: Garnier.

Rimbaud, Arthur (2005), *Rimbaud: Complete Works, Selected Letters (A Bilingual Edition),* edited by Wallace Fowlie and Seth Whidden, Chicago: The University of Chicago Press.

Scott, Clive (2006), *Translating Rimbaud's Illuminations,* Exeter: University of Exeter Press.

Shields, Kathleen (Spring 1995), 'Three Irish Translations of Rimbaud's "Bateau Ivre"', *New Comparison: A Journal of Comparative and General Literary Studies,* 19, 149–64.

Starkie, Enid (1963), *Arthur Rimbaud,* 2nd ed., London: Faber.

9

Are Beckett's Texts Bilingual?
'Long after Chamfort' and Translation

Matthijs Engelberts

'Long after Chamfort': eight short poems, a minor work perhaps, but marvellous, playful late texts for the most part – and arguably the only work in Beckett's oeuvre that has been published as a structurally bilingual text. I will attempt to put the verse renderings in English of Chamfort's French prose maxims to use by asking three rather general – and perhaps also slightly obnoxious – questions, in order to throw what I hope to be a specific, pointed ray of light on 'Long after Chamfort' – and Beckett's work more generally, indeed, as the title of this contribution indicates. Beckett's doggerel translations of the eighteenth-century maxims have been commented on in several other productive ways than what I will propose now. Here, the three questions I will ask are related to the topic of bilingualism and translation – even if the conclusions I will try to draw relate to wider issues in criticism.

Are Beckett's texts bilingual?

'Beckett's bilingualism' (Beer 1994; Mooney 2011: 8) has by now become in the words of Nadia Louar and José Francisco Fernández, a 'minor critical industry' (Louar and Fernández 2018: 2) – quite an unexpected and nonetheless apt oxymoron indeed. Much valuable work has been written on Beckett's translations of other authors, as well as, mainly, on his self-translations in French and English and in other languages.

It is, indeed, perfectly clear that Beckett is a special case in literature generally if we look at how this exceptional writer used his bilingualism to forge an oeuvre in two major languages – or perhaps two oeuvres. Several critics have underlined rightly that other bilingual authors than Beckett have not as constantly constructed a body of work that they have made available in two languages themselves.[1] The relation between these two bodies of work can be construed in different ways, and it would be useful to survey how this has so far been done in Beckett criticism, using translation theory as a background. It seems clear, however, that one of the by now most frequent views on the relation between Beckett's two works posits the existence of 'bilingual' texts that can only be read in conjunction. It has indeed become common to state in criticism on 'Beckett and translation' – in English more so than in French, it seems to me – that 'in Beckett's writing . . . neither first nor second versions attain autonomy' (Mooney 2011: 15). In 1988, one of the first books on bilingualism in Beckett was still explicitly aimed at proving that there is 'a very strong case for the autonomy and special status of the second version of Beckett's works' (Fitch 1988: 225). However, at the same time, Fitch underscores that in Beckett's case 'the literary work has become a creation unlike any other, arising . . . from the contiguity, if not the material coming-together, of two distinct unilingual texts and the interaction of two separate linguistic systems' (Fitch 1988: 228). In the same period, another critic already asserts much more radically and fiercely: 'Each [text] becomes merely a version of the other and is apprehensible as itself only by virtue of its differences from the other text' (Connor 1989: 36). In this view, it thus seems that the ineluctable mode of reading Beckett is by moving to and from French to English and vice versa; it seems that to read Beckett is to have to read the English or French texts as 'always already' – one of the most frequent expressions in criticism in the past few decades, with or without reference to the indelible Derrida (Connor 1989: 37) – undermined by their 'other' in either French or English. Haunted by its linguistic other, the text seems always askew.

The impressive results of research on Beckett's self-translations show indeed how productive the conjoined reading of Beckett's 'bilingual' texts can be. But there is, I would venture, a caveat to be made here – and it is one that the critical enthusiasm sometimes seems to circumvent. 'Beckett's bilingualism' is incontestable,[2] if by 'Beckett' we mean the author called Samuel Barclay Beckett. 'Beckett Self-Translator', whom Ruby Cohn (1961) was probably the first to comment on extensively, is equally incontestable. And even the 'bilingual work', as it has been called since Fitch, is to a certain extent also indisputable, since it is undeniable that Beckett has published work originally written in French or in English during most of his productive life, and that he has moreover translated most of his texts into English or French.

However, we should perhaps wonder who 'we' are when we read that 'we are forced into a realisation that Beckett's writings are never fully present to themselves but are radically distracted from their textual moment' (Mooney 2011: 19). My first – and maybe rather blunt – guess would be that 'we' are, here, the kind of Beckett critics who read the academic books on 'Beckett and translation' from which this quote is taken. In that sense of the plural, it is indeed to a certain extent possible to say that 'we are left slightly but significantly *beside* ourselves as readers, held at arm's length by the implications of the doubled text' (Mooney 2011: 19). But the same critic has already noted that 'only an alert bilingual reader of both texts would note differences in the paratextual apparatus of some French and English versions of certain works' (Mooney 2011: 13). Perhaps we should add to this that the mode of publication of the vast majority of Beckett's work in French and English hardly encourages readers generally – that is, other readers than a plurality of academic critics – to actually compare versions. Even Steven Connor has to admit that 'it might be claimed that all the changes that I have been discussing could not possibly be evident either to a French or English reader, for whom the text would be single and self-sufficient' (Connor 1989: 36). 'Single and self-sufficient' is probably not meant as a recommendation is this context, and Connor clearly suggests in his article that Beckett's self-translated work can only be read in two languages.

Yet, if one looks at the publication history of Beckett's work, it seems indeed hardly possible to speak of a 'bilingual oeuvre', since so few of Beckett's works have been published in bilingual French–English editions by his main publishing houses in France, the UK and the US. There are of course (mainly) early works by Beckett in English in which the reader finds occasional words or phrases from other languages in the English text of the poems or narrative prose (although generally not as much as in some works by Joyce or Pound). Bilingual editions of any self-translated work published during Beckett's lifetime, however, are rare and seem in general to have been due to special circumstances.

I know of two examples of trade editions, one published in Great Britain and one in France. Knowlson's bilingual 1978 edition of *Happy Days/Oh les beaux jours*, published by Faber, contains an editorial note, a substantial afterword, many notes and a bibliography, all written by Knowlson, that together take up more pages than the text of the two plays together, in English and French (Beckett 1978). It is, with hindsight, a precursor of the later scholarly editions that were to be published after Beckett's death by, in most cases, houses other than the general publishers that Beckett worked with during his lifetime. The French publishing house Aubier-Flammarion – not Minuit, Beckett's French publisher – issued a bilingual edition of *Words and Music*, *Play* and *Eh Joe* in 1972 in its bilingual series (Beckett 1972). Again, the 'Chronologie', the 'Introduction' (written by the 'professeur à la Sorbonne' (title page) Jean-Jacques Mayoux, a friend of Beckett) and the 'Bibliographie sommaire' add up to more pages than the bilingual text of the *three* plays in

French and English together; this is also an early sign of the beginning of the scholarly editions, and not a bilingual text published by Beckett. There is, in short, no tradition of bilingual publication of Beckett's works in regular editions in French or English.[3]

The situation is indeed far from being coincidental. Dirk Van Hulle and Pim Verhulst are quite right when they insist on Beckett's reluctance regarding projects of bilingual editions in French and English proposed by his major publishers. The critics sketch out the history of a major project of bilingual publication, which started in the early 1960s and was initiated by Calder and also involved Faber, Minuit and Grove Press. Beckett wrote to Faber in 1965 that he was 'not keen on bilingual edition either of the novels or the plays, but would not oppose it if my publishers agree it is desirable. It suggests an invitation[4] to consider the work as a linguistic curiosity, or an adventure in self-translation, which does not appeal to me' (Beckett 2014: 665). Calder apparently *did* find bilingual editions desirable, not only for *How It Is* but also for the Trilogy, and the publisher continued his efforts until the end of the 1960s; but despite Beckett's kind deference in his letter to Faber, the project did not materialise. There is, clearly, no effort made by the author to produce his self-translations as a bilingual body of texts that would allow 'the reader' to easily grasp the publication as a bilingual work in French and English; and this goes for the plays as well as for the (short) stories and novels.[5] Even for his poetry, Beckett preferred to have his own translations published 'without the original text', as he wrote to Calder in 1960! (Beckett 2014: 345).

The publication record of Beckett's self-translations at his main publishing houses in France, in the UK and in the US thus indicates to what extent bilingual publication of Beckett's texts is indeed an exception. Whether this is only due to Beckett's attitude or also to other factors related to publication cultures, or to both, is not altogether clear. On the other hand, it is rather clear that in the French and English-speaking worlds, the vast majority of Beckett's works have been published – and continue to be published today (if one excepts specialised academic editions, geared towards a limited audience) – in editions that are either in French or in English, and that are not bilingual. In other words, we might be tempted to say that the 'bilingual work' in Beckett's oeuvre is, viewed from the angle of its publication history, in the eye of the beholder. It is perfectly possible, and perfectly legitimate, of course, for the critic as well as for a non-professional bilingual reader who would feel inclined to do so, to compare the French and English versions of Beckett's work that have been published separately. It is also useful to underscore, for those who want to know, that for some texts, the translation was started by Beckett before he finished writing the text in one language (although it should also be noted that for almost all texts it is clear in which language it was written first, and which version is the translation). The influence of Beckett's mother tongue on his French is also an intriguing topic (cf. Germoni 2018), as is the effect of his French on his use of English.

Nevertheless, it is striking to what extent Beckett and his main publishers in the English and French-speaking worlds – Minuit, Faber, Calder, Grove – have finally kept his 'double work' (Louar and Fernández are among those who use this fruitful expression) distinct – without adding, as Beckett did in the case of his theatre, radio and cinema, that '[i]f we can't keep our genres more or less distinct . . . we might as well go home and lie down' (Beckett 2014: 64). Beckett's works have indisputably been published in both an English and a French version, one of which was mostly translated by the author himself; but this should not obscure the fact that these texts have been published – and have consequently been read in most cases – as two monolingual bodies of work.

It does not even seem ludicrous to me to state that there is only a single work among Beckett's texts published under his name that can be called structurally bilingual because it has virtually always been published as such: 'Long after Chamfort'. And for this particular strikingly bilingual text, we will have to note, firstly, that it is debatable whether 'Long after Chamfort' can be called 'a work', since it has never been published independently, that is, as a separate volume in French or English, as far as I know. Perhaps it can even be asked, secondly and more importantly, whether these sequels to Chamfort, exquisite and inventive translations of eighteenth-century maxims, can be considered as Beckett's 'own' work – as they have been quite often, and as I am doing here. I would venture that it is this questionable, exceptional 'work' by 'Beckett' that can be seen as the only fully bilingual text in the Beckett canon published by his main English and French publishers.

John Pilling and Seán Lawlor write that the 'Three Poems' (published in *transition* in 1948) 'are unique in SB's *oeuvre* as the only example of the first publication of his works with English and French versions set out, as they have been subsequently, on facing pages' (Beckett 2012: 402). As we noted, it is of course debatable to some extent whether 'Long after Chamfort' can be considered as part of 'SB's *oeuvre*', but it is quite intriguing that Pilling and Lawlor themselves do indeed include these late translated poems in Beckett's own work. They do not publish Beckett's Chamfort poems in the two sections of 'Translations' in their edition of Beckett's poetry, but in the section called 'Later Poems' (Beckett 2012: 195), which brings together both French and English poems written by Beckett and published for the most part in the seventies and eighties.[6] If 'Long after Chamfort' is part of the oeuvre, as it is for the editors of this edition of Beckett's poetry, then the 'Three Poems' are not unique, since the first publication of the late poems was bilingual, as are subsequent publications.

It is worth noting, moreover, that the editors of the fine 2012 edition are not entirely correct in stating that the 'Three Poems' have subsequently been published bilingually, since they point out themselves that there are at least three major anthologies of poetry that have printed the English texts only. It is true, however, that these poems from the 1940s have been published with their French versions even in the *Poems in English* that Calder and Grove Press published in the early 1960s; here, quite strikingly, one of the rare structurally bilingual publications in Beckett's work is hidden behind a façade of English monolingualism that shrouds the French texts in the *Poems in English*.

Strangely, the extremely rare bilingual work 'Long after Chamfort' has not attracted much attention in criticism on Beckett and translation or bilingualism. I readily admit that there is a vast body of important self-translations, as well as a vast body of other translations by Beckett to be researched, not to mention the huge number of translations of Beckett's texts by other translators. However, it is still surprising that criticism has sometimes delved into a supposedly self-negating, self-deconstructing, bilingual text, seemingly without paying much attention to one of the only works, if not actually the only one, that has had an uninterrupted bilingual publication history in Beckett's oeuvre.

There is another noteworthy fact about 'Long after Chamfort' with regard to its bilingual status: it seems never to have been published by a major publisher in the French-speaking world. I may be mistaken, but I do not know of any copyrighted publication in France or Francophone countries; and in any case Beckett's French publishing house, Minuit, has not – or not yet – included 'Long after Chamfort' in any edition of the 'poèmes' – which by the way do not include *any* texts in English. After Beckett's death, Minuit has published translations by Edith Fournier of texts that Beckett published in English and that he had not translated himself, but it has not yet published the bilingual Chamfort verse. A strange fate indeed: the English – speaking world has to some extent erased the French of 'Long after Chamfort', and presented them as poems by Beckett, whereas the French-speaking world has, more radically, omitted the renderings altogether. 'Long after Chamfort' is thus, from an institutional point of view, an English text. Beckett's only bilingual work, in the strict sense of a work that has been published – consistently, in this case – as a bilingual text by his major publishers, thus functions as an English text only. Strangely, even the sole bilingual work in Beckett's oeuvre has been kept distinct – as if it were not bilingual, just as the vast majority or even entirety of his work is not bilingual in the sense that it has not been published in bilingual volumes in French and English during Beckett's life by his major publishers in France, the UK and the US.

I do not wish to suggest that the case of 'Long after Chamfort' shows the extent to which publishers and perhaps others have tried to render Beckett monolingual and to obscure the bilingual work. In some instances, this may have been the case, as we have seen for the 'Three Poems'. However, it is important to be aware that Beckett did certainly not often publish his work as bilingual texts, and has even resisted bilingual publication, and that his publishers have most often worked in similar vein, following the traditions of their houses. What cases such as the 'Three Poems' and 'Long after Chamfort' show, from the perspective that I would like to open up here, is that their bilingual status is exceptional in the Beckett canon, and that they reveal the fracture lines in the monolingual publication tradition of Beckett's work, as well as the problematic of the idea of 'bilingual texts' in Beckett's work.

We, as readers, are – in texts published by Beckett and his major French and English publishers during his lifetime – not conspicuously 'held at arm's length by the implications of the doubled text' (Mooney 2011: 19). And it is not at all necessarily the case, nor does it seem very plausible for the general readership and even for most students of literature in universities, that for the readers of the published texts as they have appeared in English and French, 'Each [text] becomes merely a version of the other, and is apprehensible as itself only by virtue of its differences from the other text'. A critic's dream, so to speak, is in this case not the reader's reality. Nor, in this case, the writer's dream, since Beckett did not favour bilingual publication – a fact that I do not wish to obscure or circumvent here in order to respect the doxa that has been imposed in different – often useful – ways by Wimsatt and Beardsley, Roland Barthes and post-structuralist theory.

What does 'translation' amount to (when it is apparently not a burden) for Beckett?

'Long after Chamfort' is also an exceptional work among Beckett's published texts for another reason. Beckett's renderings of maxims from Chamfort are among the last translations he made of work that was not his own, if not actually the last. Moreover, hardly any of Beckett's translations (that are not self-translations) were made without being commissioned. The vast majority of Beckett's translations of other authors were indeed solicited by publishers[7] or editors, and Beckett agreed to do them – or asked to do them, in some cases, as seems to be the case with Rimbaud's 'Drunken Boat' (Beckett 2012: 358) – because he was paid to do the job. The Chamfort renderings, made at the end of the 1960s and the beginning of the 1970s, appear on the contrary not to have been commissioned, and were written in the last period of Beckett's career.

'Long after Chamfort' is thus an interesting case in more than one respect, with regard to bilingualism. This is all the more so since it is well known that Beckett did not have a particular preference for translating. His aversion is quite clear in the letters, and has now been often stressed, for instance in a recent article by Pascale Sardin in which she states: 'In spite of the importance of translation and self-translation in his career, Beckett never ceased to present translation as a secondary activity with regard to his "real" creation' (Sardin-Damestoy 2002: 73). It is of course possible to question the distinction between 'real' work and the supposedly secondary task of translation; however, it seems much harder to question that Beckett conceived of translation as a necessary, but far from exciting and sometimes even painful task, even in the case of his own work.

What happens if Beckett, after so many complaints about the burden of translation, and at the end of a career that has securely established him as a major European author of the twentieth century, freely – and exceptionally – chooses to render in English a French text that he has not written himself? Here is a first example.

> L'espérance n'est qu'un charlatan qui nous trompe sans cesse; et, pour moi, le bonheur n'a commencé que lorsque je l'ai eu perdu. Je mettrais volontiers sur la porte du paradis le vers que le Dante a mis sur celle de l'enfer: Lasciate ogni speranza etc.

> Hope is a knave befools us evermore,
> Which till I lost no happiness was mine.
> I strike from hell's to grave on heaven's door:
> All hope abandon ye who enter in.

First of all, I think it is clear that Beckett carefully selects the source texts, in the sense that these feature themes which he preferred in his 'own' work. This is indeed not self-translation, whether free or not, but there is a clear correspondence with Beckett's world: the topics fit his own thematic choices. There is no doubt that Beckett saw a clear connection between his postwar work and the poems of 'Long after Chamfort' – or at least one of them. Pilling and Lawlor, for instance, insist on the remarkable conversation that Beckett had with collector Henri Wenning, after which he wrote one of the French maxims in a copy of *Endgame*. Wenning had been discussing *Fin de partie* with

Beckett and said that he did not see the 'affirmations or expressions of hope' that some of his friends saw in the play. 'The author then said, in substance, "oh those hope fellows. I was reading Chamfort the other day and he had a memorable comment to make on the subject of hope. Here give me that book and I will put it in as closely as I can from memory"' (Beckett 2012: 437). From Chamfort to Schopenhauer to Beckett, or from Schopenhauer to Chamfort to Beckett perhaps, there is a lineage; Beckett, when finally translating 'freely', without being commissioned, picks his sources carefully. The combative, even pugnacious context of the genesis of the Chamfort translations is quite clear in this example. Against the dogmas of poststructuralist readings, these translations can be considered as wilful reassertions of Chamfort's ideas, in line with archival evidence about their production.

Notwithstanding this thematic congruity, however, Beckett makes the rendering stand out as a text that restates with a difference, so to speak; these are indeed overtly 'free'[8] translations. Beckett bends the phrasing to make it different from the original, while keeping it nonetheless topically in line with the source text. I think there are mainly three – perhaps quite obvious – differences.

The texts in the target language are shorter

All the 'huit maximes', as the 1977 edition of the *Collected Poems in English and French* calls them, are longer in the original versions than in Beckett's rephrasings. An obvious example:

> Vivre est une maladie dont le sommeil nous soulage toutes les seize heures. C'est un palliatif; la mort est le remède.

> sleep till death
> healeth
> come ease
> this life disease

Five maxims count roughly half the number of words of the Chamfort text, as the one quoted here; two are only a few words less, and the 'Hope is a knave' quatrain is about forty per cent shorter. Terseness is all, apparently.[9] This is striking for two reasons. First, maxims are of course a genre that is noted for its brevity, and although Chamfort's maxims tend on the whole to be somewhat longer than La Rochefoucauld's, and do not always stand out for their conciseness, they do obey the law of the genre. Beckett chooses to make Chamfort's maxims still more concise – and he succeeds in doing this even if he chooses to render them in verse. Versifying the prose originals could have prompted longer renderings of Chamfort's maxims – but not so for Beckett. He thus abides by what seems to have been Chamfort's own ideal in wording in literature, or at least in poetry, if we look at one of the most witty and self-reflexive 'caractères et anecdotes' in Chamfort's volume (none of which was translated by Beckett): 'Un poète consultait Chamfort sur un distique: "Excellent, répondit-il, sauf les longueurs"' (Chamfort 1970: 1248).

In fact, Beckett thus appears to apply Chamfort's longing for pithiness to Chamfort's own maxims, and his changes to the source text can here probably be seen as outdoing Chamfort. This can be viewed in light of Beckett's own aesthetic and thematic choices. Terseness is all, if one's endeavour has for several decades indeed been to write a literature of the – much quoted – 'unword'.[10] Terseness might furthermore be all that is left, if one presumes, as in Beckett's Chamfort maxims, that 'life and death' are 'tuppenny aches', and if one insists on Pascal's 'how hollow heart and full/of filth thou art', also in the maxims. Beckett clearly does not favour long diatribes, but prefers maxims, devoid of longueurs.

Verse

Beckett's most noticeable departure from Chamfort's phrasing is probably the verse. The doggerel poems consist of two quatrains, one of which is in regular iambic pentameter, and six couplets, most of them rhyming.

Que le cœur de l'homme est creux et plein d'ordure.

how hollow heart and
full of filth thou art

This is an odd choice for these maxims for at least two reasons. First, the tradition of the maxim that Chamfort works in is far from being poetic, in the sense that the condensed ideas one finds in maxims are generally written in prose, in the seventeenth century, as in La Rochefoucauld for instance. Maxims in verse are uncommon – and the prose poem as genre will only appear two centuries later. The other reason why Beckett's choice of verse seems striking is that the tradition of the maxim is also far from being 'poetic' in the sense that the terse ideas of the maxim are generally disillusioned, piercing, mordant observations of the behaviour of mankind and the way the world goes. Intellect and wit are features of the maxim; the acerbic analysis of society and human behaviour does not appear to induce the use of verse. I do of course not wish to suggest that verse necessarily goes together with enchantment; the history of lyric poetry in verse, and of verse generally for that matter, has shown that verse can fit any matter. For lyric poetry, the most obvious case in this respect is probably Baudelaire, whose verse and sonnets in *The Flowers of Evil* often tell cruel stories and the lyrical voice's disgust and rebellion. However, even Baudelaire is still romantic enough to think that an escape is possible, at times, and to sometimes sing the praises of love, of travels, or of cats. In Beckett's 'Long after Chamfort', hope appears to be banned and the rhythms, rhymes and regularities of verse are used solely to sing irregularities, and filth indeed. Verse has here become a contrapuntal reminiscence of what harmony used to be when it was perhaps still imaginable. Since there seems to be no harmony any more in the world sung in these short rhymes, the verse appears to have become a wry – or perhaps comic – way of stressing the absence of it. Beckett may not be the only writer to use verse in this ironic way, and he may moreover insist on the supposedly small aesthetic worth of this late verse by calling it 'doggerel' (or 'mirlitonnades' for comparable poems in French), his use of verse is nevertheless striking here, especially in the case of an adaptation of a prose text. Here, in other words, content is form, and form is content, if one is willing to be sensitive to the fact that a well-wrought urn – very small ones, in this case – can serve to ironically highlight emptiness and absence.

Humour

Regrettably, there is no time to go into this now . . .

> Le théâtre tragique a le grand inconvénient moral de mettre trop d'importance à la vie et à la mort.

> The trouble with tragedy is the fuss it makes
> About life and death and other tuppeny aches.

Let us just underline that if there is humour in the poems of 'Long after Chamfort',[11] and if there was none in the original maxims, Beckett might again be said to outdo Chamfort, instead of fundamentally undermining him by adding joking overtones. One of the maxims by Chamfort that did not make it into 'Long after Chamfort' is indeed: 'La plus perdue de toutes les journées est celle où l'on n'a pas ri' (maxim 80).[12]

Must Beckett mean what he translates (and writes)?

Long after Cavell's 'Must We Mean What We Say', it is perhaps time to ask this rather awkward question (Cavell 1969). The main reason is a paradigm in

Beckett studies that was once rebellious and largely based on 'French theory', and that has become dominant a few decades ago already, before being I would not say contested, but to some degree pushed to the background by the advent of other critical stances, that now often stress historical or archival research in Beckett studies.

There is indeed a strong tradition in Beckett scholarship, one that has become mainstream in the 1980s or 1990s at the latest, that posits the dissolution in the text itself of what is stated by the text. In 'The Exhausted', Deleuze writes: 'It is always an Other who speaks, since words have not expected me and there is no language other than the foreign" (Deleuze 1992).[13] There is of course much in Beckett's work that warrants such statements. This is especially so with regard to the 'I' that speaks, as the trilogy, and especially the Unnamable, stresses so often:

> It must not be forgotten, sometimes I forget, that all is a question of voices. I say what I am told to say, in the hope that some day they will weary of talking at me . . . Do they believe I believe it is I who am speaking? That's theirs too. (Beckett 2009: 339)

Anthony Uhlmann is thus right when he comments on this, calling it 'a non-presence always at one remove from a "true presence"' (Uhlmann 1999: 167), and refers to Derrida's concept of 'originary nonpresence'.

However, occasionally Uhlmann departs from this Derridean commentary and also hints at the possibility and perhaps even the inevitability of an I 'that can only ever be sensed': 'But might there not be said to be an originary non-phenomenality here in the realisation that I can never be identical to language?' (Uhlmann 1999: 167). The Unnamable, according to Uhlmann, 'seems to feel that this ego does not correspond to the silent self present at the core of his being' (Uhlmann 1999: 168). It seems indeed hard to deny that there has to be a nucleus of the self in the Beckettian universe that can denounce each of the discourses on the 'I' and the utterances of the 'I', without being able to state its own being but also without being able to disappear: the discourse of denial depends on the capacity of the denier.

The French critic Bruno Clément has a less poststructuralist frame of reference but insists likewise on the 'suspension du sens' (Clément 1994: 418) and on the figure of speech called *épanorthose*. Epanorthosis is a figure of speech that amends which has been stated, and for Clément it indicates the tendency of Beckett's narrators to endlessly amend and erase their discourse. Yet, Clément also stresses in his conclusion: 'On ne peut pas faire table rase de *l'inventio*' (Clément 1994: 419). Here, he uses the rhetoric terminology that structures his book to indicate that that there still is subject matter – a topic – in Beckett's work, notwithstanding the willing suspension of meaning.

What does 'Long after Chamfort' show us in relation to this by now long-standing interpretative tradition in Beckett criticism? Beckett's work is, in a way, not only the occasion but also the cause of this tradition; however, at the same time it seems to suggest, even to the proponents of this interpretative move, the limits of the self-effacing text. I have already tried to show that Beckett's 'free' translations of Chamfort's maxims might be said to improve on Chamfort – partly by adding tones of dissonance to Chamfort's prose. This is a strange, heady mixture, and it may seem that Beckett's rephrasing creates a kind of double that could easily be called 'spectral' in the interpretative tradition that I have sketched out very briefly.

However, I tend to think that this is not very noticeably the case – and again, for most readers, I would like to add, overconfidently but not without some help from an occasional critic.[14] If we look at all eight of the poems, published alongside the original French, none of them seems to fundamentally subvert or even question the crux of the themes of the original Chamfort maxims.

> Quand on soutient que les gens les moins sensibles sont, à tout prendre, les plus heureux, je me rappelle le proverbe indien: 'Il vaut mieux être assis que debout, couché qu'assis, mort que tout cela'.

> Better on your arse than on your feet,
> Flat on your back than either, dead than the lot.

It is certainly true, as Shane Weller has said, after his short discussion of 'Long after Chamfort', but speaking more generally, that 'Beckett's dispatchings of other writers appear on occasion to put considerable strain on the distinction between respect and disrespect in translation' (Weller 2006: 63). I wonder nonetheless if one should say, as Weller suggests, that Beckett's phrasing of the 'sleep till death' poem (quoted above for its terseness) is 'unethical negation of [the] original' (Weller 2006: 62).[15] Weller does not motivate his sharp judgment, that he seems to derive from Christopher Ricks, inflating the 'distance' noted by Ricks and transforming it into 'independence from' and 'unethical negation of [the] original'. It is correct that Ricks calls the two particular 'hobbled verses' that translate the Indian proverb 'Far from Chamfort' (Ricks 1993: 16); but this is because of the 'meticulous brutality' of the translation itself – and apparently *not* because Ricks thinks that the rendering negates the meaning of the source text. In the first chapter 'Death', as indeed in the rest of his book *Beckett's Dying Words*, Ricks on the contrary insists continuously on 'the wish to die' and on 'death as ease' (the titles of the first two sections), and on Beckett's 'predecessors' (and 'predeceasers', Ricks 1993: 9) in this vein. Ricks, moreover, explicitly states that 'Beckett rendered tribute to his predecessor Sébastien Chamfort' (Ricks 1993: 13). It may thus seem odd – and perhaps slightly unethical? – that Weller annexes Ricks, since the latter manifestly does not insist on negation of Chamfort or of what are, for Ricks, other predecessors of Beckett.

Even if we try not to take into account the background knowledge that most critics have, aware as they are of the influence of Schopenhauer on Beckett and, through the letters, of the way Beckett presented the Chamfort poems to his friends, it would be hard to show that the poems fundamentally detract from the Chamfort texts or destabilise these in such a way that the original, mostly disillusioned vision that they posit is 'radically distracted' and that the 'double' created by the verse undermines the significance and autonomy of the source text. The repetition that is introduced due to the virtuoso translation does not primarily transform Chamfort's radical propositions into a linguistic phenomenon that undermines or fundamentally destabilises the idea stated in the original. If one is in any way tempted by metaphors of spectrality, one might perhaps tend to say that the translation 'haunts' the original, but the ghost is, in this case, quite sympathetic to its former appearance that it so closely sides with, and not only on the page.

The title 'Long after Chamfort' is often explained as evoking the idea that the renderings have been made a long time after Chamfort's life, first of all, and that they are 'very free versions' (Pilling and Lawlor 2012: 438), secondly. However, I would suggest that there is a third dimension: the poems show that long after Chamfort, things have perhaps not much evolved, even if they can be stated somewhat differently in a late twentieth-century translation. By reusing and restating Chamfort, Beckett shows that the maxims still appear to hold: long after Chamfort, it still appears possible to reaffirm his maxims. With his doggerelised translations, Beckett is, in a way, longing after the radical propositions of Chamfort. I would even go so far as to suggest that Beckett's presentation of the maxims highlights their assertoric nature instead of undermining it: the repetition of the maxims with an – affectionate - difference turns these writings into something more than, say, the musings of an eighteenth-century misanthrope who continued an old tradition of maxims. Notwithstanding the sometimes-light tone of the doggerel, and the emphasis on how things are said that comes with the printing of both source and target text, the reiteration here also strongly suggests that the truth value of the maxim is still worth being considered today.

Negation, self-effacement, self-annihilation is indeed present in Beckett's writing; and, on the whole, his work is not manifestly inviting a reading that would reduce it to a set of general ideas on 'life', since it opposes generalisation, notwithstanding the first wave of reception that quite often focused on distilling a coherent world view from his work. On closer look, the thetic nature of Beckett's work is not very apparent. However, it is also true that recurring themes in Beckett insistently point toward conceptions that have circulated elsewhere as mutinous ontologies and ethics in sometimes more or less marginalised writings, such as those of the Gnostics, of Schopenhauer, or indeed of Chamfort.

In the case of the latter, it is of course not true that Beckett *must* mean what he translates, in the same sense that Cavell argued that we must mean what we say. Nevertheless, it seems true that Beckett *chose* to insist on the texts he rephrased when he rendered what I have, for the sake of provocation, called his only bilingual work, 'Long after Chamfort'; long after, but still very much like Chamfort indeed.

★

I have used (or misused) eight short doggerel poems to cover too much ground by considering three fundamental questions. Is there a bilingual text in Beckett's work; what is translation ideally for Beckett; and what does the structurally bilingual text 'Long after Chamfort' – and Beckett's work generally, perhaps – do to some of the ideas that it reuses. A minimal conclusion is appropriate in these conditions: the very short 'Long after Chamfort' can, as I hope to have shown, contribute to re-evaluate the answers to these general questions, and perhaps prompt us to grasp facets that some of the tenets of current criticism have tended to erase.

Notes

1. For example, Mooney (2011: 9); Weller (2006: 63). Pascale Sardin is one of the rare critics who underscores that bilingual authors are not only to be found in modernism and beyond (Sardin 2002: 13–14).
2. It would be preferable to use the term multilingualism in the case of Beckett as a linguistic subject, since he was able to express himself in more than two languages, even if he published his literary work in two languages.
3. Interestingly, in Germany, Suhrkamp published quite a few multilingual editions of Beckett's works since the 1960s and early 1970s (1960s for the two volumes of *Dramatische Dichtungen in drei Sprachen,* for instance). Most of the plays and much short prose – but not the longer prose texts – have

been issued in bilingual or trilingual editions, that contain in each case the German translation and either a French or English text, or both. My argument concerns the main publishers in English and French speaking countries in which Beckett's work was published in the two languages he wrote in (the UK, the US and France), so Germany and other countries in which Beckett's work was published in translation lie beyond this scope. It is perhaps telling that in Germany, that took a special stance on nationalism and embraced the European project after World War II, Beckett was much more promoted as a multilingual, European author than in other countries.

4. In the published letters, Beckett's motivation reads: 'It suggests an invitation', not an 'open invitation' as the quoted article has it (Van Hulle and Verhulst 2018: 36).

5. I must add that I fail to see why the publication of the two isolated bilingual editions I mentioned earlier is a reason for Van Hulle and Verhulst to state that Beckett's position changed – 'as it would on many other issues' (Van Hulle and Verhulst 2018: 37). The editors of these two exceptional, not very well-known, partly scholarly editions were friends of Beckett, and there is no structural bilingual publication of his work – that is, until the variorum and (strictly) academic editions that were published after his death. As for Beckett's changing of mind, one can choose to insist on the fact that he did on some occasions, as well as on the fact that he regretted it quite often afterwards. Beckett even stopped the publication of *More Pricks than Kicks* by Calder and Grove after signing the contract and after proofs were produced in 1964 (Beckett 2014: 633)!

6. In the preface to the volume, Pilling and Lawlor nevertheless seem to present 'Long after Chamfort' as a translation to some extent, since they explain why they have decided not to print the 'original poems *en face*' (Pilling and Lawlor 2012: xv) in the case of Beckett's translation. They go on to say that in 'the case of "Long after Chamfort" we have included Chamfort's original prose as a way of demonstrating at least in part what SB meant in giving his texts this title' (Pilling and Lawlor 2012: xv). The result is that even in this volume, 'Long after Chamfort' is a bilingual work – published as part of Beckett's original work, moreover.

7. A notable exception is probably Robert Pinget's *La manivelle*, that Beckett translated in 1960.

8. Chris Ackerley writes on one of the maxims: 'Beckett offered a free translation' (Ackerley 2010: 232.1).

9. Mary Ann Caws describes the poems as 'witty condensations' and 'joyous translations' (Caws 2006: 93).

10. Letter to Axel Kaun, 9 July 1937.

11. For more on rhyme, brevity and humour in Beckett's 'light verse', see Engelberts (1998).
12. The day most wasted is the one without a laugh (my translation).
13. Translation Uhlmann (1999: 164).
14. 'Man wird nicht behaupten wollen, Beckett parodiere Chamfort. . . . Im Gegenteil, hier wie dort herrscht dieselbe Haltung von Härte, Hohn und Klarsicht' (Rauseo 1997: 136).
15. Paul Shields comments on the same maxim as the one I quote here, calling it – rightly – a 'loose translation', but stating also: 'As late as 1975 . . . Beckett still gives voice to this desire [for death], and with a similar irreverence that is to be found within *Dream* and *Murphy*' (Shields 2006: 30).

Works Cited

Ackerley, Chris (2010), *Obscure Locks, Simple Keys: The Annotated Watt*, Edinburgh University Press.

Beckett, Samuel (1972), *Words and Music, Play* and *Eh Joe*, Paris: Aubier-Flammarion.

Beckett, Samuel (1978), *Happy Days / Oh les beaux jours*, James Knowlson (ed), London: Faber.

Beckett, Samuel (2009), *Three Novels*, New York: Grove Press.

Beckett, Samuel (2012), *The Collected Poems of Samuel Beckett*, John Pilling and Seán Lawlor (eds), New York: Grove Press.

Beckett, Samuel (2014), *The Letters of Samuel Beckett: 1957–1965*, Vol. 3, George Craig, Martha Dow Fehsenfeld, Dan Gunn and Lois More Overbeck (eds), Cambridge, UK: Cambridge University Press.

Beer, Ann (1994), 'Beckett's Bilingualism', in John Pilling (ed), *The Cambridge Companion to Beckett*, Cambridge, UK: Cambridge University Press, pp. 209–21.

Cavell, Stanley (1969), *Must We Mean What We Say*, New York: Scribner.

Caws, Mary Ann (2006), *Surprised in Translation*, Chicago: University of Chicago Press (Quoted chapter originally published in *Samuel Beckett Today / Aujourd'hui* 8, 1999, 43–57).

Chamfort, Sébastien (1970), *Maximes et pensées. Caractères et anecdotes*, Paris: Gallimard (collection Folio).

Clément, Bruno (1994), *L'Œuvre sans qualités*, Paris: Minuit.

Cohn, Ruby (1961), 'Samuel Beckett Self-Translator', *PMLA*, 76.5, 613–21.

Connor, Steven, (1989), 'Traduttore traditore: Samuel Beckett's Translation of *Mercier and Camier*', *Journal of Beckett Studies*, 11/12, 27–46.

Deleuze, Gilles (1992) 'L'Épuisé', in Samuel Beckett, *Quad et autres pièces pour la télévision*, Paris: Minuit (English translation quoted from Uhlmann).

Engelberts, Matthijs (1998), 'Beckett et le *light verse*: Les *Mirlitonnades* et *Long after Chamfort*', in *Beckett versus Beckett, Samuel Beckett Today/Aujourd'hui,* 7, Amsterdam: Rodopi, pp. 277–96.

Fitch, Brian (1988), *Beckett and Babel. An Investigation into the Status of the Bilingual Work*, Toronto: University of Toronto Press.

Germoni, Karine (2018), 'Les anglicismes de Beckett à l'époque de la "French frenzy"', *Samuel Beckett Today/Aujourd'hui*, 30.1, 97–111.

Louar, Nadia and José Francisco Fernández (2018), 'Introduction', *Samuel Beckett Today/Aujourd'hui*, 30.1, 1–4.

Mooney, Sinéad (2011), *A Tongue Not Mine: Beckett and Translation*, Oxford: Oxford University Press.

Rauseo, Chris (1997), 'Das umgekehrte Erhabene und die Umkehrung seiner sprachlichen Gestalt, Zu Beckett's zweisprachigen Humor', in Peter Brockmeier and Carola Veit (eds), *Komik und Solipsismus im Werk Samuel Becketts*, Stuttgart: M&P, pp. 131–48.

Ricks, Christopher (1993), *Beckett's Dying Words*, Oxford: Oxford University Press.

Sardin-Damestoy, Pascale (2002), *Samuel Beckett auto-traducteur ou l'art de l'«empêchement»*, Arras: Artois Presses Université.

Shields, Paul (2006), *Zone of Evaporations: Samuel Beckett's Disjunctions*, Amsterdam: Rodopi.

Uhlmann, Anthony (1999), *Beckett and Poststructuralism*, Cambridge, UK: Cambridge University Press.

Van Hulle, Dirk and Pim Verhulst (2018), 'Beckett's Collaborative Translations in the 1950s', *Samuel Beckett Today/Aujourd'hui*, 30.1, 20–38.

Weller, Shane (2006), *Beckett, Literature and the Ethics of Alterity*, Basingstoke: Palgrave Macmillan.

Part III
Beckett's Poetics of Translation

Part III

Beckett's Poems and Translations

10

Au plaisir: Beckett and the Neatness of Identifications

John Pilling

Geminal, said Camier.
Yes, said Mercier, everything double but the arse.

Beckett, *Mercier and Camier* (1970: 95)

A conversation involving an exchange of a kind, between the night-nurse and her patient in the Merrion Street Dublin Nursing-Home:

'See you later' she said.
There was no controverting this. Belacqua cast about wildly for a reply that would please her and do him justice at the same time. *Au plaisir* was of course the very thing [= 'I look forward to it'], but the wrong language. Finally he settled on *I suppose so* and discharged it at her in a very half-hearted manner, when she was more than half out of the door. He would have been very much better advised to let it alone and say nothing. ('Yellow' in Beckett 2010c: 157)

Such pleasure, shall we say – since soon enough Beckett will be moved to say it for us – that pleasure was not the word. But 'I suppose so' does not seem to be quite right either, and Beckett's lifelong struggle with 'the neatness of identifications' (Beckett 1983: 19) is obviously in full swing, even with the author not yet into his thirties, as if he had already realised that he might have to stay caught between something not quite right and something better left unsaid. There are other, even earlier, indicators where there is no suggestion of a translation – Latin, *translatio*, a drawing across – at least not between two different languages, but within the very fabric of language itself, notably in *Dream of Fair to Middling Women* (1931–32), which seems to favour 'one category only, yours' (Beckett 1992: 35) but always makes heavy weather of differentiating ('Is that neat or is that not?' (Beckett 1992: 120)). Perhaps some kind of answer is offered sixteen or seventeen years later, by Malone: 'The forms are many in which the unchanging seeks relief from its formlessness' (Beckett 2010a: 23). But the inference must be that any Beckettian 'one' must contain a 'many'.

So it seems, in letters – 'sentir plusieurs (au bas mot) tout en restant (bien entendu) unique' (Beckett 2011a: 135) – and in passages jettisoned from ongoing creative projects, in the notebooks towards *Malone meurt*, and especially in the many notebooks demonstrating how often Beckett tried out a number of variants, before he inevitably found himself obliged to choose just one, however provisionally. The ground base was a 'dualist conception of the creative act' ('B' in the third of the *Three Dialogues with Georges Duthuit*), and Beckett found dualisms wherever he looked: 'The parallels Rimbaud–Cézanne, Corbière–Goya take longer to meet then most'; 'the passage from [the alexandrine] to [prose dialogue in Molière's *La Princesse d'Élide*] is one of the great reliefs in literature'; 'In death they did not cease to be divided' [of the 'Dives–Lazarus symbiosis'] (Beckett 1983: 78, 82, 92). But it was creative dualism which mattered most: two languages (English; French) to write in, having also tried out German, though not Spanish or Italian, despite knowledge of both; at least two genres (prose fiction; plays), with poems and criticism 'suitably' occasional; and an almost continuous exercise in 'self-extension' (Beckett 1983: 19). No wonder he was intrigued by how Neary's man Cooper could, for the most part, successfully act as a 'servant of two masters' in *Murphy*, something which Beckett found ever more a challenge as time wore on, as commitments multiplied, and as 'old' work threatened to divert his attention from something new. It was all too often a case either of 'indigestion' with 'all the adventure gone' (Beckett 2011a: 407), or 'wastes and wilds of self-translation for many miserable months to come' (Beckett and Schneider 1998: 14). The backwash of 'reculer pour mieux enculer' (Beckett 1992: 120), created situations of near absurdity, as when having to translate into French the doggerel poem 'To Nelly' from *Watt* (IMEC Archive/University of Reading: letter to Jérôme Lindon of 4 March 1968), never likely to prove a cakewalk. Directing or assisting with the production of his own plays further guaranteed a succession of non-identical conversions and excursions, and the only escape from self-extension was in translating others, where there is never much 'relief' but inevitably 'many forms'. (How 'In me, civil war', as in the first of the six poems from Alain Bosquet, must have seemed a natural point of contact! (Beckett 2012: 191)).

Much of what became the norm for Beckett over the course of a long creative life is 'stated', if not 'summed' (Beckett 1992: 125), in two whiplash sentences, one from June 1929 ('The danger is in the neatness of identifications'; Beckett 1983: 19), the other from August 1935 ('The sun shone, having no alternative, on the nothing new'); and between them, in September 1934, an extended analysis of the paintings of Paul Cézanne in a letter expressing sympathy for 'the absence of a rapport that . . . would have been false for him, because he had the sense of his incommensurability not only with life of such a different order as landscape but . . . even with the life . . . operative in himself' (Beckett 2009b: 227). In the event, necessarily, even this life of a supposedly different order had to be lived, though Beckett increasingly tended to find it had for the most part to be lived in pursuit of an 'alternative' wherever such an expedient might best be found, by running 'the gantelope of sense and nonsense' (Beckett 2012: 23).

It had all begun in *Dream* with a devil-may-care *sangfroid* issuing in unanswerable questions of the 'What would Leibniz say?' – type (Beckett 1992: 179). Presumably, the putative reader was meant to supply something along the lines of

the simplicity of substance is by no means inconsistent with the multiplicity of the modifications which are to be found together in that same simple substance, and these modifications must consist in variety of relations to the things which are outside. It is as in the case of centre or point, in which, although it is perfectly simple, there is an infinite number of angles formed by the lines which meet in it. (Leibniz, *Principles of Nature and of Grace, based on Reason*, 1714: paragraph 2)

But *Dream* is of course (at least notionally) inimical to such prodigies of subtlety unless it can whistle up its own '[t]angles'. Whoever it is who is at least in principle in charge of proceedings in that novel prefers rather to think of the lead character (Belacqua) as 'at his simplest . . . trine': 'Centripetal, centrifugal and . . . not. Phoebus chasing Daphne, Narcissus flying from Echo and . . . neither' (Beckett 1992: 120).

'The dots are nice don't you think?' (Beckett 1992: 120), not because they look good, but because one begins to see here what Beckett might mean when he promises 'The experience of my reader shall be between the phrases. . .' (Beckett 1992: 137), and by extension what is at stake in the very important line in the 1931 poem 'Alba': 'a statement of itself *drawn across* the tempest of emblems' (Beckett 2012: 10. My italics). Wherever these 'many forms', singularities in groups, may manifest themselves – as poems, as prose, as translations, even as pauses – each activity is conditioned by something which precedes the moment at which language shapes itself into speech or writing, since even an idea can only become 'a statement of itself' by being 'drawn across' the divide between potentiality and actuality. But in being 'drawn across', like a

violin bow across strings or a curtain across a window, Beckett was ever ready
to show that what cannot but be to some extent relational also cannot avoid
being essentially non-relational, differential.

Understandably in the circumstances, although Beckett was ever suspicious
of 'analogymongers' (Beckett 1983: 19), he could still occasionally find fel-
lowship across the gap with a remarkably diverse gaggle of alter egos: Dante,
Schopenhauer, Jules Renard, Geulincx, Stéphane Mallarmé ('The eye, a hand',
Beckett 2012: 136), Avigdor Arikha ('By the hand it unceasingly changes the
eye unceasingly changed', Beckett 1983: 152) . . . But it was always a struggle to
come up with an image for the 'something there' (Beckett 2012: 202) that was
notionally outside the skull ('hors crâne', Beckett 2012: 201), but mysteriously
also present inside it. This is nowhere more dramatically demonstrated than in
the remarkable correspondence with the art critic Georges Duthuit, Beckett's
contributions to which explode out of the pages of volume 2 (1941–1956) of
the *Letters*, where the words *dehors, dedans* and *devant* resonate with extraordinary
frequency and intensity (Beckett 2011a: 136, 148). Here the painter Bram van
Velde is the putative focus but without the *gouffre* ('ce qui nous sépare'; Beckett
2011a: 164) between Beckett and Duthuit significantly diminishing. It effectively typifies the Beckettian position that he should resort to a foreign language
in an attempt to get his ideas across, much as he had done in the mid-January
1937 entry in his private (and still unpublished) German Diaries, notably in the
notion that Fate and Chance should be seen as one and the same thing: 'Schick-
sal = Zufall, for all human purposes' (Nixon 2011: 178). Only, however, when
those human purposes chose to rise to the challenge of translation was Beckett
able to demonstrate by example precisely how 'the desire to bind for ever in
imperishable relation the object to its representation' (Beckett 1992: 160) might
with great effort and ingenuity be at least in part mitigated by 'a continuous cir-
cumvention of textual fixity' (Van Hulle 2015: 158fn146).

Translatio was always going to be a matter of facing up to an obstacle. The
'*empêchement*' of Beckett's 1947 *hommage* to the van Veldes ('Peintres de
l'empêchement'; Beckett 1992: 133–7; its English equivalent is 'The New
Object') – a notion already beginning to emerge, without a term to give it
a name, in its predecessor of 1945 ('Le Monde et le pantalon', Beckett 1992:
118–32) – was not simply an optional extra but an intrinsic and essential element in keeping the danger in 'the neatness of identifications' nullified. This is
why, in the second of the *Three Dialogues with Georges Duthuit*, 'B' dissociates
himself from the supposed 'possessiveness' of a Leonardo, whose otherwise
admirable interest in 'disfazione' remains vulnerable to the objection that he
'knows that for him not one fragment will be lost'. For Beckett there needed
to be something lost if there were ever to be anything gained, even at the cost

of losing what has been conceived of as normal vision altogether ('Les vers qui importent sont ceux qu'on oublie . . . ça ne voit plus rien', he told Duthuit in August 1948 (Beckett 2011a: 90)). In 'Le Monde et le pantalon' Beckett makes the impossible sound as if it might even be quite easy to achieve:

> A van Velde paints the extended.
> G van Velde paints the successive.
> (Beckett 1992: 128. My translation)

But 'Peintres de l'empêchement', seeing things from the inside as it were, emphasises what this might mean in practice, and what obstacles have to be circumvented:

> The one [Geer van Velde] will say, I cannot see the object to represent it because the object is what it is. The other [Bram van Velde], I cannot see the object to represent it because I am what I am. (Beckett 2011b: 879)

★

> Weil es nicht anders kann (from Beckett's practice piece in German, 'dramatising' situations taken from Ariosto's *Orlando Furioso*; literal meaning: 'as cannot be otherwise', 'having no alternative'; Van Hulle and Verhulst 2017: 331).

In a sense, Beckett's 'new object' – an inevitable surrogate of a 'new self' – was a visual substitute for what in his 1938 piece on Denis Devlin he had thought of in narrowly verbal terms as 'the evocation of the unsaid by the said' (Beckett 1983: 92). It is as though painting – as embodied in the canvases of the van Veldes – had revealed to Beckett that, even if the subject, however objictified, never could be its own object, there nevertheless might still be a way to create an entity capable of being 'that something itself' (Beckett 1983: 27), an outside projected from inside, drawn across the tympanum between them. Beckett was prepared to engage in 'art cackle' (Beckett 2011a: 145) for so long as art could serve his essentially literary purposes. Otherwise, what could be seen was always likely to yield to the separations generated by what the mind saw. Ironically enough, his emphatically italicised phrase almost contrives to obscure the way in which 'that something itself' contains a 'that' and an 'itself' which 'show' how the essay's initial 'prospect of self-extension' (Beckett 1983: 19) has been obliged to turn outwards, towards an 'itself' in touch with a 'that'. Beckett's emphasis has rather backfired in critical accounts of his work which use this judgment as explicative of his own practice, rather than as applying to Joyce's *Work in Progress*, and the way in which the 'it is' and the 'itself' mirror each other has rarely been given its due. But as both *Dream* and the *Dialogues* demonstrate, if matters were always *verbal* for Beckett ('the word overheard' of *From an Abandoned Work*; his final text, 'what is the word', as a kind of summing up of a life's work), they were also *gestural*, and *performative*. In seeking out 'some form of Nominalist irony' (Beckett 1983: 173), the 'irony' consisted in the way that the presentation of 'something' could be made to matter as an object of perception for the subject perceiving it.

★

> Be again, be again. [*Pause.*] All that old misery. [*Pause.*] Once wasn't enough for you. (Beckett 2009a: 11)

Identifications, neat or not so neat, 'nice' or not so 'nice', are characteristically treated with suspicion by Beckett, whose preference is almost always for a separation between things, a disconnection predicated on difference. Not for him the 'total object' of Tal Coat in the first of the *Three Dialogues*; the 'partial object' is what matters, the fragment, the flotsam and jetsam (as he seems to have accepted with some relish in his German Diaries). 'The artist has acquired his text; the artisan translates it' (Beckett 1965: 84). And goes on doing so: 'The Proustian world is expressed metaphorically by the artisan because it is apprehended metaphorically by the artist: the indirect comparative expression of indirect and comparative perception' (Beckett 1965: 88). The language is philosophical: 'apprehended', 'perception' – sometimes in a manner that references Schopenhauer (Beckett 1965: 91), but one which also evokes 'the unsaid' with terms taken from Leibniz and Kant:

> He [Proust] deplores his lack of will until he understands that will, being utilitarian, a servant of intelligence and habit, is not a condition of the artistic experience. When the subject is exempt from will the object is exempt from causality (Time and Space taken together). And this human vegetation is purified in the transcendental aperception [*sic*; the spelling is the same in 1931, but 'corrected' in 'the cold comforts of apperception' in the 1934 review-essay 'Recent Irish Poetry'; Beckett 1983: 20] that can capture the Model, the Idea, the 'thing in itself'. (Beckett 1965: 90)

More economically, if also more cavalierly, expressed: 'La Chose de Kant' – the *Ding-an-Sich* – becomes a model for what is 'perfectly intelligible' and 'perfectly inexplicable' ('Le Concentrisme', Beckett 1983: 42. My translation), if never quite so perfectly expressible. The Modern Language Society at Trinity College Dublin in late 1930 were not only being given a word to the wise, but receiving a 'double response, two holes to a burrow' ('Ding-Dong', *More Pricks Than Kicks*, where the 'ding' can never be the 'dong' and *vice versa*, but where they can never wholly detach themselves from each other). 'The artist', Beckett told readers of the *Dublin Magazine* in 1936, 'takes [the thing] to pieces and makes a new thing, new things. He must' (Beckett 1983: 89). This, it turns out, is what 'the whole mind' makes of 'the sun, moon and stars' (Beckett 1983: 94), and the great virtue of the mind is 'that it can dispel mind' (Beckett 1983: 95 ('dispel' replaces 'delight' in Trinity College Dublin MS 9072 fol.10)), demonstrating how illusory wholeness is. It is by way of judgments of this separatist kind that Beckett prepares the ground for the 'simple games' which he will go on to play in a work like *Watt*, as, for example, in the observation: 'It was as he feared, earlier than he hoped' (Beckett 2009c: 198), repeated ten pages later on, though – logically enough – with 'later' replacing 'earlier'. *Translatio* can only move things 'worstward' in the longer run, 'vestiges of an old longing' (Beckett 2011a: 104) reapplying Virgil's *veteris vestigia flammae* (*Aeneid* VI) but reassigning it from love to literature. Every such reassignment requires a 'different principle of measurement at each step of [the] calculation' (Beckett 1983: 173), as per the Axel Kaun letter – which was apparently never sent (an ideally separatist gesture on Beckett's part). The letter was written close in time to when Beckett read, and took copious notes from, Mauthner's *Beiträge zu einer Kritik der Sprache* (1901-02), written to free the mind from the tyranny of words, given the way that language generates a merely illusory unity between the word and the world. The unavoidably metaphorical nature of language means that words are only ever 'vestiges' of what might have been and are not even the currency familiarity has made them seem in transactions merely conventional. A phrase from one of the Mauthner passages found in Beckett's 'Whoroscope' Notebook (taken from volume 2 of the *Beiträge*: 689–90) sums up the relationship between words and the world as a game played by coincidence. Translation did not so much change the rules of the game as subvert it by virtue of demonstrating non-coincidence.

★

L'art adore les sauts (Beckett, 'Le Monde et le pantalon', 1983: 128)

('Art loves its jump-cuts')

Criticism, even as practised by the journeyman chartered recountant (Beckett 1983: 89), also loves jump-cuts and relishes dream-dives, albeit with an irreducible tincture of lessness attached, given that the very genre itself seems to preclude any possibility of being creative, all the creativity having been performed already by someone other than oneself, as in the 'hommage' for a fellow-artist, into which – as in Mallarmé's '*Hommage à . . .*' sonnets – one's own concerns can be absorbed and enfolded, *pli selon pli*. These *disjecta*, naturally enough, tend to be ignored or soft-pedalled by the academic interpreter, as if their obsolescence were almost intrinsic to them. Yet they repay close attention, especially if you are intent on tracing either (a) translatability or (b) transactions between a given object and a perceiving subject. Far from being ephemeral pieces, Beckett's *hommages* are always, as in the *Disjecta* subsection title, 'Essays *at* aesthetics' (my italics). Hence why I now turn to 'Henri Hayden homme-peintre' (Beckett 1983: 146–47; the hyphen matters!) – on the way to seeing how we might extend our understanding of the 'homme-écrivain' Samuel Beckett both *in propria persona* and as imaginatively or otherwise expropriated by any persona impersonating him. The Hayden piece dates from January 1952 but was only published three years later, in November 1955, in the *deluxe* journal *Cahiers d'Art*. The key sentence in it has never received the praise it merits, in spite of its being one of Beckett's most carefully, and most imaginatively, crafted: 'Elle n'est pas au bout de ses beaux jours, la crise sujet-objet' (Beckett 1983: 146).

How aptly the apparent afterthought – 'la crise sujet-objet' (the 'hidden' subject masquerading as the predicate) – prolongs, so to speak, the very 'salad days' ('beaux jours') whose sharp end ('bout') cannot be so very far away, though obviously further away than this sentence seems to be prepared to go. ('One is deliberately given the sense of a moment', Peter Levi once wrote of a Platonic dialogue, 'that would not last'; Levi 1985: 340). But it is those very 'beaux jours' which currently occupy the limelight, for at least two good, unavoidably Beckettian, reasons and, arguably, one even better non-Beckettian one. It seems unlikely that Beckett could or would have forgotten his 1933 poem 'Sanies I', with its distinctively Irish dimension of the laugh and tear conjoined as expressed in the line 'happy days snap a stem shed a tear' (Beckett 2012: 12). But not even Beckett's powers of prophecy stretched almost ten years into the future to 'see' Winnie and Willie as each other's subject and object in the 1961 play *Happy Days*, however well he may have remembered his earlier use(s) of the phrase with a wry smile and a tear or two stored up for later.

Beyond Beckett, though only the French translation of *Happy Days* (*Oh les beaux jours*) takes us there, is one of his favourite subject–object disputes across the good old gender divide (compare *Play*, and the recently recovered, still unpublished 'Match Nul' poem): 'Colloque sentimental', one of the best-known poems in Paul Verlaine's *Fêtes galantes* collection: amorous awaydays.

(Beckett 1978: 128fn1, Knowlson describes this as 'expressly' recalled, and also recalls 'Sanies I', though not the Henri Hayden *hommage*). Satisfactory English equivalents for 'fêtes', 'galantes', 'colloque' and 'sentimental' are strangely hard to come by, with *faux amis* in each case and every word with something of an ironic shadow attached to it, even before one reads the poem itself. In the poem proper a couple are placing differential emphases on the possible future of their affair, 'she' supposing it effectively over, 'he' hoping it can be resuscitated. Each of Verlaine's speakers in the 'colloquy' is quite as conscious of their own selves as of the other party to the dialogue. (Kant, following Leibniz, would call this '*Apperzeption*', a consciousness of Self constituting itself as Self-Perception, which according to Beckett, only permits one to 'celebrate' its 'cold comforts'; Beckett 1983: 78). Insofar as the very form of Verlaine's poem can structurally dramatise its content, their discourses are situated alongside one another, or rather successively, as if the two parties to the 'colloquy' were parallel lines that could never meet, or – irony of ironies – could only ever meet as they are (not quite) meeting in this poem. The poem's mood – over and above its actual tenses – is subjunctive, and its 'music' (a key concern of Verlaine's) is in what Beckett calls the 'subjunctive minor' ('Spring Song'; Beckett 2012: 45).

Beckett's Hayden *hommage* situates itself at a point of pivot, at what the late play *That Time* wryly posits as a 'turning point', as if such a thing, unlikely as it might seem, were possible; and the key sentence in it, the Beckettian signature so to speak, admits as much in its very structure. The sheer casualness of the original French – with 'beaux jours' more an idiom than a statement of fact – cannot seem 'natural' in English, if it is to be 'drawn across' at all, without some reorientation of its terms, as, say, in

It has not yet reached the due date on its salad days, the subject–object dispute.

Or:

The subject–object relation has not yet given up its claim to a place in the sun.

In making such a shift the very act and fact of translation reanimates what might well have seemed tired old issues, here in a context where *ut pictura poesis* may very well be on its last legs. But perhaps Beckett's aim is not so much to end, as to give vent to 'the effort to end' (Beckett 2011a: 303): 'Finished, it's finished, nearly finished, it must be nearly finished' (Beckett 2009d: 6). Well or poorly performed, suitably 'finished' or not, *translatio* transvalues, because it is always in some sense a statement drawn across what it purports to replace. Given that there never could be a perfect epitome of this kind of substitution, a

special charm perhaps attaches to the way Beckett chose to render an utterance
of Madden's at the start of chapter 'IV' of the original (1970) text of *Mercier et
Camier* – 'les beaux jours qui ne risquent heureusement pas de revenir' (Beckett 1970: 58; written in July 1946) – some three decades later as '*the good old
days* happily gone for ever' (Beckett 2010b: 30. My italics); 'now gone for
ever' is to be found attached to 'happy days' in *Murphy* in 1935–36. Beckett
seems to have taken a special pleasure in keeping 'happily' as close as possible
to 'gone for ever' whilst at the same time leaving indeterminate precisely how
good the good old days ever actually were.

★

Words fail me, he said, to disguise what I feel. (Beckett 2010b: 32)

Beckett's Hayden piece does what Beckett can to keep Beckett himself out
of the picture, albeit without achieving the slightest success in what emerges:

On me demande des mots, à moi qui n'en ai plus, plus guère, sur une chose
qui les recuse. Exécutons-nous, exécutons-là . . . Le voilà, cela au moins,
chose faite. (Beckett 1983: 147)

('They're asking me for words, *me*, who hasn't got any, not any more, on a
subject stubbornly resistant to them. Let's give it a go, let's give it a try . . .
There you are, that much said at least, mission impossible accomplished'.
My translation)

Was compliance ever so haunted by an incapacity unable wholly to let go of a
task which can nevertheless be shown as not quite so resistant to treatment as
had apparently been feared? The stance may prompt one to compare the opening self-advertisement of 'And now here am I . . .' in 'Dante . . . Bruno. Vico.
Joyce' in 1929 (Beckett 1983: 19). But back there and back then it was as if
the sheer unlikelihood of what was being asked for gave the enterprise a helpful turn of the screw, whereas here there is greater resistance, more *empêchement*, less chutzpah. Closer in time, and in spirit, is the surprising decision in
a *foirade* (or 'fizzle') which in the event failed to deliver on its own promise
to 'let myself be seen before I'm done' ('Horn came always'; Beckett 2010d:
141). In practice, this turns out to mean that letting oneself be seen is leaving
behind the 'deep marks' of 'what it is to be and to be in face of' (Beckett 1983:
152), and of having been seen, a living concern in the notionally dead world
of 'M' in *Play*. 'Henri Hayden homme-peintre' registers relief at a job done,

however inadequately, with the meremost minimum of self in the mix, but just enough for the 'homme-écrivain' to be felt as something of a presence, perhaps particularly at moments of maximum involvement, which are never merely moments, and which are always seen in flux, in a flurry of movement rather than merely a discrete and momentary instance of occurrence:

> Étrange ordre des choses, fait d'ordre en mal de choses, de choses en mal d'ordre. (Beckett 1983: 147)

> ('A peculiarly natural order, comprising a disorder in things *and* things in disorder'. My translation, my italics)[1]

'Henri Hayden homme-peintre' gives Beckett the (not wholly unexpected) opportunity of exploring an intrinsic disharmony between one thing and another, and indeed between one kind of man and another kind of man, with the writer as it were translating the painter and his paintings in a cross-over from a 'natural' visual medium to a conflicted verbal one. Successfully? No. But by dint of effort – a few false starts, some disorder before an appropriate text emerges – Beckett finds it possible to sign off on a 'chose faite'. No doubt privately Beckett felt that there was a great gulf fixed between, on the one hand, the art seen (and to be seen) and, on the other, the words apparently unable to act adequately on its behalf. Yet insofar as this text can be said to exist as an entity establishing its own integrity and its own identity, a disabling '*empêchement*' has nevertheless permitted a few gasps to make some kind of a mark.

And how else, we might well wonder, when everything has been said and done, and given how prevalent '*empêchement*' is proving to be, is anything at all to be achieved? At least the 'homme-peintre' Henri Hayden can be seen, through however many clouds of witness, before the writer Samuel Beckett can feel it appropriate to put his pen down. The salad days of the subject–object problem have not quite taken their leave – how could they? – but the 'crise' in which they continue to be implicated has at least been tempered. Writer and painter, brothers in arms if not in the same art forms, are 'confondus dans une même inconsistence, ils se désistent de concert' (Beckett 1983: 146): conjoined in a comparable inconsistency, dehiscing in unison. They are 'from nowhere' and they are not 'kith' (Beckett 1983: 149), but they are kin.

These issues can be made to make a kind of sense in themselves, but with Beckett there is always another context which can make 'the lenitive of comment' (Ibid.) possible, if never as necessary as the commentator might wish his own comments to be. I turn now and in conclusion to two other 'lenitives' as found in two other visual (translational) confrontations, neither of which have any obvious connection to Henri Hayden, but both of which are visuals made verbal, bridging what would otherwise leave 'homme-peintre' and 'homme-écrivain' separated from one another in virtual, if not necessarily in any actual, terms.

★

> 'Do you think' she [the Ottolenghi] murmured 'it is absolutely necessary to translate it?' (Beckett, 'Dante and the Lobster', *More Pricks Than Kicks*, 2010: 12)

Almost certainly inspired by the miniature drama in Dresden in which Beckett sees (*stages*, one must say) multiple, fragmentary images of himself in a mirror (Nixon 2011) in 1937 was a passage written almost a decade later, arguably one of the more unusual examples of *translatio* in the whole of Beckett:

> Thus were engendered, though no eyes met, images of extreme complexity enabling each to enjoy himself in three distinct simultaneous versions plus, on a more modest scale, the three versions of self enjoyed by each of the others, namely a total of nine images at first sight irreconcilable, not to mention the confusion of *frustrated excitations jostling on the fringes of the field*. In all a gruesome mess, but instructive, instructive. Add to this the many eyes fastened on the trio and *a feeble idea* may be obtained of what awaits him too smart not to know better, better than to leave his black cell and that harmless lunacy [cf. Horace's '*amabilis insania*'; Beckett 1965: 91], *faint flicker* every other age or so, the consciousness of being, of having been. (Beckett 2010b: 67. My italics)

This makes fictional what in Dresden had been merely personal, and even refines upon the almost Leibnitzian 'infinite number of lines which meet' in the looks exchanged by the academic committee sitting on the case of Louit and Mr Nackybal (Beckett 2009c: 150–5), a better-known but more mechanical application of the same idea.

But once we ourselves *see* this, we are surely duty-bound to recall to the eye of the mind a single paragraph from Beckett's first published novel *Murphy*, almost ideally positioned immediately subsequent to the commentator's notes on the final (in its way, fatal) chess game between Murphy and his alter ego Mr Endon, between the who that remains 'without' and the who whose name in Greek means 'within'. I shall not quote this verbatim, but just the main points, which as it happens – or as it happens again – can in some respects be seen as 'trine':

1. An 'after image' of Mr Endon 'scarcely inferior to the original', an image which fades, allowing Murphy the 'rare postnatal treat' of seeing nothing, 'being the absence (to abuse a nice distinction) not of *percipere* but of *percipi* [= to perceive; to be perceived]' (Beckett 2009e: 154).
2. 'Murphy saw that Mr Endon was missing'[2] (Beckett 2009e: 154).
3. 'seeing himself stigmatised in those eyes that did not see him [Mr Endon's], Murphy heard words demanding so strongly to be spoken that he spoke them . . .' (Beckett 2009e: 156).

This is probably Beckett's most elaborated evocation of the unseen by the seen, at least until the culminating moment in Chapter 13 of the novel, as Mr Kelly watches his kite fly out of sight, only for it to descend upon him in a tangle of lines a few moments later. Should we think of this as the end of one of those 'happy days' which an artisan translator gets to know only too well? Or is there no such thing as a 'due date' for a perception which makes being perceived (as later in *Film*) an agony to be avoided?

★

A devouring of the without by the conditions of the without . . . a being shut away and shut off and turned inward for ever. (Beckett 2011b: 880)

In the third of the *Three Dialogues with Georges Duthuit* Beckett (as 'B') speaks rather dismissively of 'disquisitions on the nature of occasion' as being 'of scant interest', since 'It is obvious that for the artist obsessed with his expressive vocation, anything and everything is doomed to become occasion'; Beckett's hostility towards anyone with an 'expressive vocation' is no doubt in part a function of him recognising that – much as he might wish it were otherwise - he himself is equally 'obsessive' in respect of what cannot be expressed and, as he later makes clear, of 'existence at the expense of all that it excludes' (Beckett 1965: 124). Yet it is in fact far from 'obvious' exactly what Beckett meant here by 'occasion', as he seems to have come to realise when, shortly before he died, he helped Edith Fournier with her translation of the *Three Dialogues* into French. Beckett's concern was to make more 'obvious' than it had been that 'occasion' applies to 'the totality of antecedents from which the painting is supposed to arise' (Beckett 1998: 25), an explanation still typically tentative ('. . . is supposed to . . .'), but nonetheless helpful in the way it clarifies how and why the 'relation' between 'the artist' and 'the occasion' must always be 'unstable' (Beckett 1965: 124). (The emphasis on 'antecedents' resonates with the '*ante*' in the Latin tag from Donatus in the 'Addenda' to *Watt* (Beckett 2009c: 219), but with the focus shifted from what has already been said ('dixerunt') to what can ideally be seen. Every 'occasion' of translation offered Beckett an opportunity to address and reassess the apparent fixity of *a priori* conditions of possibility, the very conditions he had taken – unacknowledged, unsourced and unidentified – from De Sanctis in his *Proust* essay back in 1930 (Beckett 1965: 79), when claiming that whoever lacks the capacity to destroy ('uccidere') reality will also lack the capacity to recreate it. There were two holes to Beckett's burrow from the outset. And he seems to have surmised from the very start, in his essay for Joyce (1929), that any commitment to 'that something itself' (Beckett 1983: 27) meant in practice the surrender of the self who was doing the perceiving of the 'something'.

Beckett could of course have easily enough taken more of a 'round trip' (Beckett 1983: 65), or shouldered arms in the conviction that the struggle never could avail. But the fact that he chose to keep going, to 'call that going, call that on' (Beckett 2010e: 1) is not the least remarkable aspect of an exceptional creative life, unendangered by 'the neatness of identifications', yet very much a prey to every other kind of danger: self-torment, self-destructive impulses, self-estrangement and the conviction that ultimately, alas, there was 'nothing to be done' other than to go on saying as much, 'cela au moins' (Beckett 1983: 147).

From *au plaisir* to *au moins*? Beckett – insofar as he could ever be simply himself – would not have been himself if he had not tended to dismiss all such palaver as par for the course, as in the more or less celebrated case of Mercier and Camier:

> They did not have to face, with greater or lesser success, outlandish ways, tongues, laws, skies, foods, in surroundings little resembling those to which first childhood, then boyhood, then manhood had endured [Fr. 'endurcit'] them. The weather, though often inclement (but they knew no better), never exceeded the limits of the temperate, that is to say of what could still be borne, without danger if not without discomfort, by the average native fittingly clad and shod. With regard to money, if it did not run to first class transport or the palatial hotel, still there *was enough to keep them going, to and fro,* without recourse to alms. It may be said therefore that in this respect too they were fortunate, up to a point.
>
> They had to struggle, but less than many must, less perhaps than most of those who venture forth, driven by a need now clear and now obscure. (Beckett 2010b: 3. My italics)

Enough to keep them (and himself) going, to *and* fro, like Erskine in *Play*. So: fortunate enough . . . if only up to a point.

Notes

1. For a very early example of a natural order treated as peculiar, the largely forgotten squib 'The Possessed' (1931) offers up 'an unprecedented contest – shall we call it a competition? – . . . timed to begin from one minute to another' (Beckett 1983: 99). And, much later, *How It Is* seems to be haunted throughout by the need to 'follow I quote the natural order more or less', despite the speaker being already in part three when 'narrating' part one (Beckett 2009f: 3).
2. An *empêchement* patient of being witnessed!

Works Cited

Samuel Beckett

Beckett, Samuel (1965), *Proust* and *Three Dialogues with Georges Duthuit*, London: John Calder.

Beckett, Samuel (1970), *Mercier et Camier,* Paris: Les Éditions de Minuit.

Beckett, Samuel (1978), *Happy Days/Oh les beaux jours: A Bilingual Edition*, James Knowlson (ed), London: Faber and Faber.

Beckett, Samuel (1983), *Disjecta: Miscellaneous Writings and a Dramatic Fragment*, Ruby Cohn (ed), London: John Calder.

Beckett, Samuel (1992), *Dream of Fair to Middling Women*, Eoin O'Brien and Edith Fournier (eds), Dublin: Black Cat Press.

Beckett, Samuel (1998), *Trois dialogues*, translated by Samuel Beckett and Edith Fournier, Paris: Minuit.

Beckett, Samuel (2009a), *Krapp's Last Tape and Other Shorter Plays*, London: Faber and Faber.

Beckett, Samuel (2009b), *Letters of Samuel Beckett: 1929–1940*, Vol. 1, Martha Dow Fehsenfeld, Lois More Overbeck, Dan Gunn and George Craig (eds), Cambridge, UK: Cambridge University Press.

Beckett, Samuel (2009c), *Watt,* London: Faber and Faber.

Beckett, Samuel (2009d), *Endgame,* London: Faber and Faber.

Beckett, Samuel (2009e), *Murphy*, London: Faber and Faber.

Beckett, Samuel (2009f), *How It Is,* London: Faber and Faber.

Beckett, Samuel (2010a), *Malone Dies,* London: Faber and Faber.

Beckett, Samuel (2010b), *Mercier and Camier,* London: Faber and Faber.

Beckett, Samuel (2010c), *More Pricks Than Kicks,* London: Faber and Faber.

Beckett, Samuel (2010d), *Texts for Nothing,* London: Faber and Faber.

Beckett, Samuel (2010e), *The Unnamable,* London: Faber and Faber.

Beckett, Samuel (2011a), *Letters of Samuel Beckett: 1941–1956*, Vol. 2, George Craig, Martha Fehsenfeld, Daniel Gunn and Lois More Overbeck (eds), Cambridge, UK: Cambridge University Press.

Beckett, Samuel (2011b), 'The New Object', *Modernism/modernity,* 18.4, 878–80.

Beckett, Samuel (2012) *Collected Poems,* Seán Lawlor and John Pilling (eds), London: Faber and Faber.

Beckett, Samuel (2014), *Letters of Samuel Beckett: 1957–1965*, Vol. 3, George Craig, Martha Dow Fehsenfeld, Dan Gunn and Lois More Overbeck (eds), Cambridge, UK: Cambridge University Press.

Beckett, Samuel (2016), *Letters of Samuel Beckett: 1966–1989*, Vol. 4, George Craig, Martha Fehsenfeld, Daniel Gunn and Lois More Overbeck (eds), Cambridge, UK: Cambridge University Press.

Beckett, Samuel, and Alan Schneider (1998), *No Author Better Served: The Correspondence of Samuel Beckett and Alan Schneider*, Maurice Harmon (ed), Cambridge, MA: Harvard University Press.

Manuscripts:

HRHRC MSS 7–2 and 7–4 (*Malone meurt*); TCD MS 9072 fols. 10–13 ('MacGreevy on Yeats'); UoR MS 3000 ('Whoroscope' Notebook).

Other:

Leibniz, Gottfried W. (1898), *The Monadology and Other Philosophical Writings*, translated by Robert Latta (ed), Oxford: Clarendon Press.

Levi, Peter (1985), *A History of Greek Literature*, London: Viking.

Nixon, Mark (2011), *Samuel Beckett's German Diaries 1936–1937*, London: Continuum.

Van Hulle, Dirk and Pim Verhulst (eds) (2017), *The Making of Samuel Beckett's En attendant Godot/Waiting for Godot*, Antwerp: UPA.

11

A Poetics of the Doppelgänger: Beckett as Self-Translator

Dirk Van Hulle

Self-translation in Beckett's works is more than only a linguistic matter. It goes to the heart of an important theme in his oeuvre, the doppelgänger, which is a topic that already appears in some of the pre-war poems. This essay therefore starts by establishing the presence of this theme in Beckett's works and manuscripts; then proceeds to examine the connection with self-translation; and ends with the way Beckett deployed self-translation to develop this theme, thus turning translation into a tool in his poetics of the doppelgänger.

The *Doppelgänger* Motif

In *Damned to Fame*, James Knowlson pointed out that Beckett's decision to start writing in French did not coincide with the end of the Second World War because he already wrote in French before the war (Knowlson 1996). Among Beckett's French poems of 1937–39, published in *Les Temps Modernes* in November 1946 ('Poèmes 37–39' in the *Collected Poems* edited by Seán Lawlor and John Pilling (Beckett 2012)), the poem 'Arènes de Lutèce' works with a technique known as *dédoublement*, as Lawrence E. Harvey points out: 'Much of the pathos and discreet nostalgia that 'Arènes de Lutèce' elicits comes from the two visions made possible by the experience of *dédoublement*' (Harvey 1970: 206). Harvey speaks of a 'split between the two selves', which 'acquires a dualistic resonance' (Harvey 1970: 205) linked to the setting: Lutèce is the old Roman city on which Paris was built, so the arena represents a city within the city, ancient Lutèce and modern Paris. From this temporal perspective, this doubling effect implies that the 'I' never entirely coincides with its past or future self; that the 'we' of the first line (seated above the bleachers) is the 'we-in-the-present' and the other 'we', entering from the Rue des Arènes, is the 'we' of the past or the future:

De là où nous sommes assis plus haut que les gradins
je nous vois entrer du côté de la Rue des Arènes,
hésiter, regarder en l'air, puis pesamment
venir vers nous à travers le sable sombre
                                        (Beckett 2012: 101)

'We' are sitting and we see 'us' coming towards us. 'Nous' are apparently a couple, 'je' and 'elle'. A dog crosses the arena, and 'elle' looks at the dog. When 'elle' turns back, 'je' has already moved on. 'Elle' hesitates, then follows 'me' ('puis me suit'). Then the 'I' has a shiver, because 'je' realises that 'it is I that joins me': 'J'ai un frisson, c'est moi qui me rejoins' (Beckett 2012: 101). The 'je' turns back and sees a face that is referred to by means of a third-person pronoun ('Je me retourne, je suis étonné / de trouver là son triste visage'), which (grammatically) could be – and has been – interpreted as referring to either the female or the male protagonist. Ruby Cohn interprets it as the face of 'elle'; Philip Nikolayev translates it as 'I turn back, amazed / to find there his sad face' (Beckett 2008: 388). This poetic instance is a nice evocation of Arthur Rimbaud's famous line 'Je est un autre', but it is perhaps even a more direct reference to Heinrich Heine's poem 'Der Doppelgänger' (Heine 1827), put to music by Franz Schubert in a *Lied* that was one of Beckett's favourites. The opening stanza evokes a silent night and a house in which the poet's or the first-person narrator's beloved used to live. The second stanza describes the crucial moment:

Da steht auch ein Mensch und starrt in die Höhe
Und ringt die Hände vor Schmerzensgewalt;
Mir graust es, *wenn ich sein Antlitz sehe* –
Der Mond zeigt mir *meine eigne Gestalt*.
                                        (Heine n.d. [1827]: 146)

('A human being is standing there as well, looking up / And wringing his hands out of pain; / I am horrified when I see his face – / The moon shows me my own shape'.) (My translation)

After this scene, the third and last stanza addresses the lookalike directly: 'Du Doppelgänger, du bleicher Geselle!' ('Doppelgänger, pale companion!'), asking him why he imitates the pain (*Liebesleid*) that has tormented him so often in the past. The poem is part of Heine's *Buch der Lieder*, of which Beckett had a copy in his library.[1] Whether Beckett consciously had Heine in mind when he wrote 'Arènes de Lutèce' is hard to tell, but he certainly did have 'Der Doppelgänger' in mind while he was working on other works, notably during the writing process of *Film*. As Rosemary Pountney already pointed out, in the manuscripts, Beckett notes: 'If music unavoidable Schubert's *Doppelgänger*' (*BDMP8* MS-UoR-1227-7-6-1, 06v; Beloborodova 2019: 302; Pountney 1988: 125).

In the context of *Film*, with Object and Eye (O and E) as protagonists and Berkeley's 'esse est percipi' as motto, this choice of music would have made perfect sense, for the German origin of the notion is a footnote on the slightly differently spelled neologism 'Doppeltgänger' in Jean Paul's novel *Siebenkäs* (1796) explaining it as the term for people who see themselves ('So heißen Leute, die sich selber sehen') (Jean Paul 1959: 67). This definition obviously applies to E and O in *Film*.

About the crucial moment in the film, when O sees his own face, looking at E, Beckett specifies in the manuscript that the last image should be a 'non-mirror' image (*BDMP8* MS-UoR-1227-7-6-1, 05v), which suggests that it seems to avoid any direct connection with the 'mirror stage' in Jacques Lacan's sense of the notion (see Brown 2016; 2019). O should be wearing the eye patch on the right eye and should not be smiling, while E should be wearing the eye patch on the left eye, and should be smiling, according to Beckett's notes. E is O's alter ego, or as Beckett puts it in his manuscript: 'E = alter O' (*BDMP8* MS-UoR-1227-7-6-1, 05v), which suggests that, of the two characters, O is the 'ego' and E (Eye) his self-awareness.

Self-Translation

Having established the presence of this theme of the doppelgänger in Beckett's works, the next question is: how does it relate to the act of self-translation? Is it more than just a metaphor for self-translation? In the remainder of this essay, I will try to argue that, as the doppelgänger motif denotes self-perception and self-awareness, self-translation is part of a poetics, a way for Beckett to show rather than tell how this self-awareness works. To examine this phenomenon, I would like to analyse the first instance of Beckett's practice of self-translation, which took place a few years before the Second World War, shortly before Beckett wrote the poem 'Arènes de Lutèce', when he translated his own poem 'Cascando' into German in August 1924, calling it 'Mancando' (Beckett 2012: 351). The occasion for the poem was the brief love Beckett felt for Betty Farley Stockton, an American friend of Mary Manning Howe's. In his German

Diaries (7 February 1937), Beckett refers to this period of his life as 'the Farley episode' (Nixon 2011: 210). In the poem this occasion is presented as follows:

> why not merely the despaired
> of occasion of
> wordshed (Beckett 2012: 57)

In a letter to Thomas MacGreevy (15 July 1936) these opening lines were a bit more explicit and less elliptic:

> Why were you not simply what I despaired for
> an occasion of wordshed. (Beckett quoted in Hunkeler 1999: 34)

The German translation is closer to this version from the letter than to the published version:

> Konntest du nicht
> jene blosse Gelegenheit zum Wortvergiessen,
> jene goldene
> einfach sein? (Beckett 2012: 249)

'Cascando' and 'Mancando' are forms of 'decrescendo'. In that sense, one could read the title as an attempt to write the opposite of James Joyce's literary project, since 'work in progress' was always growing, 'crescendo'. But self-translation, at least at this moment of Beckett's career, was not (yet) a means to reduce the number of words. On the contrary, the English version has 37 lines, the German has 62. What does become more explicit in the German version is Beckett's linguistic scepticism. The English version reads:

> *saying* again
> if you do not teach me I shall not learn
> *saying* again there is a last
> even of last times
> last times of begging
> last times of loving
> of *knowing not knowing pretending*
> > (Beckett 2012: 57. Emphasis added)

In the German version, Beckett indicates explicitly that the words (*Worte*) are grey (*grau*) and stale or vapid (*schal*).

> Die grauen *Worte*
> > Lehrst du mich nicht,
> > Lerne ich nie.

Die schalen *Worte*:
> Es gibt ja ein letztes
> auch von letzten Malen,
> eine letzte letzter Bitten,
> eine letzte letzter Lieben.
> Es kommen doch zu Ende
> *Wissen, Zweifel, Trug*,[2]
>> (Beckett 2012: 250; Hunkeler 1999, 32. Emphasis added)

What Beckett does in the last line of the quotation is interesting against the background of his essay 'Dante . . . Bruno. Vico.. Joyce' (1929). According to Beckett, the English language had been 'abstracted to death' and Joyce had found a way to de-sophisticate it (Beckett 1984: 28). The example he gives is the term 'doubt', which according to him is much more abstract than for instance the German word 'Zweifel', in which you can still recognise 'two' (*zwei*), as in being in two minds. In *Finnegans Wake*, Joyce makes the concept of 'doubt' less abstract by means of the expression 'in twosome twiminds', thus letting the language show rather than tell: 'Here, form *is* content, content *is* form', Beckett famously commented: 'His work is not *about* something, *it is that something itself*' (Beckett 1984: 27). Beckett may have tried very hard to distinguish himself from Joyce, but he has always appreciated this form of literary enactment in Joyce and never stopped finding alternative ways to apply it in his own works. At first sight, the German self-translation of 'Cascando' is not exactly the most successful attempt in this regard. He uses one abstract concept after the other: 'Worte . . . Worte . . . Wissen, Zweifel, Trug', whereas the English version uses verbs: 'saying . . . saying . . . knowing not knowing pretending'. The 'doubt' is evoked by 'knowing not knowing' – another solution to de-abstract the notion of doubt, different from Joyce's, but with the same effect: the text is not *about* something, it is that something itself. At first sight the enactment is better in the English version than in the German self-translation.

But if we take a closer look at the German text, Beckett does apply a similar technique of enactment. In an early version of the English poem, in a letter to MacGreevy, the text reads:

> the churn of stale words dans the heart again
> love churn of old thud of the plunger
> pestling the
> inalterable whey
> of words
>> (quoted in Hunkeler 1999: 36)

The German text repeats the word 'Worte' three times in short succession, thus showing rather than telling how empty these words are:

> Es dreschen des Herzens Flegel die faulen *Worte*,
> die schalen *Worte*,
> die unablässige
> Spreu von *Worten*.

The words enact the beating of the flail on the chaff. In his translation, Beckett changes the image of the English version (churning) into a totally different metaphor: the words are the empty chaff, and no matter how long and how hard you keep flailing, there is not a single grain in them anymore. As a result, the images in the two languages are different, but what they have in common is the insistence of the beating or the thuds of the plunger. The repetition of 'Worte . . . Worte . . . Worten' enacts this beating. In the published English text, Beckett eventually chose to use words to a similar effect, but instead of the 'words' it is 'love' that is repeated three times to enact the thuds of the plunger, changing 'love churn of old' (see above) into 'love love love':

> the churn of stale words dans the heart again
> *love love love* thud of the plunger
> pestling the unalterable
> whey of words

> (Beckett 2012: 57)

All these variants create an interesting tension between the English and the German self-translation, the so-called 'original' and its *Doppelgänger*.

Self-translation as Enactment of the Doppelgänger Motif

The next step in the development of Beckett's poetics of self-translation was that he used the act of self-translation to enact the theme of the doppelgänger. To some extent, this theme was already introduced in Beckett's collection of poems *Echo's Bones and Other Precipitates*. Thomas Hunkeler reads the myth as an allegory of repetition, a reflection both of and on reflection, 'une réflexion de la réflexion en même temps qu'une réflexion sur la réflexion' (Hunkeler 1997: 162–3), a reflection on the same and on the other. Both these mythical figures question identity. Narcissus's mirror image in the water is only an illusion and therefore does not stand for the self's coincidence with itself, but actually undermines it. Similarly, the slightly distorted repetition of Echo's words is not emblematic of self-identity but undermines it.

Not only Beckett's poems but also his stories and novels are often narratives of non-identity. While Daniel C. Dennett argues that telling stories is 'our fundamental tactic of self-protection, self-control, and self-definition' (Dennett 1993: 418), and Jonathan Gottschall claims that storytelling – as 'a crucial evolutionary adaptation' – 'allows us to experience our lives as coherent, orderly, and meaningful' (Gottschall 2012: 102), Beckett does not see this as a reason to commend the human storytelling impulse. Instead, he constantly questions it, making it fail to render identity coherent or meaningful. More often than not, his narratives constitute a repudiation, rather than an affirmation, of identity. For this literary project, he often uses philosophies of identity as a scaffolding, which he then undermines. One of these philosophies of identity is being thematised in *Murphy* through Bishop Berkeley's motto: 'esse est percipi (aut percipere)' – to be is to be perceived (or to perceive). According to Berkeley, whatever exists, only exists because it is perceived by a mind – a philosophy that is alluded to in *Murphy*, when, at the Magdalen Mental Mercyseat, Murphy attains a state of bliss and begins 'to see nothing, that colourlessness which is such a rare postnatal treat, being the absence (to abuse a nice distinction) not of *percipere* but *percipi*' (Beckett 2009a: 154). He then looks Mr Endon in the eyes: 'Murphy kneeled beside the bed, . . . took Mr Endon's head in his hands and brought the eyes to bear on his, or rather his on them . . . *Approaching his eyes still nearer Murphy could see* the red frills of mucus, a large point of suppuration at the root of an upper lash, the filigree of veins like the Lord's Prayer on a toenail and in the cornea, horribly reduced, obscured and distorted, by *his own image*' (Beckett 2009a: 155–6) (Emphasis added). The image of seeing oneself in another eye is further developed in an entry in Beckett's German Diaries, written in early January 1937:

> When I take off my glasses and bring my face as close to the mirror as my nose permits, then I see myself in my right eye, or alternatively my reflection's left eye, half profile left, and inversely. If I squint to the left I am full face in left eye, and inversely. But to be full face at once in the mirror + in my eye, that seems an optical impossibility. But it is not necessary after all to take off my glasses. By keeping them I see myself 3 times at once, in the mirror, in my glasses and in my eyes. (German Diaries, 3 January 1937; Nixon 2009: 39)

After his journey through Germany, Beckett developed the doppelgänger theme in several novels and plays, by means of pairs of characters: Murphy and Mr Endon; Watt and Sam; Mercier et Camier; Didi and Gogo; Molloy and Moran. The theme becomes less obvious in *Malone Dies*, because Malone is really alone, me-alone. So, at first sight, this seems to be a comforting narrative of identity, when the ego coincides with itself. But even when Beckett's characters are alone, they start doubling themselves. Thus, Malone starts talking about Sapo. After a while, he cannot call him Sapo anymore, and so he tries to find another name, a name that needs to start with an M. Eventually M will become Macmann, but in the manuscripts Malone cannot immediately find a name (*BDMP5*, FN2, MS-HRC-SB-7-4, 37r). Similarly, a few pages earlier in the manuscript, when Malone is about to mention his own name for the first time, Beckett does not have one for him yet, he only knows that it needs to start with an M (*BDMP5*, FN2, MS-HRC-SB-7-4, 29r). Both instances are marked by a hiatus in the manuscript. In other words, Beckett creates a character, M, who eventually becomes Malone, who in his turn creates a character, M, who eventually becomes Macmann, his doppelgänger.

In the Sapo story, the French manuscripts speak of the Louis family, whereas in the English version they are called the Lamberts. The intertextual reference to Balzac's novel *Louis Lambert* only works when the original and the self-translation are juxtaposed. It is not unimportant to know that the pun was created only late in the translation process, so it can be read as a deliberate commentary on the status of Beckett's self-translation (Van Hulle and Verhulst 2017: 270). In the early manuscript fragment of his English translation (held at Trinity College, Dublin), Beckett still used the name 'Louis' for the family of peasants that Sapo visits from time to time. He did not change their name to 'Lamberts' until the typescript stage. Since the intertextual pun only works when you take the French and the English text together, this suggests that the one is incomplete without the other. As a result, *Malone Dies* becomes the doppelgänger of *Malone meurt*. And in the manuscript, this Doppelgänger motif is also developed on a smaller scale. A jotting at the back of the second notebook indicates the relationship between Lemuel (who at that point is still called Samuel) and Macmann, by comparing it to the relationship between Murphy and Mr Endon:

Samuel: ~~Macm~~ Macmann : : Murphy : Endon (*BDMP5* FN2, 152r).

And when the patients of the asylum where Lemuel works are enumerated, they are presented as pairs:

Murphy [who was previously paired to Mr Endon; see above]
Watt – Quin
Mercier – Camier
Molloy – Moran
~~Macmann~~
Malone – Macmann
               (*BDMP5* FN2, f. 100v)

This list appears underneath an addition to an interesting passage where Samuel (Lemuel) goes to the kitchen with a bucket. Beckett changed this into two buckets 'avec ~~un~~ les deux seaux' (*BDMP5* FN2, MS-HRC-SB-7-4, f. 101r) and added on the verso: 'l'un ~~dans~~ enfermé dans l'autre' (100v). The *dédoublement* of the characters is similar to the situation in 'Arènes de Lutèce': the bucket within the bucket, the city within the city, the ancient Lutèce in the modern Paris. But this image does not fit the act of self-translation. A self-translation is not one bucket inside another; it is one thing next to or in relation to another. As Brian Fitch has argued, the traditional relationship of 'dependence' between a translation and its source text becomes a relationship of 'interdependence' in the case of self-translation (Fitch 1988: 107). A more fitting image is that of the doppelgänger in its original definition: 'So heißen Leute, die sich selber sehen'. The self-translation looks at the so-called original, but as soon as something changes in the self-translation, the original also becomes dependent on the self-translation: the Louis are not just the Louis anymore, they are the counterpart to the Lamberts, and only together do they become an intertextual allusion.

Some fifteen years after the writing of *Malone meurt* and twenty-five years after *Murphy*, starting again from Berkeley's 'esse est percipi' motif, Beckett described the doppelgänger motif when he explained the plot of *Film* to Barney Rosset:

> The point of departure is the old metaphysical doctrine to the effect that being consists in being perceived and that without some perceiving intelligence there would be nothing . . . I often imagine a naive human being involved in [this] situation, so unphilosophically minded as to take it literally, seeking ingenuously to be as nothing by withdrawal within a space stripped of all perceiving organs and running foul of himself as perceiving organ . . . It is therefore the old theme of *split personality*, . . . *between conscious and non-conscious being*, between the *being that is perceived* and the *being that perceives*. And in order that this may be shown (on a screen) the two halves are given shape, . . . in the form of a *fleeing* object and a *pursuing* eye. (21 June 1963; Beckett 2014a: 549–50)

Described in this way, Beckett's explanation of the tension between perceiving and perceivedness sounds like the visual transposition of a musical fugue, which suggests another element that plays a role in Heine's 'Der Doppelgänger': time. The perceiver or 'alter O' perceives 'O' from a point in time that is always just a bit 'too late' as it were to coincide with him.

This factor of time also plays a role in Beckett's 'Film Vidéo-Cassette' project (University of Reading MS 2928, ff. 13r-14v; written in Paris in November

1972), in which the protagonists are called 'F1' and 'F2' (Nixon 2009: 32). Ruby Cohn has given the piece the title 'F1 et F2' (Cohn 2001: 321). The first note on the manuscript specifies the doppelgänger motif: 'F2 = F1? + tard' (F2 = F1? later). The project consists of two films. Film I shows a woman (F1) sitting on a two-seat chair and waiting (apparently for someone), but in vain. In Film II, F1's 'alter O' (F2) watches a video recording of Film I. This is almost a literal evocation of what Daniel C. Dennett calls the 'Cartesian Theatre', his caricature of Descartes' explanation of consciousness. According to Descartes, the soul interacts with the body through the brain's pineal gland, which Dennett presents as a theatre in the brain where a small homunculus observes all the sensory data projected on a screen. The idea of such a homunculus inside the skull is visualised in one of Beckett's doodles in the manuscript of *L'Innommable* (*BDMP2* FN2, MS-HRC-SB-4-1, f. 21r). The homunculus hypothesis, however, raises the question how this homunculus's consciousness works; according to the same logic, it would require an even smaller homunculus in its brain, who watches the 'film' in its turn, and so on *ad infinitum*. This 'ad infinitum' aspect is also suggested in the 'Film Vidéo-Cassette' sketch, for towards the end Beckett introduces 'F3': 'Egalement possible F3 regardant F2 regardant F1 avec 3 GP [gros plans] juxtaposés à la fin' (quoted in Nixon 2009: 40). As Nixon notes, the 'key moment' (Nixon 2013: 184) is when F2 stops the video of 'Film I' during a close-up of F1. At that moment, 'Film II' shows a close-up of F2 watching a close-up of F1, which turns into a juxtaposition of the two in a mirror (UoR MS 2928, 14r).

    I propose to read this sketch against the background of Heine's 'Der Doppelgänger'. The lookalike mimics the first-person narrator's 'Liebesleid', literally: 'love pain'. This 'heartache' is also the theme of a sonnet by Louise Labé, the last stanza of which appears in the bottom margin of folio 14r of the 'Film Vidéo-Cassette' sketch. The sonnet opens with the line 'Ô longs désirs, ô espérances vaines' ('O long desires, o vain hopes'). This hope is thematised in Film I and its vanity in Film II. While F2 is an isolated figure sitting on a single chair, F1 is still hopefully sitting on a two-seater. F2 has abandoned all hope, it seems; she locks the door, window and shutters, whereas F1 leaves the door and window ajar, albeit only just: 'Porte entrouverte (à peine)'. This 'à peine' echoes the 'peines' (heartache) in the second stanza of Labé's 'Sonnet 3': 'Ô cruautés, ô durtés inhumaines, / . . . / Estimez-vous croître encore mes *peines*?' ('Oh cruelties, oh harsh inhuman rigour, / . . . / have you resolved to make my burdens bigger?') (Labé 1983). This is the final question before the volta, which indicates that it is impossible for Eros to add more pain to her heartache, followed by the final stanza, which Beckett noted in the bottom margin:

Car je suis tant navrée en toutes
parts que plus en moi une nouvelle plaie
pour m'empirer ne pourrait trouver place.
(University of Reading MS 2928, f. 14r; Nixon 2013: 186)

For now I bleed so much in every part
that should he seek again to strike me hard
he'll find there's no place left to wound me worse.
(Labé, tr. Peter Low 2005)

Labé's French term for 'wound me worse' is 'm'empirer', similar to the 'wors-ening' principle that underlies the dynamics of *Worstward Ho*, the work Beckett famously claimed he could not translate. Here, the doppelgänger motif is no longer directly related to heartache, but certainly to pain in general. Not unlike the 'Film Vidéo-Cassette' sketch, based on Labé, *Worstward Ho* also starts from an intertextual reference: Shakespeare's line 'The worst is not / So long as one can say, This is the worst', excerpted from *King Lear* in his 'Sottisier' Notebook (University of Reading MS 2910). Whereas Labé's son-net concludes by stating that the current situation is the worst, impossible to worsen ('empirer'), Shakespeare's line challenges this statement by giving it a self-perceptive twist. The utterer becomes his own hearer, as in *Company*, where 'Hearer' (A) plus 'Inventor' (B) plus 'Voice' (V) equal Company (C): 'C = A + V + B' (UoR MS 1822, f. 20v), or as in its precursor 'VERBATIM' (the initial plan of which states regarding the speech by A, overheard by B and described to C, that A, B, and C are one and the same); or as in *Ohio Impromptu* (whose stage directions specify that Listener and Reader should be as alike in appearance as possible). As soon as one claims this is the worst, self-perception kicks in, reminding oneself that as long as one is still able to utter this thought, it can still get worse. Instead of saying that explicitly, however, Beckett chooses to show it, by creating a doppelgänger for the utterance. Even though he claimed that he could not translate *Worstward Ho* he did produce a doppelgänger, a translation of a 'sample' assembled with fragments from paragraphs 19, 20 and the end:

> Bit by bit an old man and child. In the dim void bit by bit an old man and child. Any other would do as ill. // Hand in hand with equal plod they go. In the free hands – no. Free empty hands. Backs turned both bowed with equal plod they go . . . Slowly with never a pause plod on and never recede. [§19–20] . . . Nohow less. Nohow worse. Nohow naught. Nohow on. // Said nohow on. (Beckett 2009b: 84; 103)

Peu à peu un vieil homme et un enfant. Dans l'ombre vide peu à peu un
vieil homme et un enfant. N'importe quoi d'autre ferait aussi mal l'affaire.
Main dans la main ils vont tant bien que mal d'un pas égal. Dans les mains
libres – non. ~~Dans~~^{Vides} les mains libres ~~rien~~. Dos courbés vus de dos ils
vont tant bien que mal d'un pas égal. Lentement sans pause tant bien que
mal s'en vont et jamais ne s'éloignent. Moins ne se peut. Pire ne se peut.
Néant ne se peut. Plus loin ne se peut. Dire plus loin ne se peut. (FSB,
16BKT/9/0; Van Hulle 2015: 58; Cordingley 2017)[3]

He sent it to Jérôme Lindon with a note, presenting it as a sample ('échantillon')
of what he was sparing him ('ce dont je vous fais grâce'; FSB, 16BKT/9/0; Van
Hulle 2015: 58; Cordingley 2017). Whereas the English text ends with a past
participle, suggesting that the worst (nohow on) has been 'said', the French
doppelgänger uses the infinitive, implying a self- reflexive mood, an 'F2' looking at the 'film' of an 'F1', who claims this is the worst and observing that what
he is doing is just 'saying again' as it were (as in the poem 'Cascando'), saying
that it is the worst – not 'said nohow on' but 'saying nohow on'.

Conclusion

The French term for 'self-translation' is 'autotraduction'. It is sometimes translated as 'autotranslation' (Grutman 1998), but this notion also refers to 'automatic
translation' or 'machine translation', which makes it less appropriate for a discussion of Beckett's poetics of self-translation. Moreover, as Anthony Cordingley
notes, the term 'self-translation' denotes 'an exploratory, creative act, a positive
discovery or negotiation of multiple "selves", even the emancipation of one or
many identities within the self' (Cordingley 2013: 81). As this essay has tried to
show, Beckett's act of self-translation problematises these notions of 'identity' and
'self', especially in the manuscript of *Malone meurt*. Moreover, this manuscript is
followed by a sort of 'Coda', a two-page draft of a text that never made it into
publication. A first-person narrator expresses the wish to define himself 'totally':
'Si je pouvais me définir totalement, en tant que corps se décomposant . . . je
connaîtrai[s] l'étendue de mon exil' ('If . . . I could define myself completely, as
the body decomposing . . . I would know the extent of my exile'; *BDMP5* FN2,
f. 111r). The first-person narrator subsequently tries to define himself: 'But I
myself have always been the one I am nostalgic for, who has never had language
or consciousness' (*BDMP5* FN2, f. 111r), 'which gives an annoying impression of
2 people . . . whereas it is just one person present in two irreconcilable varieties,
that of the life which I know, badly but well enough, and that which the habit
of life prevents me from naming . . . and which in the life that I know is called
death' (*BDMP5* FN2, f. 112r).

Here, the 'fugue' between perceiving and perceivedness is connected to being and non-being. The coda is 'about' *dédoublement*: one person presented as two persons, not unlike the confidants in Racine, which – according to Beckett's lectures at TCD – served to express 'division in mind of antago-nists' (Rachel Burrows' notes, TCD MIC 60; Le Juez 2008: 59): the division that is implied when people see themselves, the division that is implied in doubt, *Zweifel*, being 'in twosome twiminds'. In a manner that is quite dif-ferent from Joyce's, Beckett eventually found his own way to enact this idea by self-translating his own texts. As a consequence, his twin texts are not *about* self-perception, they *are* self-perception. Whereas the Coda tells us about *dédoublement*, the self-translations take this a step further; they show it at work; they are *dédoublement*.

The Coda's attempted self-definition is preceded by a so-called 'image', the image of a set of terms covering a space that had better remained blank: 'Image: termes . . . impropres venant se placer là où . . . un blanc ferait mieux l'affaire' ('Image: inadequate terms coming to place themselves where a blank would be better suited'). Since this is about self-definition, the *image* of the self turns out to be never 'still'. It is always stirring. This instability is reflected in *Stirrings Still*, Beckett's penultimate text, which he wrote in two languages alternately, translating himself while he was writing it (*BDMP1* MS-UoR-2934). The text again uses the technique of *dédoublement*: 'One night as he sat at his table head on hands *he saw himself* rise and go'. (Beckett 2009b: 107). As soon as this idea was written down in English, Beckett turned around his notebook and started his French translation from the back. And throughout this text about an old man who sees himself rise and go there are slight differences between the English and the French that make the 'image' stir continuously, turning it into what Beckett called 'a *fleeing* object and a *pursuing* eye' (cf. supra).

The notion of the fugal self-translation, which – like Zeno of Elea's hare that can never catch up with the turtle – is always just 'too late' to coincide with 'O' (as in the 'Original'). In this sense, Beckett's self-translations are much more than only a linguistic matter. They enact a central theme in Beckett's poetics, the theme of human self-awareness, in a most uncanny or *unheimlich* way, which can best be captured in a multilingual edition that presents the self-translations as an inherent part of Beckett's oeuvre. For Beckett's works never fully coincide with themselves and are crucially not entirely at home in any language. If they are 'at home' at all, it is only in the sense of being 'heimlich'. As Sigmund Freud notes, 'heimlich' can mean homely but also secretive. It denotes something that is enclosed in a 'home' and therefore kept from sight, so that others do not get to know about it, thus becoming 'uncanny': in other words, 'heimlich is a word the meaning of which develops towards an ambivalence until it finally coin-cides with its opposite, unheimlich' (Freud 1917–19: 226). That is the image evoked by Heine's 'Der Doppelgänger': the home (*heim*) or house in which the beloved used to live becomes *unheimlich* through a process of self-perception and *dédoublement*. Instead of telling about the way in which self-perception constantly creates an alter ego or 'alter O', Beckett's self-translations show how this mechanism works. This sustained enactment of self-perception is a fundamental aspect of Beckett's poetics of the doppelgänger.

Notes

1. *Beckett Digital Library*, BDL, https://www.beckettarchive.org/library/ HEI-BUC.html
2. The text of the *Collected Poems* (Faber 2012) omits the word 'letzte'. The typescript at Dartmouth College, on which Thomas Hunkeler's transcription in *Samuel Beckett Today/Aujourd'hui* 8 (Hunkeler 1999, 32) is based, reads 'eine letzte letzter Bitten'.
3. In Edith Fournier's translation this corresponds with: 'Peu à peu un vieil homme et un enfant. Dans la pénombre vide peu à peu un vieil home et un enfant. N'importe quoi d'autre ferait aussi mal l'affaire. // Main dans la main ils vont tant mal que mal d'un pas égal. Dans les mains libres – non. Vides les mains libres. Tous deux dos courbé vus de dos ils vont tant mal que mal d'un pas égal . . . Lentement sans pause tant mal que mal s'en vont et jamais ne s'éloignent. . . . Plus mèche moins. Plus mèche pire. Plus mèche néant. Plus mèche encore. // Soit dit plus mèche encore' (Beckett 1991: 14–15; 62).

Works Cited

Beckett, Samuel (1972), [manuscript] 'Film Vidéo-Cassette projet', Beckett International Foundation, The University of Reading, UoR MS 2928.

Beckett, Samuel (1984), *Disjecta*, Ruby Cohn (ed), New York: Grove Press.

Beckett, Samuel (1991), *Cap au pire*, translated by Édith Fournier, Paris: Les Éditions de Minuit.

Beckett, Samuel (2008), 'Arènes De Lutèce', translated by Philip Nikolayev, *Poetry* 191.5, 388–90, www.jstor.org/stable/20608015 (Accessed on 24 November 2019).

Beckett, Samuel (2009a), *Murphy*, J.C.C. Mays (ed), London: Faber and Faber.

Beckett, Samuel (2009b), *Company, Ill Seen Ill Said, Worstward Ho, Stirrings Still*, Dirk Van Hulle (ed), London: Faber and Faber.

Beckett, Samuel (2012), *Collected Poems*, Seán Lawlor and John Pilling (eds), London: Faber and Faber.

Beckett, Samuel (2014a), *The Letters of Samuel Beckett: 1957–1965,* Vol. 3, George Craig Martha Dow Fehsenfeld, Dan Gunn and Lois More Overbeck (eds), Cambridge, UK: Cambridge University Press.

Beckett, Samuel (2014b), *L'Innommable/The Unnamable: A Digital Genetic Edition, Beckett Digital Manuscript Project* 2, Dirk Van Hulle and Shane Weller (eds), Brussels: University Press Antwerp, www.beckettarchive.org. Referred to as BDMP2.

Beckett, Samuel (2018), *Malone meurt/Malone Dies: Digital Genetic Edition, Beckett Digital Manuscript Project* 5, Dirk Van Hulle, Pim Verhulst and Vincent Neyt (eds), Brussels: University Press Antwerp, www.beckettarchive.org. Referred to as BDMP5.

Beckett, Samuel (2020), *Play/Comédie* and *Film: A Digital Genetic Edition, Beckett Digital Manuscript Project* 8, Olga Beloborodova and Vincent Neyt (eds), Brussels: University Press Antwerp, www.beckettarchive.org. Referred to as BDMP8.

Beloborodova, Olga (2019), *The Making of Samuel Beckett's 'Play'/'Comédie' and 'Film'*, London: Bloomsbury.

Brown, Llewellyn (2016), *Beckett, Lacan and the Voice*, Stuttgart: Ibidem.

Brown, Llewellyn (2019), *Beckett, Lacan and the Gaze*, Stuttgart: Ibidem.

Cohn, Ruby (2001), *A Beckett Canon*, Ann Arbor: University of Michigan Press.

Cordingley, Anthony (2013), 'The Passion of Self-Translation: A Masocritical Perspective', in Anthony Cordingley (ed), *Self-Translation: Brokering Originality in Hybrid Culture*, London: Bloomsbury, pp.81–94.

Cordingley, Anthony (2017), 'Samuel Beckett and Édith Fournier Translating the "Untranslatable" *Worstward Ho*', *Journal of Beckett Studies,* 26.2, 239–56.

Dennett, Daniel C. (1993), *Consciousness Explained*, London: Penguin.

Fitch, Brian T. (1988), *Beckett and Babel: An Investigation into the Status of the Bilingual Work*, Toronto, Buffalo, London: University of Toronto Press.

Freud, Sigmund (1917–19), 'The Uncanny', in: *The Standard Edition of the Complete Woks of Sigmund Freud*, Vol. 17, translated by James Strachey, in collaboration with Anna Freud, assisted by Alix Strachey and Alan Tyson, London: The Hogarth Press and the Institute of Psychoanalysis, pp. 218–53.

Gottschall, Jonathan (2012), *The Storytelling Animal: How Stories Make Us Human*, New York: Houghton Mifflin Harcourt.

Grutman, Rainier (1998), 'Autotranslation', in M. Baker (ed), *Routledge Encyclopedia of Translation Studies*, London & New York: Routledge, pp. 17–20.

Harvey, Lawrence E. (1970), *Samuel Beckett: Poet and Critic*, Princeton, NJ: Princeton University Press.

Heine, Heinrich (n.d. [1827]), *Buch der Lieder*, Leipzig: Insel Verlag.

Hunkeler, Thomas (1997), *Echos de l'ego dans l'œuvre de Samuel Beckett*, Paris: L'Harmattan.

Hunkeler, Thomas (1999), '"Cascando" de Samuel Beckett', *Samuel Beckett Today/ Aujourd'hui*, 8, 27–42.

Jean Paul (1959), *Sämtliche Werke*, 10 Bände in 2 Abteilungen, Vol. I/2, *Siebenkäs; Flegeljahre*, Norbert Miller (ed), München: Carl Hanser Verlag.

Knowlson, James (1996), *Damned to Fame: The Life of Samuel Beckett*, London: Bloomsbury.

Labé, Louise (1983), *Oeuvres poétiques*, Paris: Gallimard.

Labé, Louise (2005), *The 25 Sonnets of Louise Labé*, translated by Peter Low (Brindin Press), Virtual Book 37, http://www.brindinpress.com/vb37cove. htm. (Accessed 6 December 2019).

Le Juez, Brigitte (2008), *Beckett before Beckett*, London: Souvenir Press.

Nixon, Mark (2009), 'Samuel Beckett's "Film Vidéo-Cassette projet"', *Journal of Beckett Studies*, 18.1–2, 32–43.

Nixon, Mark (2011), *Samuel Beckett's German Diaries 1936–1937*, London: Bloomsbury.

Nixon, Mark (2013), 'Samuel Beckett, Video Artist', in Peter Fifield and David Addyman (eds), *Samuel Beckett: Debts and Legacies: New Critical Essays*, London: Bloomsbury, pp. 177–190.

Pountney, Rosemary (1988), *Theatre of Shadows: Samuel Beckett's Drama, 1956–1976*, Gerrards Cross: Colin Smythe.

Van Hulle, Dirk (2015), 'Translation and Genetic Criticism: Genetic and Editorial Approaches to the "untranslatable" in Joyce and Beckett', *Linguistica Anverpiensia New Series – Themes in Translation Studies*, 14, 40–53.

Van Hulle, Dirk, and Pim Verhulst (2017), *The Making of Malone meurt/Malone Dies,* Brussels: UPA.

12

Tuning Absent Pianos: *Watt* and the Poetics of Translation

Fábio de Souza Andrade

Le devoir et la tâche d'un écrivain sont ceux d'un traducteur.

Marcel Proust

The duty and the task of a writer (not an artist, a writer) are those of a translator.

Proust (translated, commented and quoted by Beckett)

In Beckett's works, missed encounters are often the expression of an unbridgeable abyss between the world and the words, the body and the mind, presence and representation, as different examples such as the asynchronous timetable in *Mercier et Camier* or the always postponed meeting with Godot attest. They point out how '*empêchement*' should replace positive '*correspondence*' in Beckettian poetics as a whole, translation included. In *Watt*, one may find many allegorical expressions of this permanent gap, so significant in his work, as well as in translation's tasks and objectives. I will concentrate particularly in the Galls' piano tuning episode – and the semantic crisis it causes – as a critical metaphor of the limits and possibilities of translation in a Beckettian perspective.

The novel provides a meticulous consideration of the fissure that divides the character's memories of the Galls' visit to Knott's house – amounting to a flow of vividly recollected perceptions – from his frustrated efforts, a posteriori, to attribute a recognisable verbal shape and a stable linguistic translation to such an elusive and magmatic mnemonic material. My concern is to examine how far this passage in the novel may be read as a 'philosophical image' (cf. Anthony Uhlman 2006), of a particularly significant instance of 'misencounters' in Beckett's works, deeply related to other crucial Beckettian poetical and philosophical issues, such as his long term defence of a non-relational art, not only in his postwar art criticism, but in early writings as well, or the central place translation occupies in his creative process.

Beckett's readers deal with what might be called a 'poetics of appointed misencounters', a route of programmed near collisions, on which his notion of an unbridgeable gap between perception and expression, language and experience, subject and object, body and mind, present and past, presence and representation builds up. Beckett's work carries from birth an inner call for permanent mobility. Such a dominant drive, both translation itself and Beckett's own complex and close connection with translation do emulate and mirror. The refusal of neat distinctions and a permanent instability of limits play an essential role in the forge of his personal path and there is no way to dissociate them from the just mentioned gap. His writing process is one of continuous recreation, autographic self-rectification, a persistent trait that can be grasped in many different layers, all of them connected to the translation process: in his very singular routine of self-translation, from English to French, from French to English, and back, which bilingualism imposes; in the plurality of scenic translations to which his drama, deprived of precise historical references, invites to; in his works' openness to intersemiotic translation, leading to a free stray between different arts and supports, from prose to stage, from stage to screen, and so on; in his strained-to-the-limit language, consistently eroding conventions and traditions of each new genre it adopts; in the way his works naturally appeal to remote cultural contexts, implying new receptions, new Becketts for each new translation.

Already in his youth essay on *Proust*, the determinations of habit and memory (linguistic habits, for sure, but also the artistic conventions and genre traditions), challenged, are central in the formulation of a Beckettian poetics, Bergson and Schopenhauer resonating in many concrete aspects of the further development of his work. Beckett's faith in the impossibility of the harmonic correspondence, hand and glove, between names and signs, on the one hand, and the experienced world, on the other, originates from this early convincement, as does his urgent need of a new form of art – the so called 'literature of the unword'. What he has in mind is a new kind of mimesis, which not only takes seriously the obstruction and opacity that lie beneath any expressive gesture, but also leaves behind the illusion of an unlikely Baudelairean forest of symbols, aiming at an art that is no longer under the spell of improbable correspondences and echoes, nor of the feasible.

From the very beginning, Beckett refuses an epiphanic aesthetics as well as the totalising and positive aspects of the Proustian madeleines, considerably distant from his personal artistic goals. Those are better understood in the neighbourhood of the antinomic 'expression that there is nothing to express, nothing with which to express, nothing from which to express, no power to express, no desire to express, together with the obligation to express', as he phrases it in his *Three Dialogues* with Duthuit (Beckett 2006c: 556). Evolving from the modernist ruptures, his project reacts to the figurative, to romantic tonalism, to finalist realism, but refrains from any loud and affirmative kind of protest, choosing rather to resist by desistance, by the potency of no. In one word, the task is to arrange a paradoxical poetics of impediments, which comes true only by means of a patient and attentive, a caring reflection on the nature (and naturality) of the obstacles, the noises, the friction that language, as imperfect adjustment, will always produce.[1]

If language is better used when ill-used, the keyword in Beckett must be impasse and, in this sense, his own work provides us with many extremely useful, self-descriptive critical metaphors, as the mentioned appointed misencounter, an emblematic deviation in which chance plays a minor role. Self-conscient and self-imposed, the apparently restrictive becomes a delivering starting point for creation, deliberately accepted, even looked for. As the well-known and significative, famous or infamous, 1937 German Letter to Axel Kaun states, the artist resembles the mathematician discarding successive methods on his way, only because he is absolutely sure that the perfect match of subject and object is a lie, ignorance of how deeply both are submitted to time's changing action.

Risky as a periodisation of Beckett's work may be, there seems to be reasons to speak of at least three distinct moments in his making of as an author, considering the different literary fronts he elects to fight in as well, as the different grades of radicalism in dismissing traditional conventions he adopts, namely:

1. The years of heroic modernism carrying the sign of parodic writing, dominated by an intertextual irony contesting naturalist tradition, embodied in its most representative form, the novel, and relying on an omniscient and witty third person narrator;
2. The postwar period, when the French novels announce a deliberately simplified literary form, an inner deconstruction of narrative prose and modern drama to the very bottom of their structural elements; this radical intratextual erosion comes together with a first-person narrator, in act and self-conscious;
3. A late style, based on a linguistic turn, a critical reconstruction of the representational drive, founded on a new conscience of the propositional structure of reality and a new kind of mimesis implied; this effort is brought to the extreme in the invention of an intensely self-reflective language, paired by a 'last person' narrator, and hybrid minimal texts, in-between genres.

Throughout this development, the multiple forms the recurrent and inevitable appointed 'misencounters' assume highlight a common core of Beckett's negative poetics, bringing together the intent of undoing and the praise of the unfinishable in his art. Logically and chronologically, the first and most elementary variation is the physical divergence, prevailing in the early novels and plays, visible in the strict domain of comical disagreements between act and will, body and mind. This physical inconsistency rules the routines and choreographs the unusual gestures and strange attitudes of his protagonists, unable to anchor in stable plans their spatial journeys.

If the best known instance is the unaccomplished meeting with Godot, the same dynamics leads also the (unsuccessful) generalised quest for Murphy in Beckett's London; the elaborate physics involved in Watt's peculiar gait or in the intriguing alternatives that conduct his entering Mr Knott's house; the ruinous progress of Molloy to his mother's room, paralysed leg, dismantling bike, crawling through the forest included; not to mention *Quad*'s late choreography, bodies on the verge of collision, deviating at the last moment, avoiding each other and the forbidden centre, or Buster Keaton worries in *Film*, dealing with incoming and outgoing cats and dogs, in his solipsist refuge.

The asynchronous timetable of Mercier's and Camier's reunion just before launching their journey, postponing the necessary gathering of the first Beckettian uneven pair, illustrates the impersonal paradigmatic forces operating beneath this pattern:

> They had consulted together at length, before embarking on this journey, weighing with all the calm at their command what benefits they might hope from it, what ills apprehend, maintaining turn about the dark side and the rosy. The only certitude they gained from these debates was that of not lightly launching out, into the unknown.
>
> Camier was first to arrive at the appointed place. That is to say that on his arrival Mercier was not there. In reality Mercier had forestalled him by a good ten minutes. Not Camier then, but Mercier, was first to arrive. He possessed himself in patience for five minutes, with his eye on the various avenues on the approach open to his friend, then set out for a saunter destined to last full fifteen minutes. Meantime Camier, five minutes having passed without sight or sign of Mercier, took himself off in his turn for a little stroll. On his return to the place, fifteen minutes later, it was in vain he cast about him, and understandably so. For Mercier, after cooling his heels for a further five minutes, had wandered off again for what he pleased to call a little stretch. Camier hung around for five more minutes, then again departed, saying to himself, Perhaps I'll run into him in the street. It was at this moment that Mercier, back from his breather, which as chance this time would have it had not exceeded ten minutes, glimpsed receding

in the morning mist a shape suggestive of Camier's and which was indeed none other. Unhappily it vanished as though swallowed up by the cobbles, leaving Mercier resume his vigil. (Beckett 2006a: 383–4)

Beckett's intuitive willingness to recognise divergence as a norm, a parted and twisted axis of modern condition, multiple and unavoidable by nature, constantly deferring rest and exasperating tension, is also figured by the counterpoints between voice and presence, memory and fiction, light and darkness that animate his final drama and fiction. One might evoke the pale 'tangle of tatters', a blurred vision that materialises Amy's absent presence in *Footfalls* (Beckett 2006b: 430); or even the clashes between Krapp and his past versions he would like to bury, but still ghost him; the same motif as retrieved in television plays such as *Eh Joe* and . . . *but the clouds.* . . or in *Film*; and even the chamber of silences and voices, shrine of the divided self, sculptured in *Company*, can be remembered in that context. These variations deal with the unlikeness of soothing encounters, not only in the perspective of fleeing time, but also of fleeting words and images, normally taking place in 'profounds of mind' or 'of mindlessness', as in *Ohio Impromptu* (Beckett 2006b: 476). They could perfectly be described in terms of Beckett's early readings of Schopenhauer, acutely revived in his late works.

The sharpest aspect of 'misencounter' in Beckett's *écriture* seems to be an expressive-cognitive one and I would argue it is hard to find a more eloquent and emblematic presentation of this matter in his novels and plays than the piano tuners' episode in *Watt*.[2] The incident triggers a serious semantic crisis, which interferes with the character's perception of the world's phenomenological structure and confronts him with the eventual correspondence, or lack of correspondence, between the stubborn fixedness of names and the instability of experienced reality. Nevertheless, this crisis can, unpredictably, reveal itself productive, by making explicit and visible these oscillating borders and, therefore, insinuating a bunch of new negative possibilities. Moreover, it might suggest how extensively translation as a whole (and particularly when Beckett's oeuvre is concerned) is an example of permanently denied or postponed 'semantic succour'. The artist and the translator share the same never-ending struggle for a satisfying expression, always out of reach. The experience of the translator mirrors the writer's, as far as both of them try to express, by other means, 'almost the same', whether read in a foreign language or perceived in the world, as Umberto Eco puts it, stressing the almost (Eco 2008). To this minimal gap, an abyss of possibilities and frustrations, are we fated.

In *Watt*, Beckett rises new critical and interpretative issues directly related to the translation act. Looking for some meaning in a trivial episode – the

Galls, father and son, tuning the piano, in Knott's house – the storyteller reminds us that Watt 'had not seen a symbol, nor executed an interpretation since the age of fourteen or fifteen, and [who] he had lived, miserably it is true, among face values all his adult life, face values at least for him'. In many different ways, translators certainly feel as helpless as this protagonist, in bad need of any 'semantic succour' at sight, when compelled to elect a few among many fleeting, elusive, if not conflictive, possible meanings. The passage itself, exemplary of the cognitive operations involved in the task of translators, is considerably brief: Gall senior, a blind man, and Gall junior are admitted to the music-room, the young man works on the piano, observed by the elder, concludes his task, gathers his tools, they exchange a few comments on the miserable condition of the instrument and leave. Watt's consideration of the affair, though, is considerably longer:

> This was perhaps the principal incident of Watt's early days in Mr Knott's house.
>
> In a sense it resembled all the incidents of note proposed to Watt during his stay in Mr Knott's house, and of which a certain number will be recorded in this place, without addition, or subtraction, and in a sense not.
>
> It resembled them in the sense that it was not ended, when it was past, but continued to unfold, in Watt's head, from beginning to end, over and over again, the complex connexions of its lights and shadows, the passing from silence to sound and from sound to silence, the stillness before the move-ment and the stillness after, the quickenings and retardings, the approaches and separations, all the shifting detail of its march and ordinance, according to the irrevocable caprice of its taking place. It resembled them in the vigour with which it developed a purely plastic content, and gradually lost, in the nice processes of its light, its sound, its impacts and its rhythm, all meaning, even the most literal.
>
> Thus the scene in the music-room, with the two Galls, ceased very soon to signify for Watt a piano tuned, an obscure family and professional relation, an exchange of judgements more or less intelligible, and so on, if indeed it had ever signified such things, and became a mere example of light commenting bodies, and stillness motion, and silence sound, and comment comment.
>
> The fragility of the outer meaning had a bad effect on Watt, for it caused him to seek for another, for some meaning of what had passed, the image of how it had passed. (Beckett 2006a: 225–6)

If here Beckett's growing mistrust in words and affirmative art, his literary project of unwording the world, speaks out, it is certainly due to the book's open structure, a deliberately confusing and misleading one. What emerges from a supposedly candid attempt of providing simple answers to unpretentious logical questions (who, when, where, what, why) gradually becomes a baffling maze of senses, archetypical of all narratives, *mise en abime* of narrators and voices, defying conventional syntax and grammar. The cancerous spreading of the enumerations, for instance, paradoxically results in a demonstration of the umbilical shortcomings of the logical quest the narrator confesses being at their origin.

When translating, one should at the same time be aware of this essentially ironical, paradoxical move into which Watt is swallowed. It is not just about 'obscure locks and simple keys', as Ackerley named, after Beckett, his annotated *Watt* (Ackerley 2010). The changing matter of experience is analogue to the moving textual meanings the translator faces. As the Galls compare the piano they presently examine to its former image, gone but not completely, by writing and translating in-between languages, aware of the interval between perception and expression, Beckett keeps hearing an absent piano, even when playing the new one: pressing the keys at his hand, he probably suffers the reaction of a ghost instrument, the corresponding ruined dampers still at work.

Watt is an unfinished and virtually unfinishable work, in other words, a novel that makes room in itself for flaws and broken bits, as the addenda, the textual incongruities, or the extravagant footnotes may well suggest. They testify how far Beckett refuted the idea of well performing and successful writing. Failure, a predictable and even desirable feature of his work, assumes from here on its leading role, another instance of the unavoidable 'misencounters', now taken for necessary, no longer disasters, their signal, swapped.

A writer, as well as any translator, must acknowledge to be installed in the heart of a 'poetics of indeterminacy', to speak as Marjorie Perloff, a poetics that impels a new meaning on the oath to be precise, the inclination to translate the marked by the marked, the unmarked by the unmarked, and so on. Uncertainty and instability must be welcomed and twisted in favour of the translation process. As 'in the beginning was the pun' acts as a (temporary) simple key for the reader of *Murphy*, 'no symbols were none intended' does for *Watt*.[3] The ambiguity of the original in its double negation, at the same time a specification and its refusal, recalls the importance of *epanorthosis*, which Bruno Clément took for the key rhetorical device in Beckett's 'style without a style' (Clément 1994). The constant self-correction, modulation, annulation and rephrasing of what has just been stated seems effectively to be an important propelling force in his writing and translating.[4]

Having *Watt* and the Gall's episode in mind, we are distant from the symbolic metaphoric resonance, from meaning circles well tied to one and only irradiating centre. In fact, signification here seems to convey from remains, from what escapes classical hermeneutics, *Echo's Bones*. Being a deferred presence, phantasmatic, meanings are only insinuated, dependent on hypothetical and denied vanishing points, visible in the opacity of the obstacles, expressive and linguistic, that at the same time resist their complete accomplishment. One cannot sufficiently insist on how much this poetics is founded on Beckett's belief that rather than representing conveying or mirroring an objective world, words constitute and invent the world relying on an essential, but imperfect tool, language. Experience, objective and subjective, though not totally apprehended in linguistic form, is only to be grasped in the materiality of expression. Indeed, specifically in what exceeds language as an effort to produce efficient expressive form, oozing or leaking from the cracks of the verbal surface. In a Beckettian point of view, this *parti pris* brings writing closer to the task of the translator, torn between source and target languages, multiplying originals into new versions, feeling the phantom pain of an amputated limb, but also being able to foresee the sensitivity of a new imagined one, as scholars devoted to Beckett, bilingualism and self-translation could not help noticing.[5] According to Uhlmann, *Watt* seems to be a turning point in his work, announcing a new understanding and a different use of images. From this point on, they are no longer strictly symbolic, a bridge between communicating and fusing elements: they are rather an index of a failure, revealing the impossible correspondence between the (ill)-achieved linguistic expression, the made up 'pillow of old words', and its objective pretext, the events/perceptions it somehow tries to formulate (Uhlmann 2006).[6] In that sense, the Gall's episode is exemplary. If missed encounters indeed became more central and emblematic in Beckett's work from *Watt* on, they must also be a symptom of a much earlier originated Beckettian concern: Beckett's reluctance towards a relational and representational art, an art based on the conciliation of disjunctive poles, subject and expressive will, on one side, object and aesthetic material, on the other, dating from his very first critical formulations and considerably important in determining the paths he picked in European modernism.

Although Beckettian prose and drama developed by systematically mining traditions, conventions and singularities of naturalism, mobilising the gender-specific attention demanded by every different medium or support he adopted (the page, the stage, the screen), Beckett never ignored a major aesthetic issue common to all fronts he engaged in: the gap between perception and expression, which language is unable to dissolve, and the consequent need to re-found an inherited (and no longer sustainable) relationship between subject and object. This need was prematurely formulated by him and consistently pursued in all his subsequent critical and creative advances.

The stages of his ideas on this crucial topic can be followed throughout his critical writings, in his essays, private notebooks and correspondence. From the beginning, Beckett never failed to recognise that all authentic art must stand on the interrogative – therefore, critical – approach. As Mark Nixon recalls, already back in 1931, during his classes at Trinity College Dublin, he praised André Gide for 'refus[ing] to abdicate as a critic in his novels'; in 1936–7, systematically discovering German museums' collections, he justified his fondness for a particular painting by Cézanne as 'at last the reassertion of painting as criticism, i.e. art' (Beckett quoted in Nixon 2015: 74). The consequences of such an equivalence, between art and criticism, he analytically developed in exploring a foreign artistic territory, that of the visual arts. Writing about contemporary aesthetic impasses, Beckett always revolved round a few obsessive themes, 'questions of perception, the image, the rupture between subject and object, and the related failure of language to adequately give voice to these tensions', as well as 'the role of the artist to negotiate this challenge' (Nixon 2015: 74).

In a review on 'Recent Irish Poetry', published under a pseudonym, in *The Bookman's* special Irish Number, in 1934, as part of the commissions that supported him while his career as a writer did not take off, Beckett once again states his decisive aesthetic question. The filter that distinguishes the poets who truly matter from the 'antiquarians', a category in which he includes W. B. Yeats, is the recognition that 'a new thing has happened' in modern art, 'the breakdown of the object', 'a rupture in the lines of communication, introducing a void between subject and object', which forces the contemporary artist to become aware of 'the space that intervenes between him and the world of things', a space that Beckett calls 'no man's land' (Beckett 1983: 70).

Beckett's postwar art criticism essays acutely develop this theory of an incommensurability between subject and object, particularly in the *Three Dialogues with Georges Duthuit*, further repudiating relational art and suggesting the artist had no alternative but to welcome failure and impotence.[7] Nevertheless, renouncing pre-constituted subjects and objects, besides blurring the distinction between the inside and the outside world, casts a doubt on the efficiency of images, by nature, expressive, substantial and relational, even if in a minimum degree.

In *Samuel Beckett and the Philosophical Image* (Uhlmann 2006), Uhlmann examines how certain quotes, fragments carefully collected from his readings of manifold philosophers, so distinct as Arnold Geulincx or Zeno of Elea, were incorporated into Beckett's novels and plays as metonymical, concrete evocation of the abstract ideas or puzzling conceptual problems they once embodied. Uhlmann argues that these 'philosophical images' simultaneously maintain a sensitive memory of the complexity, either formal or thematic, present in their original context, qualities related to the intellectual architecture from which they stem, and acquire different meanings and functions in the fictional and aesthetic regime into which they are brought. Beckett takes advantage of their direct appeal to the readers' nerves for ironic, interrogative or lyrical consideration of these borrowed ideas.

Converting them into expressive, linguistic material, he achieves concrete resonance for otherwise very abstract issues, without endorsing the philosophical systems they were taken from, which remain only in the aspect of traces. The lividness of the crisis triggered by Watt's pursuit of meaning in the Gall's episode owes something to a similar procedure. Rather than representing the aesthetic ideals behind Beckett's works, it enacts, performs them in language and in situation.[8] Translation and writing, an inseparable couple in Beckett's eyes, should also share this performative treat.

In a letter to Georges Duthuit (9 June 1949), Beckett dreams of an imageless art: 'Does there exist, can there exist, or not, a painting that is poor, undisguisedly useless, incapable of any image whatever, a painting whose necessity does not seek to justify itself?' But, as he himself acknowledges, in *Watt*, 'the only way one can speak of nothing is to speak of it as though it were something',[9] as the persistent memory of the Galls facing the ruined piano may well warn us.

Notes

1. In order to understand how important Beckett's writings were on visual arts in the development of such aesthetical premises, see Mark Nixon's 'Ruptures of the Visual: Beckett as Critic and Poet' (Nixon 2015) and Anthony Uhlmann's book on *Samuel Beckett and the Philosophical Image* (Uhlmann 2006).

2. In 'Towards a Creative Involution', Stanley Gontarski analyses the same episode from a philosophical perspective, in close proximity to Bergson and Deleuze, which is very revealing of Beckett's uneasiness with traditional representative art, refuting the usual relation between subject and object, singling him out among other modernists: 'We can thus characterise something of a philosophical genealogy, a line of flight that has neither need for nor interest in the periodisation of Modernism, a line of which Beckett (even reluctantly) is part. Murphy et al. are deterritorialised as much as Beckett's landscapes are, and so he/they become a "complexification" of being that manifests itself in Beckett not as represented, representative, or a representation, since so much of Beckett deals with that which cannot be uttered, known, or represented, but whose image the works (and its figures) have become, a thinking through of negativity, becoming and multiplicity through non-Newtonian motion, of being as becoming, where every movement brings something new

into the world, but in something of a reverse Darwinism that moves from complex to simple organism, from Murphy to Watt, or Watt to Pim, . . . an "involution"' (Gontarski 2015: 101).

3. 'No symbols were none intended' is one of the fragments Beckett incorporated as addenda to *Watt*, unable either to completely blend them in the novel, or to discard them, once and for all. Beckett's French version of the motto, 'Honni soit qui symboles y voit', would deserve a paper on its own, totally devoted to the singularities of Beckettian self-translation.

4. Examining Beckett's abandoned attempts to translate *Worstward Ho* into French, Anthony Cordingley (Cordingley 2017) and Dirk Van Hulle (Van Hulle 2015a and 2015b) make clear the decisive role played by this continuous drive towards rewriting in his work, not only as a writer, but also as a self-translator, common sign of a 'work in -gress', rather than in progress, always in want and on the move, refusing a definite form.

5. Cf. Nadia Louar, 'De la mémoire involontaire de Proust au bilinguisme de Beckett' (2008); Brian Fitch, 'The Relationship between *Compagnie* and *Company*: One Work, Two Texts, Two Fictive Universes' (1990); Raymond Federman, 'The Writer as Self-Translator' (1990); Marjorie Perloff, 'Une voix pas la mienne: French/English Beckett and the French/English reader' (1990).

6. In a similar context, Daniel Katz refers precisely to the same Gall's episode: 'This passage is remarkable for a number of reasons. First of all, it asserts that the purpose of linguistic representation is less to convey meaning or information than quite simply to alleviate suffering, by the very construction and solidification of meaning – any meaning – in and of itself . . . Language and representation, then, have a function beyond that of conveying information or solidifying knowledge, but act in and of themselves as a palliative, or to use another Beckettian term, a calmative, possessed of powers which seem to border on the somatic . . . And indeed, this leads to a second crucial implication of how these passages from *Watt* represent what is anterior to language and representation in the first place: not as a primal experience, or an ineffable feeling or impression, but rather as something which is not only "unspeakable" (or unnamable, perhaps) but also quite literally "unthinkable", as such or in itself. In this way, Beckett marks a clear difference with certain sorts of phenomenological or existentialist thinking prominent at the time *Watt* was written, as he refuses to posit anything, with the very important exception of suffering, as pre-representational at all. That is to say, for Beckett "experience" is almost always already *within* the regime of language and representation, and not a prior essence which gives rise to them. And this in turn implies that if language must be viewed as suspect, it is not

because it is in some way insubstantial with regard to what it represents, as in the classic realist critique, but quite on the contrary; it is not insubstantial enough'. (Katz 2013: 365–66).

7. 'To be an artist is to fail, as no other dare fail, that failure is his world and the shrink from it desertion, art and craft, good housekeeping, living' (Beckett 1983: 145).

8. 'Expression as ooze means language, failing as subjective mirror or voice (which is all to the good, even all to the better) exists expressively as trace . . . In this way, the tracing language for Beckett is as much indexical as symbolic; a mark and not a representation of its source' (Katz 2013: 368).

9. 'Does there exist, can there exist, or not, a painting that is poor, undisguisedly useless, incapable of any image whatever, a painting whose necessity does not seek to justify itself?' (Beckett quoted in Nixon 2015: 81).

Works Cited

Ackerley, Chris. J. (2010), *Obscure Locks, Simple Keys: The Annotated Watt*, Edinburgh: Edinburgh University Press.

Beckett, Samuel (1983), *Disjecta: Miscellaneous Writings and a Dramatic Fragment*, Ruby Cohn (ed), London: Calder.

Beckett, Samuel (2006a), *The Grove Centenary Edition, Vol. 1: Novels. Murphy; Watt; Mercier and Camier*, Paul Auster (ed), New York: Grove Press.

Beckett, Samuel (2006b), *The Grove Centenary Edition, Vol. 3: Dramatic Works*, Paul Auster (ed), New York: Grove Press.

Beckett, Samuel (2006c), *The Grove Centenary Edition, Vol. 4: Poems, Short Fiction, and Criticism*, Paul Auster (ed), New York: Grove Press.

Clément, Bruno (1994), *L'Oeuvre sans qualités: Rhétorique de Samuel Beckett*, Paris: Seuil.

Cordingley, Anthony (2017), 'Samuel Beckett and Edith Fournier Translating the "Untranslatable" *Worstward Ho*', *Journal of Beckett Studies*, 26.2, 239–56.

Eco, Umberto (2008), *Experiences in Translation (Toronto Italian Studies/Emilio Goggio Publications Series)*, Toronto: University of Toronto Press.

Federman, Raymond (1990), 'The Writer as Self-Translator', in Alan Friedman, Dina Sherzer and Charles Rossman (eds), *Beckett Translating/Translating Beckett*, University Park and London: Pennsylvania State University Press, pp. 7–16.

Fitch, Brian (1990), 'The Relationship between *Compagnie* and *Company*: One Work, Two Texts, Two Fictive Universes', in Alan Friedman, Dina Sherzer and Charles Rossman (eds), *Beckett Translating/Translating Beckett*, University Park and London: Pennsylvania State University Press, pp. 25–35.

Gontarski, Stanley (2015), *Creative Involution: Bergson, Beckett, Deleuze*, Edinburgh: Edinburgh University Press.

Katz, Daniel (2013), 'Language and Representation', in Anthony Uhlmann (ed), *Samuel Beckett in Context,* Cambridge, UK: Cambridge University Press, pp. 361–69.

Louar, Nadia (2008), 'De la mémoire involontaire de Proust au bilinguisme de Beckett', in Carvalho and Rui C. Homem (eds), *Plural Beckett Pluriel*, Porto: FCT, pp. 171–89.

Nixon, Mark (2015), 'Ruptures of the Visual: Beckett as Critic and Poet', in Dirk Van Hulle (ed), *The New Cambridge Companion to Samuel Beckett*, Cambridge, UK: Cambridge University Press.

Perloff, Marjorie (1990), 'Une voix pas la mienne: French/English Beckett and the French/English Reader', in Alan Friedman, Dina Sherzer and Charles Rossman (eds) (org.) *Beckett Translating/Translating Beckett*, University Park and London: Pennsylvania State University Press, pp. 37–48.

Uhlmann, Anthony (2006), *Samuel Beckett and the Philosophical Image*, Cambridge, UK: Cambridge University Press.

Van Hulle, Dirk (2015a), 'Plus loin ne se peut: Beckett et la genèse de *Nohow On*', *Roman*, 20–50.60, 11–26.

Van Hulle, Dirk (2015b), 'Translation and Genetic Criticism: Genetic and Editorial approaches to the "Untransatable" in Joyce and Beckett', *Linguistica Antverpiensia, New Series: Themes in Translation Studies*, 14, 40–53.

13

'The absolute impossibility of all purchase': Property and Translation in Beckett's Postwar Prose

Martin Schauss

Introduction

In *Monolingualism of the Other*, Jacques Derrida refers to the 'impossible property of a language' (Derrida 1998: 63) in relation to the prosthetic qualities of speech. This, he maintains, is not a universal position that neutralises difference, but the opposite. It is a position that allows us to repoliticise language. It helps us understand how language conceived as property, how language 'appropriation', is really an aggressive instrument for nationalist, imperialist, and mono-culturalist hegemonies. Writes Derrida:

> Where neither natural property nor the law of property in general exist, where this de-propriation is recognised, it is possible and it becomes more necessary than ever occasionally to identify, in order to combat them, impulses, phantasms, 'ideologies', 'fetishisations', and symbolics of appropriation. Such a reminder permits one at once to analyse the historical phenomena of appropriation and to treat them *politically* by avoiding, above all, the reconstitution of what these phantasms managed to motivate: 'nationalist' aggressions (which are always more or less 'naturalist') or monoculturalist homo-hegemony. (Derrida 1998: 64. Emphasis original)

Forms of language property have allowed a range of critics to read the catachrestic and prosthetic quality of language in Beckett's work. For example, commenting on Malone's failure to account for his possessions, Daniel Katz notes how in *Malone Dies* '[the] problem is not whether the pots "really belong" to Malone or not – "Malone" here is not even capable of the self-identity that would be prior to any claim of agency' (Katz 1999: 15). The 'subjective' rift between possessive and first-person pronoun precedes, here, the socio-economic definition of Malone's 'property'. Especially in *The Unnamable* and many subsequent works, language is rehearsed as a 'thing', external, prosthetic, and not belonging to the narrator or speaking 'subject'. This is property understood on an individual, bodily, phenomenological level, connecting among many things Beckett's concerns with expression, voice, the idea of the monad, and our ability to establish any kind of meaningful relation.

More recently, such readings have in turn informed political approaches to Beckett, in relation to issues of authority, power, nation-building, and colonialism in the French, Irish, German, Spanish, and more broadly European context. Especially when it comes to Beckett's postwar oeuvre, this critical conversation stresses the impossibility to index stable political and historical referents. What is often called Beckett's particularism (his refusal of a systematic philosophy of history) can be understood as another form of dispossession. In his German Diaries, Beckett laments the reifying animistic and novelistic tendencies of rationalist historiography: 'the anthropomorphisation of the inhuman necessities that provoke the chaos'[1] (Beckett quoted in Nixon 2011: 177–8). What he wants from a historical work 'is the straws, flotsam, etc., names, dates, births & deaths, because that is all I can know' (Beckett quoted in Nixon 2011: 177–8). This essay seeks to add to the political approaches that focus on Beckett's labour of indetermination, with specific reference to the intersection of property and translation in Beckett's short stories written in 1946 (published, with *Premier amour* omitted, in 1955 by Les Éditions de Minuit as *Nouvelles*, together with *Textes pour rien*). The essay explores how Beckett registers (dis)possession in the political sense through the 'impossible' property of language as indexed by translation and cultural-linguistic instabilities. The tramp's exclusion from normative, bourgeois discourse (and his residual rehearsal of it) is read through a larger multilingual framework whereby nationalist discourses (Irish, French, German, Spanish) are grounded in the violent marginalisation of the other's language. This political conception of Beckett's self-translation must, however, be viewed itself as a kind of deprivation, whereby Beckett denies the historical 'purchase' of his work in a way that echoes his narrators' historical exclusion through language.

Crossing Borders: Beckett Translating

In *Beckett's Political Imagination* (2017), Emilie Morin makes one of the most convincing cases for translation as key to registering the political and historical interventions of Beckett's postwar work. Writes Morin: 'Conceptualisations of politics as a totality that functions dialectically and involves shifting patterns of legibility are particularly pertinent to the diverse European moments to which

Beckett's work of displacement and translation is sutured' (Morin 2017: 7). Morin's study shows how Beckett's translation of other writers marks the intersection of translation, politics, and a world-literature space. For instance, some of his translations for Octavio Paz's *Anthology of Mexican Poetry* (1958), according to Morin, 'strengthen a historical dimension that is only half-stated in the original poems and bring together coded signifiers of colonial conquest and imperialist custom' (Morin 2017: 27). The translations of committed négritude essays and poetry for Nancy Cunard's 1934 *Negro* anthology are arguably even more noteworthy for how Beckett accentuates colonial trade, forced labour, strategic cruelty, imperial authority and claims to legitimacy. The translations are not neutral and transparent. For instance, in his translation of Benjamin Péret's essay, Beckett 'grants added significance to Péret's depiction of colonial trade and alters the text slightly to draw attention to the strategic use of starvation and forced labour' (Morin 2017: 99). Other translations stress the structures of colonial authority and claims to legitimacy. Beckett even politicises the terminology of essays on sculpture, which did not in fact deal with racial politics directly, giving a different slant on aesthetics and commitment than that commonly associated with him.

The comparison with Beckett's own writing begs, where we are accustomed to intrusive cultural and linguistic markers in otherwise decontextualised settings. In the works that Beckett wrote during his 'frenzy of writing'[2] (1946–51), wartime and early postwar European borders are suggested, time-honoured in that sense, only to be dismantled and scattered. The role of language in the inconsistency and playfulness of Beckett's world is undeniable, extending to cultural and geographical referents. Throughout one finds Anglicisms in the French and Gallicisms in the English. The texts undermine their own authority this way; Sam Slote notes, for example, that the parrot's bilingual swearing in the French *Molloy* destabilises its own claim as original version because it implies the translation of a prior, virtual English version (Slote 2011: 209). Another example is *Premier amour* (published in 1970 alongside *Mercier and Camier*), in which we are told that neither Loulou nor the narrator are French or francophone, whereas the English *First Love* (1973) completely leaves out any reference to the characters' (non-) belonging to the text's language. While the question of geographical and historical location remains largely indeterminable, self-conscious or contradictory cultural traces proliferate, especially in the original French. The inconsistency of this register betrays the politics of inclusion and exclusion that undergird the thematic content of the stories: the socio-economic expulsion of the dehumanised narrator within a historical time on its last legs.[3]

The formative importance of Beckett's travels in 1930s Germany has been acknowledged in this context; the reappearance of German coordinates throughout Beckett's work (including the poetry) will remain central to the inclusive disjunction of political meaning (especially regarding propaganda and censorship), interpolated with the residual tension between French and Irish (and British) nation states. Malone recalls: 'Tiepolo's ceiling at Würzburg, what a tourist I must have been, I even remember the diaeresis' (Beckett 2010a: 63). That moment (in which Malone identifies with Beckett the diarist and art critic in 1930s Germany) is followed by the ejaculation 'Up the Republic!', begging the question for the reader: which republic? Ireland, France, Germany, Spain? James McNaughton notes how the slogan does not so much describe Beckett's political identity as an analysis of political polysemy and 'the inertia that besets cultural and political thought, a lesson learned . . . from Beckett's experience in Free State Ireland' (McNaughton 2010: 57).[4] In the stories, the place names Lüneburg heath and Ohlsdorf, and the 'Stützenwechsel' of the Saxon church add ambiguous German coordinates to the stories from in and around Hamburg, where Beckett arrived by boat in October 1936 (Beckett 1995: 50, 27, 68). Lüneburg and Ohlsdorf reach into the more remote parts of the narrator's memory, and it is uncertain how far he has come since. Beckett himself would do a lot of solitary walking in the strange city of Hamburg and visit numerous churches (Knowlson 1997: 231–2). He kept extensive diaries during his stay and made tentative plans for a longer work entitled 'Journal of a Melancholic' (Nixon 2011: 110–31). As Mark Nixon finds, a lot of details, especially in *First Love*, correspond to diary entries (Nixon 2011: 115). Lüneburg heath (northern Lower Saxony), which Beckett visited, now evokes the WWII battlefront, the site of partial surrender of the German forces in the northwest on 4 May 1945; the nature reserve also enclosed the Bergen–Belsen concentration camp. What constitutes a broken biographical index forms within the context of the stories' world and publication a highly evocative, paradoxical historical framework.

It is then notable that, as Morin has shown, those texts 'that allude most clearly to the murky period of political transition in France after 1944 are those that were most ruthlessly modified in translation' and revision (Morin 2017: 144). Morin has in mind *Mercier et Camier* (1970; written 1946), severely shortened and emended in the (for Beckett) unappealing process of translation, and the play *Eleutheria* (written 1947, posthumously published and translated). But even in the translation, numerous references or idioms in *Mercier and Camier* evoke the Nazi occupation, French collaborationism and resistance: names like Clappe[5] or Gast, the spy-like Mr Conaire and his singular toilet humour: 'In Frankfurt, when you get off the train, what is the first thing you see, in gigantic letters of fire? A single word: HIER'[6] (Beckett 2010b: 40).

Like the *Nouvelles*, *Mercier and Camier* puts wartime and notions of geographical and cultural frontiers to the test, while its Irishness is largely added in

Beckett's translation (Kennedy 2010c: viii). Consider the characters' 'journey' in the opening paragraph: 'Physically it was fairly easy going, without seas or frontiers to be crossed, through regions untormented on the whole, if desolate in parts. Mercier and Camier did not remove from home, they had that great good fortune' (Beckett 2010b: 3). Despite their 'journey', they do not leave home; the crossing of borders is retracted. The regions remain 'untormented'. By whom? They are 'desolate'. In what way? We continue: 'They did not have to face, with greater or lesser success, outlandish ways, tongues, laws, skies, foods, in surroundings little resembling those to which first childhood, then boyhood, then manhood had inured them' (Beckett 2010b). Again, a sealed-off cultural region is evoked only for Mercier and Camier to be later confronted with foreign tongues. 'He takes us for globe-trotters', says Mercier as an innkeeper speaks, 'in a tone of tentative complicity', the German word for 'comfortable': '*gemütlich*' (Beckett 2010b: 33). Did the innkeeper mistakenly identify a fellow collaborationist? Beckett had always been generous with foreign language quotations, including German, notably in the poems and early prose. While earlier manifestations are in the vein of modernist multilingualism, humorous or classical or both (often direct dialogue), the foreign words of the postwar prose combine with other intrusive referents to haunt the urban and rural wasteland in the absence of geo-cultural demarcations, with resonances of wartime invasion, occupation, persecution and ruination.

Beckett regularly lessens the historical index in his auto-translations from French into English, neutralising explicit references to the police and welfare state, or to wartime contexts. As a rule, Beckett's emendations meant cuts and contraction, rather than additions, and it is due much more to these revisions than to a progressive lessening in Beckett's *oeuvre* that its politico-historical dimensions are destabilised. This is especially true for works that remained untranslated for many years. The *Nouvelles* take on a special status in this respect; in them, translation adopts a particularly ambiguous role, not least because they mark the very moment of Beckett's transition from English to French. In *First Love*, which Beckett translated as late as 1972–73, the French 'asile' (shelter/asylum) becomes 'cover'.[7] Possible, disharmonic connotations of peril, refuge, charity and institutionalisation disappear as the text moves into English. In 'The Calmative', translated in 1967, a reference to the Salvation Army is cut; whereas in 'Le Calmant', the narrator considers asking a 'salutiste' (Beckett 1955: 69) (member of the Salvation Army) for the way, in the English, there is no mention of that institution of unimpeachable Victorian Protestantism. By comparison, the much earlier translation of *Molloy* (with Patrick Bowles in 1953–54) does not evacuate original encounters with charitable bodies and retains its Nietzschean distrust of liberal philanthropy. Morin has shown how 'Suite' (later to become 'La Fin') originally suggested the homecoming of a survivor ('un absent'), describing 'infected wounds' and implying 'symptoms of malnutrition'.[8] Historicising Beckett's 'refugees' from a human rights angle, Lyndsey Stonebridge notes how the charity worker's use of 'refouler' [turn away] in 'La fin' evokes

> The legal principle that permitted nations to return refugees back to the country they had left last throughout the war (and beyond). The first ever convention on refugees in 1933 had contained an article prohibiting *refoulement*, but this had explicitly excluded refugees fleeing Nazi Germany. *Refoulement*, as Beckett no doubt knew all too well, had meant death for thousands of fleeing refugees since then. (Stonebridge 2018: 130)

Specific biopolitical and historical markers become sparser as Beckett returns to translate the stories. Acknowledging such minute but consequential alterations, however, it becomes necessary to show how the stories' political and historical index is already dislocated and translated in the first place ('disowned' if you will). The critic Rebecca Walkowitz has defined works that oscillate between languages, cultures, nations, as 'born-translated', referring to modernism in relation to the classical tradition and cosmopolitanism (Walkowitz 2015: 3). By comparison, the sense that arises from Beckett's texts, from their unstable linguistic index, the self-translation and revisions, is, to borrow from *Watt* via Jung, much more that of a work that has 'never been properly born translated' (Beckett 2007: 248).

The Purchase of Translation

Beckett's *Nouvelles* pose material dispossession, socio-economic expulsion and rejection as a precondition. Pre-empted by the title 'L'Expulsé'/ 'The Expelled', the stories, it seems, can only begin as each narrator is 'ejected' from his house or shelter, already far removed from the dominant marketplace and economy (Beckett 1995: 48). The expulsion is not the 'drama' but the setting. In the case of 'The Calmative', the narrator has already died; he is the narrator closest to *Texts for Nothing*, can no longer tell the difference between den and ruins, and think of little reason to stir other than having been thrown out. The *Nouvelles* still represent the conditions and violence of the expulsion itself, if by way of scrappy memory, whereas later works proceed by *fait accompli*.[9] Early into 'The Expelled', when the narrator is still pondering his forced removal, he recounts how the occupants of the house start cleaning after they threw him out: 'A thorough cleansing [nettoyage] was in full swing. In a few hours they would close the window, draw the curtains and spray the whole place in disinfectant [pulvérisation au formol]' (Beckett 1995: 49[17]). The racial and

anti-Semitic undertones of the English 'cleansing' can be powerful for a contemporary reader: while Beckett was extremely sensitive to the dehumanising
discourses of racial purity and Nazi propaganda, the French 'nettoyage' undermines the specificity of that interpretation. However, the thorough cleaning
with formalin (as the French specifies) of his former den also designates the
tramp's status as vermin. Kafka's *ungeheures Ungeziefer* springs to mind, and
while it adds little to suggest an intertextual reference, one can see Beckett's
environments as a world in which the metamorphosis has already occurred, in
which the surprise held by the violent transformation has been neutralised by
historical recurrence.[10]

Property is in the *Nouvelles* very much 'real', in its relationality, its abstraction of material properties. But property is also metaphorical, not so much in
the symbolic sense, as in the sense of translation, insofar as it can be seen as
an element that 'secretly governs the whole', to borrow Brian Dillon's words
(Dillon 2017: 105). Property is 'real' then insofar as it dissolves into all of
its implications, as it names the equivalences and relations that allow us to
'repoliticise' language in Beckett's stories. It is in this (Derridean) sense that we
can understand Beckett's *aporia* of translation, the untranslatable translation, as
'*[making] things happen', faire arriver,* as 'producing [illegible] events in a given
language' (Derrida 1998: 66. Emphasis original). Two such moments of translation 'making things happen' in the stories gain particular significance. The
first occurs in 'L'Expulsé': 'Le grand inconvénient de cet état, qu'on pourrait définir comme l'impossibilité absolue d'acheter, est qu'il vous oblige à
vous remuer' (Beckett 1955: 26). The English (translated by Richard Seaver
in 1962 with Beckett heavily involved)[11] reads: 'The great disadvantage of this
condition, which might be defined as the absolute impossibility of all purchase, is that it compels you to bestir yourself' (Beckett 1995: 54). Framed in
this way, the narrator reduces his expulsion from the socio-economic domain
down to the want of money, which in turn propels the 'necessary' narrative
movement – the drifting, looking for shelter, the odd job or begging and
the many anxious encounters. 'Acheter' (buying) becomes 'all purchase' in
the translation. The English totalises the impossibility of acquiring 'property',
while the French remains tied somewhat more closely to cash flow.

If we conceive of the historical 'purchase' of Beckett's text itself, it is indeed
money that offers a picture of an inherently translated environment. Money
is strangely traceable throughout the stories: from small inheritances to penni-
lessness to the allowance issued by custodians (lost in a scam). The class of the
money-makers is evident: Lulu, the prostitute, a cabby, drug dealer, swindler
from Greece/Turkey, and a man with an ass selling 'sand, sea-wrack, and shells
to the townsfolk' (Beckett 1995: 87). In Beckett's words: the 'same deadbeats'

(Beckett 2011: 48), remains of the realist financial-motive protagonist. Meanwhile, in the original French, monetary currency stays firmly Anglo-Irish. Talking 'purchase' in the French runs something like: 'Un shilling, dit-il, six pence' (Beckett 1955: 63). This means that in 1946, right after the war, two years after the Bretton Woods agreement and the foundation of the International Monetary Fund (IMF), Beckett's narrators summon German landmarks (while traversing what is possibly an unnamed Dublin and its environs), deal in British coins, and all this in his new-found French prose.[12] Despite its physical existence as coinage or bills, money typically functions virtually, as a pure form of mediation, a universal law of equivalence. In Beckett's *Nouvelles*, however, money is foreignised; it interrupts rather than levels, confusing coordinates. In the French, the currency makes money appear not only out of place but downright useless, a thing among things, as its signifying function is dislocated to an elsewhere. Money becomes universally equivalent insofar as it appears from, and disappears into, nothing. The question, more so in the French than in the English: what is the exchange value of money, the value of value? Yet money also becomes oddly uneven and politicised within the immediate context of composition. To turn this sentiment on its head: foreign signifiers – like Anglicisms in the French and Gallicisms in the English – become foreign currency, registering both some residual historical recuperation and the impossibility of its 'purchase', Beckett's negation of historical 'value'.

The publication history of 'La Fin'/'The End' helps put a spin on this negation through translation and dislocation. Beckett's first forays into publishing in French were defined by a sense of dispossession of language and content. Jean-Paul Sartre and Simone de Beauvoir's *Les Temps Modernes* had published the first part of 'Suite' (1946), alongside a report on the Nuremberg trials and an essay on the controversial involvement of Marcel Petiot in the French resistance but refused to publish part two of what would become 'La fin' (translated by Seaver in 1954). Sartre's postwar 'canard' (Beckett 2011: 34) published fiction, testimonies, essays and personal accounts of the bombings, camps, and resistance groups, with a particular enthusiasm for fragmented forms.[13] Beckett's spat with de Beauvoir is well documented, his letter from 25 September 1946 reading: 'Vous m'accordez la parole pour me la retirer avant qu'elle n'ait eu le temps de rien signifier'. [You are giving me the chance to speak only to retract it before the words have had the time to mean anything] (Beckett 2011: 40–2). What is lost in the English is the ambiguity of the French double negation (ne rien), which recalls Beckett's famous exchange with Georges Duthuit about the impossible necessity of expressing nothing. Beckett seems to imply here that de Beauvoir took away his speech before it had the time not to signify anything. One can sense Beckett intimating that his story will always only signify nothing in the company of the engaged literature and expressive testimony that the socialist commitment of Sartre and de Beauvoir's journal favoured.

It is fitting that Beckett's satire of the Marxist orator and the communist law of equivalence can be found in the rejected second part of 'La fin'. 'Union . . . brothers . . . Marx . . . capital . . . bread and butter . . . love. It was all Greek to me' (Beckett 1995: 94). The French, in place of 'bread and butter', reads 'bifteck', as in: 'gagner son bifteck', bringing home the bacon (Beckett 1955: 102). The class-based expression referring to the living wage crosses from English to French, and back to English, bifteck/beefsteak. 'Je n'y comprenais rien' becomes 'It was all Greek to me'. The absence of comprehension is codified by reference to another, civilisation-grounding language. As David Weisberg notes, Beckett's ersatz communist would not have gone unnoticed by the Parisian Left at the time (Weisberg 2000: 60). Meanwhile, Beckett's *Lumpenproletarier* is not idealised but rather complicit, and implies a critique of the type of Marxism that was blind to this abject group; what Marx called 'Verkommene, Verlumpte, Arbeitsunfähige' (Marx 2013: 673). While Beckett, like Baudelaire or Céline, 'takes the side of the social misfits',[14] his weakness for the discarded life, the human *déchet*, is not a sentimental case of giving a voice to the voiceless. Complicity, passivity, laughter, violence and misogyny are among Beckett's tramp's chief characteristics: 'thoughts came to me of cruelty, the kind that smiles' (Beckett 1995: 63).

If the tramp has any 'property' in the stories, it is inherited: cash, the hat, greatcoat, but also language. His speech consists of a desperate medley of bourgeois judicial and devout idioms, a class-based social lexicon that is inherited and studied. 'Pardon monsieur, pardon monsieur, la porte des bergers, par pitié'. [Pardon me your honour, the Shepherd's Gate for the love of God] (Beckett 1955: 56[69]). David Weisberg describes the scene as 'a grotesque affront to bourgeois standards of propriety and self-respect, yet locked into the "tone" of "polite conversation"' (Weisberg 2000: 55). Such Flaubertian *idées reçues* capture what the narrator of *Premier amour* calls his 'âme bourgeoise',[15] but also a history of clashes with institutional bodies. The same narrator clarifies that these ejaculations happen only on rare occasions:

> I was so unused to speech that my mouth would sometimes open, of its own accord, and vent some phrase or phrases, grammatically unexceptionable but entirely devoid if not of meaning, for on close inspection they would reveal one and even several, at least of foundation. But I heard each word no sooner spoken. Never had my voice taken so long to reach me as on this occasion. (Beckett 1995: 41)

This socio-economic inflection regarding property of language is both internalised and dispersed in later works, such as *Texts for Nothing*, in which the ghost-like Mother Calvet still mutters, 'Your highness! Your honour!' (Beckett 1995: 105–6). The material dispossession of Beckett's tramps is inseparable from the property of narrative and language that characterises the later prose so strongly, a correlation indexed not least by the remains of bourgeois cliché and realist description. Towards the end of 'The End', the narrator comments on the social limits of his ultimate expulsion: 'You become unsociable, it's inevitable. It's enough to make you wonder sometimes if you are on the right planet. Even the words desert you, it's as bad as that. Perhaps it's the moment when the vessels stop communicating, you know, the vessels' (Beckett 1995: 97). In anticipation of his suicide, the narrator has retreated from the comfort of treating words like things and things like words, as he does in 'The Calmative': 'words to carry away with me to my refuge, to add to my collection' (Beckett 1995: 65). The tramp's exclusion from bourgeois discourse is performed by his residual rehearsal of it, the wider historico-political mood emerging from the entanglement of nationalist discourses and the violent marginalisation of the other's language.

In slightly later works like *Malone Dies* and *The Unnamable*, the depletion of material resources cannot really be separated from the depletion of language. Nor do language, voice, first-person pronoun and possessive any longer 'belong' to the narrator or speaking 'subject'. To quote Katz again: 'The first-person pronoun no longer expresses a self in either its plenitude or poverty, but rather becomes itself an "object" which must be endlessly re-appropriated for any designation of "proper" attributes to occur' (Katz 1999: 15). Names and initials – *le nom propre* – have become, by the time of Beckett's Trilogy, principal signifiers to think 'language property' and displace 'subjectivity'. Murphy, Watt, Molloy, Moran, Malone, Macmann, Worm: we get the impression that Beckett's characters are exchangeable 'M's and 'M's turned upside down 'W's, part of the same family of dispossessed placeholders. This is the contradictory exchange value grounding Beckett's propertied world: the abject, 'improper' tramp is thoroughly exchangeable but has also lost his currency and ability to offer something in exchange. If the tramp's multiple expulsions and his continual encounter with borders formulate a stubborn resistance regarding culturally and morally homogenous nation-building, we can similarly see the dispossession of language – the tramp's language and the splintered, irreconcilable linguistic pluralism of the stories – in terms of political expression and resistance. Later plays like *Rough for Radio II* and *Rough for Theatre II* make this gesture more overtly, thematising political repression through the violence of language: torture to extract testimony and denunciation, or torture *through* testimony and denunciation. The Algerian War offers the most vivid context, with both plays written around 1960 (published in 1975/76) and Beckett closely following the conflict at home and abroad.[16]

'cette horreur chosesque/what nightmare thingness'

A second event of ambiguous translation highlights the ethical–political stakes relating to material deprivation, inclusion in the world, possession of (social and mental) faculties, the right to property. In 'The Calmative', the narrator, speaking from the dead, seeks refuge in a church. His respite is short-lived, and he is quickly disturbed by activity in the church: 'I sprang up from the mat on which I lay before the altar . . . I found myself at the foot of a spiral staircase which I began to climb at top speed, mindless of my heart, like one hotly pursued by a homicidal maniac' (Beckett 1995: 68). This earns him run-ins with various unwitting 'wild-eyed' visitors, and leads him to wonder: 'Quelle est cette horreur chosesque où je me suis fourré?' (Beckett 1955: 55). In Beckett's own translation: 'Into what nightmare thingness am I fallen?' (Beckett 1995: 69). The question suggests on a primary level the estrangement from transcendental spheres, a Cartesian or spiritualist discomfort with a Hobbesian or materialist worldview. While the passive English 'am I fallen' carries a lapsarian connotation, the active pronominal verb in the French 'je me suis fourré' is more humorous: the narrator feels this is a mess he got himself in. The English reverses the relationship between language and matter, matter and world. What stopped Beckett from translating 'horreur chosesque' into 'thinglike' or 'thingly' 'horror'? It is not like the French 'chosesque' was lexically sounder. The French implies an immaterial world, thing-like only in semblance, 'in a skull', as the narrator says, a sceptical idealism (Beckett 1995: 70). By contrast, the inversion of adjective and noun in the English implies a nightmarish material world, and has, arguably, stronger political resonances. The mystical, social, and spiritual estrangement that is implied in the French, diverting Dostoyevsky, Hamsun, Céline, is expanded in the English by a more concrete sense of *Verdinglichung*, or thingification. And if at the end of 'La Fin' Beckett's tramp is disqualified even from the specifically Marxist understanding of reified labour, and certainly from the committed politics of the Left, his 'nightmare thingness' remains firmly outside sublimation. The philosophical indetermination that arises for the tramp's world in translation may matter little with regards to the individual text, yet it signals the inadequate relation – or collapse – of language and matter. Translation and Beckett's multilingualism play a key role in registering the very problem of politics in his work, displacing the already unstable cultural referents once over.

Let us return to the scene. The worldly irony of uttering the words 'nightmare thingness' in a church evokes the Catholic symbolic of matter impregnated with the Spirit. More literally, the passage speaks to the narrator's fear of discovery tied to the institutional body. He is an inhuman parasite in the church's sanitised environment, which cannot stand up for the abjectness of the destitute it purports to protect. The scene betrays the historical connection between vagabondage and heresy, as from the Middle Ages, the vagabond was identified with rebellion, heresy and secular non-conformity, and persecuted as a result. Whether he (mostly a 'he') was an active heretic or not mattered little. Vagabondage was already a welcome, actively fostered, result of market expansion, feudal and then capitalist; its identification with heresy similarly a product of the rule of law, producing 'rebels' in turn.[17]

These what we could call 'biopolitical' implications of the narrator's 'nightmare thingness' inform the way in which the stories resist or 'disown' their national and cultural coordinates. Reading the church scene through Beckett's uncomfortable position as a member of the Protestant upper-middle classes in Ireland, the starving vagrant becomes on the one hand both a prod-uct and a figure of resistance against the landed ascendency's rule, and on the other hand a stand-in for Beckett's unease toward the power of the Catholic Church. Beckett's outsider position within a privileged Protestant minor-ity, amid a sectarian, republican Catholic hegemony, has offered a key point of departure for historicising criticism regarding the 'politics' of his work, regarding the sense of non-belonging (that contributes in this narrative to his 'exile' in France) and his critique of the nationalist ideology. Both *Endgame*, for instance, and Beckett's reworking of the Irish Big House trope (the Knott household in *Watt*, the ruin in 'The End') have been read as an indirect com-ment of the Protestant Ascendancy's culpability during the Irish Famine.[18] We can understand 'nightmare thingness' then as a highly politicised expres-sion – and an instinctive historical resistance – with a long past, opposing the expelling institution and the expelled creature, the socially abject and crimi-nalised life. However, the text itself also resists this historical labour.

It is not a stretch to suggest that 'nightmare thingness' – rather than being tied to one determinable context – is precisely the confrontation of multi-ple, irreconcilable and spectral contexts. Spectral not simply because they are haunted by the past, but because the spectre expresses, in the Derridean sense, the future that has not yet arrived. We might consider then how the imme-diate environment preceding the stories' composition – the Nazi and Vichy regimes, their language of propaganda tied to persecution and extermination – is precisely one in which borders, identities, and communities become violently unfixed. Regarding the church scene: Beckett would have been conscious of the echoes of religious persecution for a European audience during the post-war years. And while he would not yet have known the accurate extent of the Holocaust, he had witnessed the persecution of German Jews during his travels and perceived with revulsion the rife anti-Semitism in Ireland (aimed also at his Jewish uncle William Sinclair and his family). The *Nouvelles* – like *Mercier and Camier* and *Molloy* – evoke a contemporary imaginary registering the perils of movement, of deportation and repatriation. Beckett's friend Alfred Péron died in Switzerland, on his return journey after his liberation from Mauthausen in 1945 (Beckett 2011: 16). Beckett had himself repeatedly complained to the Irish Legation about his inability to travel freely in 'Free France' (Beckett 2011: xvii). From Roussillon, he writes to Cornelius Cremin, the First Secretary of the Irish Legation in Vichy:

> Have had prolonged interviews with the local Gendarmes . . . My history almost day by day from my first setting foot in France. They can't believe that I can be called Samuel and am not a Jew. Yesterday they took away my identity card I suppose to see if it had not been tampered with. My movements are restricted in the extreme, radius of ten kilometres about. (Beckett 2011: xvii)

A subsequent appeal reinforces the sense of Beckett's acute concern with the bureaucracy of movement, restriction, identity, and interrogation (Beckett 2011: xviii). At the same time, the immediate postwar work, full of gendarmes recalling the French police state, come as de Gaulle heralds a heroic and mythic united France and nationalist moral order.[19] As Anthony Uhlmann notes, what the Third Republic, Vichy government and postwar governments (Fourth and the Gaullist Fifth Republic) all had in common was an appeal 'to the notion of La France, to the unchallengeable good of the French nation state to justify the actions of their governments' (Uhlmann 1999: 103). The same national-ist vision and moral order that Beckett knew all too well from his country of birth. His tramp becomes a foreign body in both national discourses. We can ask what kind of sense of place and nation emerges from the narrator's night-marish encounter in the church. Patrick Bixby talks of Beckett's 'no man's land', suggesting: '[Beckett's] form of unwriting does not . . . abandon all rela-tions with a material political geography for an extra-ideological textual space', but instead 'marks the haunting return of pastness and placidness in traces that cannot be completely elided even by the space-clearing gestures of his unwrit-ing' (Bixby 2009: 174–5). Focusing like Bixby on Beckett's dismantling of Irish nationalism, Nels Pearson similarly argues for a pervasive but unresolved origin in Beckett's stories, an Irish context that can never be simply eschewed:

'numerous details of the topography, dialect, and culture strongly imply the environs of greater Dublin in the 1920s and 1930s while its coastal scenes imply the seaside Protestant suburbs of south Dublin' (Pearson 2015: 117). Both Bixby and Pearson's illuminating studies cannot help but overdetermine the Irish context of Beckett's prose, proving largely disinterested, for instance, in French as the primary language of the postwar texts and in their immediate Francophone audience and intellectual milieu. This is where the linguistic instability that arises within, and in-between, the original French and the English translation 'makes things happen', or indeed makes things 'arrive'. For the spectral indeterminateness of Beckett's landscapes surely can only be historical insofar as it expresses the conflict of coordinates, including what Beckett calls in 'The Capital of the Ruins' a 'time-honoured conception' of France 'in ruins' (Beckett 1995: 278).

The spectre of modern warfare, espionage, and totalitarianism haunts the vocabulary of the Trilogy. The material reality of checkpoints and curfews could not be more relevant to the Europe of Beckett's 'siege in the room' (Gibson 2010: 119). Molloy relates a typical day: 'Morning is the time to hide ... Yes, from eight or nine till noon is the dangerous time. But towards noon things quiet down ... there have been a few survivors but they'll give no more trouble, each man counts his rats' (Beckett 1995: 67). Like Molloy, the narrator of 'The Calmative' enters a city with ramparts and a checkpoint-like gate: 'Cyclopean and crenelated, standing out faintly against a sky scarcely less sombre, they did not seem in ruins, viewed from mine, but were, to my certain knowledge' (Beckett 1995: 63). While the streets of the city are unpopulated, the narrator is reminded 'that the houses were full of people, besieged, no, I don't know' (Beckett 1995: 76). Such particulars recall Beckett's reality in occupied France while also unravelling under the narrator's failing memory and crisis of naming. The ghostly city that the narrator enters through the pastorally named 'Shepherd's Gate', with its trams and buses, running, 'but few, slow, empty, noiseless, as if under water', recalls a post-catastrophic scene (Beckett 1995: 64). He overcomes his reticence to fill us in on more than just a 'few remarks', so that the emptiness and stillness of the city – it might well be nighttime – is repeatedly asserted (Beckett 1995). Shadows, ghostly cyclists, fleeing prostitutes: what remains of the modernist cityscape are its nightmares, its delinquents in spectral form. Dispossession, flight, checkpoints and ramparts, references to warfare, these tie the Nouvelles, if indeterminately, to the recent past of the repeated re-demarcation of national borders and the parsing of Germany into four occupied zones, and to the mass displacement of people across Europe. The implications of these descriptions, what Marjorie Perloff called 'Beckett's brilliant indirection, his ways of not- saying and yet saying',

(Perloff 2005: 100) for a French audience at the time of the *Nouvelles'* publication cannot – and, paradoxically, must not – be overstated.

In *Molloy*, the well-known contrast between the Molloy Country and Moran Country mocks the ideological discourse surrounding borders, jurisdiction and nationhood. A letter to his German translator Erich Franzen in 1954 shows how this issue comes up in the translation process: 'I prefer Gegend to Gebiet precisely because it is vaguer (limits never determined by Molloy) and somehow less administrative. Gebiet is a Moran word, not a Molloy word' (Beckett 2011: 458). (*Gegend* is a region defined in relation to a specific point, but without the officially drawn borders of *Gebiet*.) Famously, the only papers Molloy carries with him are the ones he uses to wipe himself. This becomes an issue when he has to identify himself upon entering a town (again, he is an automatic rebel in a sanitised, demarcated space). The identity document within the context of border control is replaced in this episode by excrement, the allegorical counter translated by the abject index. In psychoanalytic terms, the instability of Molloy's self through the arrival of the non-self (bodily excretion) carries over into the conceptualisation of a homogenous national culture (the latter allegorised through Moran's moral censorship).[20] For our present purposes, it remains to recognise that Beckett's insistence on 'Gegend' is emblematic of how translation registers the historical and political murmurs of his postwar writing, how it rehearses issues of borders, territory, property, possession and belonging.

Conclusion

Beckett's auto-translation performs a kind of deprivation or negation, denying at once its own historical 'purchase' and the narrators' historical inclusion through language. 'Disjointed from land, labor, and law' (Nail 2015: 147), the vagabond becomes in Beckett's prose the emblem of political resistance, understood not in terms of active political commitment, but insofar as his impossibility of 'purchase' translates into national, cultural and linguistic border crossings. This resistance informs the sense in which Beckett's stories both sustain and 'disown' the possibility of their historical content. His auto-translation sustains the problem of how politics and ethics enter his border-crossing worlds, registered by the tramp's deprived complicity.

They describe an inadequate, translated relationship between Beckett's negative narrative mode and various possible histories: an Irish colonial history of mass expropriation, criminalisation of 'delinquent' tenants and land 'wasters', controlled starvation and Malthusian politics, a fervent Irish republicanism tied to the powerful Catholic Church of Ireland, a postwar moment in Western Europe marked by mass deportation, extermination of the infirm, and redrawing of national borders, as well as a dominant mythical appeal to the moral good of French nationhood. While Beckett's alterations in the English are subtle, they do nevertheless - and at times paradoxically – reinforce the sense of socio-economic exclusion and historical persecution in the stories' world.

Notes

1. Beckett quoted in Mark Nixon (2011: 177-8).
2. Beckett quoted in James Knowlson (1997: 358).
3. Beckett had made a habit of speaking of the four stories in one breath, as 'a book of long short stories' ready for publication: Samuel Beckett (2011: 55). The running order in *Nouvelles et Textes pour rien* (1955) – 'L'Expulsé'/'Le Calmant'/'La Fin' – is both indicative and treacherous, and one should be wary of attributing too much continuity. In 1977, John Calder published all four stories as *Four Novellas*.
4. Leslie Hill notes: 'Already . . . in 1936, the slogan [Up the Republic!] had begun to migrate, undecidably, from Ireland to Spain, from English to Spanish and back, affirming nationalism only to the extent that nationalism is itself always already an internationalist principle' (Hill 1997: 926n10). See also Morin (2017: 105–10).
5. 'Klappe!' in German translates as 'shut up!'
6. Samuel Beckett (2010b: 40). 'HIER' (German for: here) refers to the location of the 'conveniences' whose relation to Frankfurt is playfully suggested as somehow metonymical. The 'letters of fire' conjure the continual air raids by the Allied Forces on Frankfurt-am-Main, with its medieval city centre completely annihilated.
7. See Morin (2017: 142).
8. See Morin (2017: 169).
9. In *Texts for Nothing*: 'Someone said, You can't stay here . . . I could have stayed in my den, snug and dry, I couldn't. My den, I'll describe it, no, I can't' (Beckett 1995: 100).
10. Beckett already knew Kafka's work well. See Beckett (2011: 22).
11. Seaver translated 'La Fin' and 'L'Expulsé', Beckett revising the translations substantially. Seaver noted that Beckett seemed less concerned with correcting his English translation than with revising the original itself (Seaver 2006: 105).
12. Note that the German Northwest that Beckett had visited became the British Occupied Zone until 1949. The *Reichsmark*, the currency in Germany from 1924–1948, had a *Pfennig*, penny, but no shilling or six pence.
13. See Morin (2017: 139–40).

14. 'Schlägt sich auf die Seite der Asozialen.' (Benjamin 1991: 54. My translation).
15. A social commentary somewhat flattened by the English translation as 'mean soul'. (Beckett 1970: 23[32]).
16. See Morin (2017: 220–7).
17. See Nail (2015: 145–7).
18. See Seán Kennedy's essays: 'Introduction: Ireland/Europe . . . Beckett/ Beckett', in *Beckett and Ireland*, (Kennedy 2010a: 1–15, specifically 11–13); '"In the street I was lost": Cultural Dislocation in Samuel Beckett's "The End,"' in *Beckett and Ireland*, (Kennedy 2010b: 96–113); '"Bid Us Sigh on from Day to Day": Beckett and the Irish Big House', in *The Edinburgh Companion to Samuel Beckett and the Arts* (Kennedy 2014: 222–36).
19. A favourite exclamation of the narrator is 'Exelmans!' in reference to the French soldier (Beckett 1995: 80).
20. See Schauss (2016: 193–216).

Works Cited

Beckett, Samuel (1955), *Nouvelles et Textes pour rien. 'L'Expulsé'/'Le Calmant'/'La Fin'*, Paris: Les Éditions de Minuit.
Beckett, Samuel (1970), *Premier amour*, Paris: Les Éditions de Minuit.
Beckett, Samuel (1995), *The Complete Short Prose, 1929–1989*, S. E. Gontarski (ed), New York: Grove Press.
Beckett, Samuel (2007), *Watt*, New York: Grove Press.
Beckett, Samuel (2010a), *Malone Dies*, London: Faber and Faber.
Beckett, Samuel (2010b), *Mercier and Camier*, London: Faber and Faber.
Beckett, Samuel (2011), *The Letters of Samuel Beckett: 1941–1956*, Vol. 2, George Craig, Martha Fehsenfeld, Daniel Gunn and Lois More Overbeck (eds), Cambridge, UK: Cambridge University Press.
Benjamin, Walter (1991), *Gesammelte Schriften*, 5: 1, Rolf Tiedeman (ed), Frankfurt: Suhrkamp.
Bixby, Patrick (2009), *Samuel Beckett and the Postcolonial Novel*, Cambridge, UK: Cambridge University Press.
Derrida, Jacques (1998), *Monolingualism of the Other; or The Prosthesis of Origin*, translated by Patrick Mensah, Stanford: Stanford University Press.
Dillon, Brian (2017), *Essayism*, London: Fitzcarraldo.
Gibson, Andrew (2010), *Samuel Beckett*, London: Reaktion Books.
Hill, Leslie (1997), '"Up the Republic!": Beckett, Writing, Politics', *MLN*, 112.5, 909–28.
Katz, Daniel (1999), *Saying I No More: Subjectivity and Consciousness in the Prose of Samuel Beckett*, Evanston: Northwestern University Press.

Kennedy, Seán (2010a), 'Introduction: Ireland/Europe . . . Beckett/Beckett', in Seán Kennedy (ed), *Beckett and Ireland,* Cambridge, UK: Cambridge University Press, pp. 1–15.

Kennedy, Seán (2010b), '"In the Street I was lost": Cultural Dislocation in Samuel Beckett's "The End"', in Seán Kennedy (ed), *Beckett and Ireland,* Cambridge, UK: Cambridge University Press, pp. 96–113.

Kennedy, Seán (2010c), 'Preface', in Samuel Beckett, *Mercier and Camier,* London: Faber and Faber, pp. vii-x.

Kennedy, Seán (2014), '"Bid Us Sigh on from Day to Day": Beckett and the Irish Big House', in S. E. Gontarski (ed), *The Edinburgh Companion to Samuel Beckett and the Arts,* Edinburgh: Edinburgh University Press, pp. 222–36.

Knowlson, James (1997), *Damned to Fame: The Life of Samuel Beckett,* London: Bloomsbury.

McNaughton, James (2010), 'The Politics of Aftermath: Beckett, Modernism, and the Irish Free State', in Seán Kennedy (ed), *Beckett and Ireland,* Cambridge, UK: Cambridge University Press, pp. 56–77.

Marx, Karl (2013), *Das Kapital: Erster Band,* Berlin: Dietz Verlag.

Morin, Emilie (2017), *Beckett's Political Imagination,* Cambridge, UK: Cambridge University Press.

Nail, Thomas (2015), *The Figure of the Migrant,* Stanford: Stanford University Press.

Nixon, Mark (2011), *Samuel Beckett's German Diaries 1936–1937,* London: Continuum.

Pearson, Nels (2015), *Irish Cosmopolitanism: Location and Dislocation in James Joyce, Elizabeth Bowen, and Samuel Beckett,* Gainesville: University Press of Florida.

Perloff, Marjorie (2005), '"In Love with Hiding": Samuel Beckett's War', *The Iowa Review,* 35.1, 76–103.

Schauss, Martin (2016), 'The Censor's "Filthy Synecdoche": Samuel Beckett and Censorship', *Sanglap: Journal of Literary and Cultural Inquiry,* 2.2, 193–216.

Seaver, Richard (2006), 'Richard Seaver on Translating Beckett', in James and Elizabeth Knowlson (eds), *Beckett Remembering, Remembering Beckett: A Centenary Celebration,* New York: Arcade Publishing.

Slote, Sam (2011), 'Continuing the End: Variation Between Beckett's French and English Prose Works', in Mark Nixon (ed), *Publishing Samuel Beckett,* London: The British Library, pp. 2015–18.

Stonebridge, Lyndsey (2018), *Placeless People: Writings, Rights, and Refugees,* Oxford: Oxford University Press.

Uhlmann, Anthony (1999), *Beckett and Poststructuralism,* Cambridge, UK: Cambridge University Press.

Walkowitz, Rebecca (2015), *Born Translated. The Contemporary Novel in an Age of World Literature,* New York: Columbia University Press, 2015.

Weisberg, David (2000), *Chronicles of Disorder: Samuel Beckett and the Cultural Politics of the Modern Novel,* Albany: SUNY Press.

Part IV

Commentary

Some Remarks on a Sentence in
A Piece of Monologue

Antoni Libera

The sentence: 'Parts lips and thrusts tongue forward. Birth'.

This sentence describes the action employed by the organs of speech in articulating the word *birth*. Parting the lips is both a condition for and a result of pronouncing the plosive consonant *b*; thrusting the tongue forward, more precisely, pushing it out through the parted lips and teeth, describes in turn the action involved in pronouncing the sound *th*.

The translation of this sentence therefore depends on the pronunciation of the word *birth* in the given language. In my Polish translation the word *birth* for various reasons is rendered in the verbal form as *urodził się* ('he was born'). The form *urodził się* consists of eight sounds: *u, r, o, j, e, w, sh, e*. Thus, either the articulation of all these sounds should be described, or, following the author's example, that of only a few, namely those most characteristic for pronouncing the form *urodził się*.

Unfortunately, neither the complete version nor the simplified one provides an adequate solution. On the one hand, such description would be too long and so disturb the rhythm of the text; on the other hand, it would say too little, since articulation of the form *urodził się* is not as distinctive as that of the word *birth*. Above all, it would not fulfil the function of the original, i.e., it would not reveal the specific connection between the word *birth* and its articulation, since the same connection does not exist in the case of *urodził się*. The connection links the parting of lips and thrusting forward of the tongue, necessary for the articulation of the word *birth*, with the actual act of birth. In other words, the pronunciation of this word is simultaneously the image or symbol of that which it signifies. Using still other words, in a sense this word *is* that which it signifies.

By placing the description of this word's articulation in the text, and thus revealing this connection, the author intends to evoke associations with the myth of creative power of the word, so deeply rooted in European culture. The word *birth* presents a phenomenon in which the abstract mystery of the transformation of the Word into a Thing, moreover the dependence of the Thing on the Word, appears quite directly, as something concrete and tangible. In the case of the word *birth*, meaning mixes with object, the signifier with the signified. This provides a natural model of prototype of the mythical 'orality' (verbality) of the flesh (body), the idea that the world is something spoken, that all reality is form and function of speech, that all being is Logos fulfilling itself (making itself real). Apart from being primal and possessing the power of creation, the Word as, indirectly, the source of the light:

> In the beginning was the Word, and the Word was with God, and the Word was God . . . All things were made by him; and without him was not anything made that was made. In him was life; and life was the light of man. And the light shineth in darkness; and the darkness comprehended not. (St John I, 1–5)

In the fragment under consideration the author also takes this aspect of the myth into account. He does this by making use of the verb *to part* in reference to lips as well as darkness: 'Parts lips', 'Parts the dark', 'Dark parts'. In this way poses a condition or rather an equivalence between opening the lips to utter a word and scattering darkness. Uttering the Word-Life is equal to scattering darkness.

The fact that the author omitted the fragment here discussed in the French version (and consequently the entire 'birth' motif) indicates that he did not find any analogous substitute. Probably none of the words then at his disposal could fulfil the conditions set by the English *birth* and *to part*.

The question thus arises, whether this fragment should be translated into Polish, which similarly lacks a word which completely corresponds to *birth*. If I have decided to include the fragment, it was with the conviction that such a peculiar and interesting linguistic and poetic phenomenon is worth reproducing even if only halfway (with a full explanation in the form of commentary) rather than ignoring it altogether.

The solution I have chosen: 'Wysuwa wargi i tworzy między nimi niewielki otwór' ('He rounds his lips and opens them slightly') presents a description of the articulation of the first sound only (*u*) of the Polish phrase 'urodził się'. This suggests that the turning-point, as well as the most difficult and most dramatic moment, is found in the movement of the mouth as it prepares to utter the first syllable. The uttered sound *u* may also by associated with the screams of a woman in labor. I have translated 'Parts the dark' with the phrase 'i już się coś jawi' ('and right then something came to light') with recognition, that given its immediate adjacency to the phrase 'urodził się' these words express the fundamental idea.

The Third Language of Translation

Gabriele Frasca

The last letter I received from Samuel Beckett was dated 20 June 1988. It was the only one of our brief exchange not written in his own hand. His already poor health was to precipitate in a month. But at the time I did not know that and therefore I was surprised to find myself reading not the usual card in English or French but a sheet of Éditions de Minuit letterhead, signed by Jérôme Lindon. The publisher closest to him wrote on that occasion: 'Samuel Beckett, un peu souffrant actuellement, asked me to tell you . . .'. What was he so anxious to tell me? Nothing important. It was something concerning one of my translations, and I still find it extraordinary that in such circumstances Beckett would decide to dictate his observations to Lindon in order to answer my letter. I have never known a man of such exquisite kindness. I realised that I should no longer disturb him from then on.

Although in our slim correspondence (two letters a year from 1983 on) we had sometimes touched on other issues, nonetheless the main topic between us were my translations. At the time I had not been officially entrusted with the task of translating anything written by him yet (my first Einaudi translation, *Watt*, would have been published in 1997), but I had practiced on his poems and also, somewhat recklessly, on some of his most experimental prose pieces such as *Company/Compagnie*. For me it was pretty much a critical exercise: by translating I had the chance of delving into the text thus widening my knowledge of Beckett that would result in *Cascando*, my first monograph on him, published precisely in 1988. I was very much used to sending him the provisional outcomes of my exercises, and I am still amazed at how much of his precious time he spent revising those poor early attempts of mine. Beckett knew Italian well, because it was the language of his beloved Dante, and all his life he went on reading and re-reading the *Commedia*. But he also liked practicing spoken language when he spent his holidays in Italy.

But, to go back to the letter signed by Jérôme Lindon, on that particular occasion I had pushed myself too far indeed. What I had sent him was nothing less than my first version of *Worstward Ho*, unaware as I was that it would become Beckett's only setback in his long career in self-translation. And equally unaware of the great number of different versions I was bound to produce in the following twenty years before I could handle such a difficult text. 'Samuel Beckett', Lindon went on, 'does not consider the possibility of translating *Worstward Ho* and he deems the text – ne serait-ce qu'en raison du premier mot, on – untranslatable into a Romance language'. As a matter of fact, in 1983, when *Worstward Ho* was published, he had already written to another translator, the great Antoni Libera, that he could not turn his prose into French. However, as we know, later on he did not discourage Edith Fournier from accomplishing the task. Apart from the personal anecdote, the issue is a crucial one: how should a translator react to such a declaration of impotence on behalf of the author who, in the course of the twentieth century, had translated his own works most frequently? To answer the question by stating the work's right to untranslatability once more would not solve the problem, which is even more radical than it appears to be. For, paradoxically, the problem remains the opposite: not how to translate a supposedly untranslatable text since we can always proceed by approximation, but rather, how to tackle the translation of a text which, ever since its genesis, has already been inextricably interwoven with its translations, as sometimes happens to Beckett's oeuvres. This is the real issue with the Irish author.

In his case, in fact, we cannot just choose to translate from the language of the first version neglecting the second one, especially when the phases of composition are so close in time as to overlap, which could prove to be a costly mistake. I realised this when I first tried to translate *Company*. Beckett started the French *Compagnie* (manuscript dated 3–27 August 1979) right after completing the first English version (whose manuscript is dated 5 May 1977–27 July 1979), so that it is easy to find in *Company*'s second typescript (undated but going back to the end of 1979 and consequently written after *Compagnie*), some variants clearly deriving from his French translation. In conclusion, the issue can become particularly thorny for a possible third translator: it is as if, while working on the critical edition of a text, they had to deal with two witnesses of a missing original – a condition well known to the philologist and a highly unwished – for one in addition, since without the third, whether witness or stemma of the tradition, it is the philologist who is called upon to choose, relying on his own competence. And this leads us to a conclusion only apparently unexpected, which nonetheless seems to be in line with Benjamin's view of translation: whatever it is, Samuel Beckett's true language is always a third language.

From *All that Fall* to *Stirrings Still*

Erika Tophoven

It was in January 1957 that Samuel Beckett opened for the first time the door of his flat to his German translator in company with a young German student, who had just finished her English studies in Munich and had come to Paris to complete her studies in French. They had met recently at a birthday party of a German friend living in Paris, and Top, as his friends called him, had asked her to have a look at a radio play, written in English, that he pulled out of his waistcoat. It was Samuel Beckett's first radio play *All That Fall*. English was less familiar to Top than French, the language in which had been written *Godot* in 1953, the novel *Malone meurt* in 1954 and the third volume of the trilogie *L'Innommable* that Top was still working on. Erika Schöningh, the name of his companion, later referred to as Kiki, had accepted to make a first draft in German of the play, although she found the text rather queer. Top and Kiki met several times to polish the German version, sitting upstairs in the well-known café Flore in St Germain-des-Prés, until Top thought it fit for a final revision with the author. He asked Beckett for a meeting as he used to do, since Beckett liked to follow up his work in German, being fluent in that language.

There we were, the two of us, 6 rue des Favorites, top floor, on a cold January afternoon, at 3 p.m. I didn't feel particularly excited, not aware at the time of the importance that this meeting would have for me for the rest of my life. I see Beckett very tall, standing in the door frame, welcoming his translator as well as his companion, putting them at ease and showing them into the study. I remember the room, not very spacious, but with a high ceiling and a narrow staircase, leading to a gallery. When we had a chance, twenty years later, to move into a flat, less comfortable than our little Levitt-house in the suburb, but with a gallery, I felt it had been a dream for me all the time to find such a place in memory of rue des Favorites.

We sat down at a small square wooden table and Top started reading the translation aloud, Beckett listening very concentrated, interrupting only when there seemed to be a problem of vocabulary, syntax, rhythm, repetitions or variations. I don't remember any particular difficulties, but it was the first time that I learnt to be attentive to alliterations, assonances and especially the choice of expressive words and their sound – *All that Fall* is a radio play.

The place of the action is Ireland, but there are quite a number of references to Germany, musical references as Schubert's *Der Tod und das Mädchen*, linguistic references as Mr. Rooney's remark: 'Fir as they call it now, from Vir Viris I suppose, the V becoming F, in accordance with Grimm's Law', and literary references, especially to the German writer Theodor Fontane (1819–98) and his novel *Effi Briest*:

> Mr. Rooney: Let us hasten home and sit before the fire. We shall draw the blinds. You will read to me. I think Effie is going to commit adultery with the Major. (Beckett 2006: 189)

We did not discuss the 'e' added to Effi in the original, I took it for a misprint and cut it out. Two years later the name came up again in the monodrama *Krapp's Last Tape*:

> Scalded the eyes out of me reading *Effie* again, a page a day, with tears again. Effie. . . . [*Pause.*] Could have been happy with her, up there on the Baltic, and the pines, and the dunes. [*Pause.*] Could I? [*Pause.*] And she? [*Pause.*] Pah! [*Pause.*] Fanny came in a couple of times. (Beckett 2006: 222)

I admit that I did not realise at the time what there was behind the two names: *Effie* and *Fanny*.

1963 another radio play: *Embers*. There is a passage where Addie is playing E instead of F.

> *Resounding blow of ruler on piano case. Addie stops playing.*
> Music Master: [*Violently.*] Fa!
> Addie: [*Tearfully.*] What?
> Music Master: [*Violently.*] Eff! Eff!
> Addie: [*Tearfully.*] Where?
> Music Master: [*Violently.*] Qua! [*He thumps note.*] Fa!
> > [*Pause. Addie begins again, Music Master beating time lightly with ruler. When she comes to bar 5 she makes same mistake. Tremendous blow of ruler on piano case. Addie stops playing, begins to wail.*]

Music Master: [*Frenziedly.*] Eff! Eff! [*He hammers note.*] Eff! [*He hammers note.*] Eff!

[*Hammered note, 'Eff!' and Addie's wail amplified to paroxysm, then suddenly cut off. Pause.*] (Beckett 2006: 258–9)

Now it became evident, remembering the importance of 'echoes' in Beckett's work, that in *Effie* is also inherent the musical note F/EFF and the 'e' added refers to the fact, that Addie plays 'e' instead of 'eff' in the opening bars of Chopin's Fifth Waltz in A Flat Major. Chopin – Chopinek – Chopinetto (*Dream of Fair to Middling Women*). Another echo is to be found in EFFie – FAnny in the Krapp-passage. Finally, Addie's question 'What? . . . Where?' finds an echo in the title of Beckett's short scene written in 1983, dedicated to Vaclav Havel *Quoi Où*. I have chosen this example because Fontane was particularly present in Germany last year for his 200th anniversary. The novels of Fontane were present in Beckett's mind since 1928 when he read or saw Peggy reading *Effi Briest* in Kassel. Oh, the happy memories, Winnie would say.

One of the treasures in our archives is the translation manuscript of *Happy Days*. Exceptionally we did not meet Beckett for a final revision because I gave birth to our first son at the time and I got the manuscript back while still in the clinic. There are quite a number of corrections, suggestions and clarifications, delicately noted in pencil on the border of the leaves, in particular two remarks: 'shorten' and 'same word', important to remember for later work. His subtle remarks proved once again, how well he mastered the German language.

After thirty years of working in common I felt not at all sure to continue alone in 1989. Top and I had attacked *Worstward Ho* together, but he was finally too ill to continue and Sam no longer able either to revise the translation. So, I went to England for three months and stayed with friends near Reading, where I found a helping hand, although most of Beckett's archive material was still in boxes at the library. *Worstward Ho* was published in a beautiful bilingual edition, and finally two years later *Stirrings Still*, trilingual, the French translation, still by the author, had been published in 1989.

There were some other prose texts left aside up to then, 'Le Monde et le pantalon', concerning the paintings of Geer and Bram van Velde; 'Le Concentrisme'; 'L'Image'; an essay of Gilles Deleuze 'L'Épuisé'; and the poems 'Neither' and 'what is the word'.

When, at the end of the 1990s, Beckett's *German Diaries* became known, it kindled my curiosity to the utmost. Edward Beckett entrusted me the Hamburg

Diary for transcription and a limited illustrated publication, then the Berlin Diary as basis for my book *Beckett's Berlin*.

Since Summer 2019 our Beckett archives are completely set up in the Tophoven family house in Top's hometown Straelen (near the Dutch border), where we intend to develop further projects and welcome scholars for research. There are still stirrings . . .

Works Cited

Beckett, Samuel (2006) [1986], *The Complete Dramatic Works*, London: Faber.

Beckett Translating

Alan W. Friedman

Co-coordinating an international conference on Samuel Beckett in 1984, my colleagues Charles Rossman (English Department), Dina Sherzer (French), and I called it *Beckett Translating/Translating Beckett*, the same name as the book of the conference we edited and published three years later. *Beckett Translating*, as we then wrote, 'regards translation not as a secondary production but rather as a fundamental, dynamic process that involves interpretation, adaptation, trans-formation, and transposition – activities requiring strategies and techniques for transcoding on the part of the translator' (Friedman et al. 1987: 1). We envisaged translation in broad terms, including not only translation from one language to another but also from page to stage, especially under Beckett's own direction, and from one medium to another. Almost everything that Beckett wrote in either English or French he translated himself, or reconceived and offered as interpretation, in the other language. And although he incorporated aspects of such disparate disciplines as art, music, philosophy, science, mathematics and vaudeville into his writing, his attitude toward genre, at least initially, was quite parochial and proprietorial – as he insisted that what he wrote in one medium (whether prose, verse, drama, radio play or TV play) must remain untranslated from it. Yet at times he not only allowed but even aided translations between various forms of dramatic expression.

Symptomatic of his ambiguity, in 1959 Beckett turned down an offer of $25,000 from Burt Lahr and Paramount Pictures for a film adaptation of *Waiting for Godot*, although he reluctantly accepted the BBC's 1961 version. In August of 1962 he signed a contract with Keep Films, Ltd. for a film of *Godot* with Peter O'Toole; but he had second thoughts and, after much negotiation, managed to rescind his permission. In the 1980s he vetoed all-female produc-tions of the play on the grounds that, since women do not have prostates, they couldn't properly portray Didi's urinary problem. Not until 1991, two years after Beckett's death, was the ban lifted by a court injunction that enabled an all-female cast to perform the play at the Avignon Festival. Beckett was consistently firmer with *All That Fall*, his first radio play, repeatedly refusing to allow it to be staged even though it is one of his most dramatic works. He rejected, for instance, Ingmar Bergman's request to stage *Fall* (along with *Embers*) in 1963, and yet he had allowed RTF to adapt *Tout ceux qui tombent* earlier that year (Knowlson 1996: 449–50). Not until 2012 did *Fall* appear on a British stage, the Jermyn Street Theatre, London, with Eileen Atkins and Michael Gambon as the Rooneys, and even then, it was performed as a staged radio play, with actors carrying scripts; props and gestures kept to a minimum; and microphones hanging from the ceiling to simulate a 1950s studio. The director, Trevor Nunn, called it a 'visualised radio play', and the conceit is that the audience are eavesdroppers at a studio recording (Moss 2012). Beckett was almost always accommodating with those he trusted. When Alan Schneider was invited to direct *Godot*, he immediately went to Paris to confer with Beckett, a meeting that expanded to include a trip to London to view Peter Hall's production of the play at the Arts Theatre Club. In his subsequent letter to Schneider, the first of many, Beckett wrote, 'I feel my monster is in safe keeping' (Harmon 1998: 1), though Beckett included a copy of a letter he had written to Hall offering direction in excruciating detail. Still, when Schneider subsequently queried him regarding staging details, Beckett expansively responded, 'Anyway you like, Alan', a catchphrase and compliment that Schneider used as a title for a piece he wrote on working on productions with Beckett (Schneider 1975). With similar generosity, Beckett worked closely with Jack MacGowran, one of his favourite actors to whom he was deeply loyal, on a one-man show adapted from both dramatic writings and prose. Initially called *End of Day*, MacGowran's anthology was staged in Dublin and London in October of 1962. With Beckett's further assistance, MacGowran reprised the revised and retitled work, *Beginning to End: A Television Exploration of the World of Samuel Beckett*, on Irish TV in 1965, on BBC1 in 1965 and 1967, and on stage in New York (1970), Paris (1970) and Berlin (1971).

Not I was a pivotally translated play for Beckett. As written for the theatre (and performed by Billie Whitelaw in 1973 and 1975), it features a mouth 'about 8 feet above stage level, faintly lit up from close-up and below' and a mute Auditor standing downstage, 'dead still throughout but for four brief movements' (Beckett 2006: 405): 'he would raise his arms, then lower them' (Whitelaw 1995: 123). But while working to translate *Not I* to BBC TV in 1977, Beckett abandoned two elements he had initially conceived of as crucial to the work: both the Auditor and the elevated, distant mouth. Instead, he had Mouth fill the entire screen. 'It looked', according to Whitelaw, 'strangely sexual and glutinous, slimy and weird, like a crazed, oversexed jellyfish'.

Beckett's one-word comment on this extraordinary, if unintended, image 'of a large, gaping vagina' that differed strikingly from his original conception was 'Miraculous' (Whitelaw 1995: 132). Musical transpositions were congenial for Beckett, a talented musician himself, and they worked both ways.[1] For example, *All That Fall* incorporates both Psalm 145 and Schubert's *Death and the Maiden* (the second movement of his *String Quartet No. 14*). *Ghost Trio* takes its title and central motif from Beethoven's *Piano Trio in D major, opus 70, no. 1*, known as *The Ghost*, and deploys it like a prop. Krapp in *Krapp's Last Tape* attempts to sing the Lutheran hymn, 'Now the Day is Over', although in productions he directed Beckett excised it as being 'too self-conscious and artificial'.[2] Both *Words and Music* and *Embers* portray harsh music-masters putting recalcitrant pupils through their paces. And Beckett, who often rehearsed his plays as if he were conducting, using such musical terms as 'piano', 'fortissimo', 'andante', 'allegro', 'da capo', 'cadenza', usually responded generously to requests to set his work to music, countenancing at least six musical settings or operas in 1976–77. As Knowlson writes, 'his attitude to musicians who wanted to adapt his work was much freer than it was to stage or film directors wishing to do the same thing' (Knowlson 1996: 577).

In 1991, two years after Beckett's death, Dublin's Gate Theatre, under the auspices of the Beckett Centenary Festival committee chaired by Michael Colgan, produced nearly all of Beckett's stage plays (omitting only *Human Wishes* and *Eleuthéria*) in conjunction with Trinity College and RTÉ. After reprising the program at Lincoln Center, New York (1996) and London's Barbican Centre (1999), the Gate Theatre produced *Beckett on Film*, a four-DVD box set. Most were quite faithful to Beckett's original intentions, but some varied significantly. Perhaps the most strikingly successful variation is the filmed production of *Ohio Impromptu*, which was translated from stage to screen to stunning effect, as R and L, whom Beckett wanted 'As alike in appearance as possible' (Beckett 2006: 473), were both played by Jeremy Irons, thereby becoming literally identical.

Since 1996, the Irish theatre company, The Gare St Lazare Players, has adapted and performed some two dozen of Beckett's works, mainly prose fiction, in some sixty Irish venues and in over seventy-five cities in thirty other countries.[3] Considering themselves heirs of Jack MacGowran, Judy Hegarty Lovett, director, and Conor Lovett, leading actor, comment that 'Beckett himself had staged elements of his prose works in a one-man show performed by Jack MacGowran'. Conor Lovett maintains that his staging is a form of translation that can enhance the original: 'when an actor or artist is invested in the language and empathises with the writing, there is potential for their delivery to release the text from the page and allow it to live in three dimensions as a live act'. The gains, he finds, have been great, mostly in terms of orality:

'Staging the novels has illuminated Beckett's writing for me and offered a way into the work via a voice that is itself the subject of many of his works. Hearing Beckett's novels on the stage is another way to meet his work and may even offer a chance to access the writing on a whole new level'. But the Lovetts remain fully cognisant that such transposition risks not only arousing the ire of the Beckett estate, which has vigilantly safeguarded the legacy that has been entrusted to it, although it has become somewhat more relaxed and accepting in recent years. Perhaps even more constraining has been the Lovetts' determination to remain faithful to the texts they portray: 'In dramatising the novel, we explored the text and, through trial and error, we discovered how to make the words work in three dimensions. For me, the prose and the plays are from the same world and the same song. In singing it, to paraphrase Molloy, 'Godsend we don't make a balls of it' (Lovett 2018). Of their April 2018 production of *Here All Night*, an anthology of excerpts from *Watt*, *First Love* and the *Trilogy* set to music, Peter Crawley of *The Irish Times* writes that the performance 'can twist a traditional Irish air into something startlingly spare and new (Beckett would approve) and is allowed to stray and improvise, free from strictures (Beckett would not approve)' (Crawley 2018). Still, their staging has been so successfully faithful in its way that it has gone unchallenged. Perhaps it, like MacGowran's, would even have received Beckett's own imprimatur, or at least acceptance, were he still here.

Notes

1. See Friedman, 'Beckett's Musicals' (2006).
2. Knowlson (1992: 26). It remains, however, in subsequent editions, such as Beckett (1984: 62) and Beckett (2006: 225, 229).
3. In addition to numerous plays, The Gare St. Lazare Players have adapted and staged many of Beckett's prose works, including the following (listed according to date of first performance): *Molloy* (1996); *Malone Dies* (1999); *The Unnamable* (2000); *Lessness* (2002); *Enough* (2004); *Texts for Nothing* (2005); *Worstward Ho* (2005); 'The End' (2008); *First Love* (2008); 'The Calmative' (2010); *Here All Night*: comprising *Watt*, *First Love*, *The Trilogy*, *Words & Music*, and 'The End' (2013); *How It Is* (2015).

Works Cited

Beckett, Samuel (1984), *The Collected Shorter Plays of Samuel Beckett*, New York: Grove.

Beckett, Samuel (2006), *Samuel Beckett: The Grove Centenary Edition*, 4 vols., Paul Auster (ed), New York: Grove.

Crawley, Peter (2018), 'Gare St Lazare's *Here All Night*: Sparing, Cerebral and Sensuous', *The Irish Times,* 17 April, https://www.irishtimes.com/culture/stage/theatre/gare-st-lazare-s-here-all-night-sparing-cerebral-and-sensuous-1.3463693. (Accessed 24 June 2019).

Friedman, Alan Warren (2006), 'Beckett's Musicals', *Études Anglaises,* 59.1, 47–59.

Friedman, Alan Warren, Charles Rossman and Dina Sherzer (eds) (1987), *Beckett Translating/Translating Beckett,* University Park and London: Pennsylvania State University Press.

Harmon, Maurice (ed) (1998), *No Author Better Served: The Correspondence of Samuel Beckett & Alan Schneider,* Cambridge, MA: Harvard University Press.

Knowlson, James (ed) (1992), *Theatre Workbook I. Samuel Beckett: 'Krapp's Last Tape',* London: Faber.

Knowlson, James (1996), *Damned to Fame: The Life of Samuel Beckett,* New York: Simon and Schuster.

Lovett, Judy Hegarty (2018), 'Why put Beckett's novels on stage if they were meant to be read?', *The Stage,* May 3, https://www.thestage.co.uk/opinion/2018/judy-hegarty-lovett-put-becketts-novels-stage-meant-read/. (Accessed 22 June 2019).

Moss, Stephen (2012), '*All That Fall*: the Samuel Beckett stage play that isn't', *The Guardian,* 7 November, https://www.theguardian.com/stage/2012/nov/07/all-that-fall-samuel- beckett. (Accessed 2 July 2019).

Schneider, Alan (1975), '"Anyway You Like, Alan": Working with Beckett', *Theatre Quarterly,* 5.19, 27–38.

Whitelaw, Billie (1995): *Billie Whitelaw . . . Who He?,* London: Hodder and Stoughton.

Index